3.65

=

AUTH

TITL

ACC

D1582590

Documents from Edwardian England
1901–1915

Documents from Edwardian England

1901–1915

by

DONALD READ

Reader in Modern English History, University of Kent

HARRAP LONDON

First published in Great Britain 1973
by George G. Harrap & Co. Ltd
182–184 High Holborn, London WC1V 7AX

© *Donald Read* 1973

ISBN 0 245 51090 7

*Composed in Monophoto Baskerville by M. & A. Thomson Litho Ltd., East Kilbride
and printed by Redwood Press Ltd., Trowbridge and London
Made in Great Britain*

Contents

Introduction

The following extracts are almost all taken from documents dating from the Edwardian period itself. This exclusiveness is deliberate. It would have been possible to have quoted extensively from reminiscences of the period written after, sometimes long after, the event. This has been avoided here because such retrospective accounts must always suffer from the effects of the passage of time, not only in errors of detail but also in distortions of interpretation. In the case of memories of the atmosphere before the First World War such distortion can prove particularly damaging. Accounts are necessarily diffused by after-knowledge of the war's terrible impact, terrible in its destruction of life, equally shattering in its destruction of confidence. The effect of 'the deluge' was traumatic, as Sir Philip Gibbs (1877–1962), novelist and war correspondent, emphasized in a book called *Ten Years After, A Reminder*, published in 1924. 'One has to think back to another world in order to see again that year 1914 before the drums of war began to beat. It is a different world now, greatly changed, in the mental outlook of men and women, in the frontiers of the soul as well as the frontiers of nations.'[1]

Two forms of distortion have proved particularly common in reminiscences of this old world. Some have remembered the Edwardian period as a 'golden age'; others, contrastingly, have depicted it as an epoch lurching inevitably towards Armageddon. Both interpretations are sadly twisted by later regret and disgust. Golden ages have never existed except in hindsight. Yet some surviving Edwardians, fortunate in their circumstances before 1914, who had enjoyed the even and comfortable lives then possible for the middle and upper classes, later found it easy to conclude, amid the turmoil of one or two world wars and their aftermaths, that their younger days had

[1] P. Gibbs, *Ten Years After* (1924), 7–8; A. Marwick, *The Deluge, British Society and the First World War* (1965), 9–12; A. Marwick, *Britain in the Century of Total War* (1968), chs. I–IV.

been passed in especially favoured times. 'Those who did not know this land before 1914 never knew it at all. Those who did not live before then ever (*sic*) saw this country at its greatest, its height, its Imperial might, its wonderful security and its wonderful peace.' Thus rhapsodized W. Macqueen-Pope in *Twenty Shillings in the Pound, A Lost Age of Plenty, 1890–1914*, published in 1948.[1] Europe did indeed enjoy a long, even if accidental, span of peace between 1878 and 1913, based upon coal and steel prosperity at home and upon the safety-valve of imperialist expansion overseas. Nevertheless, peace in Europe grew increasingly uncertain after the opening of the twentieth century, as did the maintenance of social and political peace at home in Britain. Uncritical 'golden age' interpretations forget this, and thereby lose all sense of proportion in retrospect. They are too partial in both senses of the adjective. The shadows upon the Edwardian scene matched the sunlight, as was natural and as Edwardians in their day realized. If London's West End was dazzling, its East End was squalid. Alongside the great country houses stood the rural slums. If the gold sovereign ruled world finance, one in three or four Edwardians still lived below the poverty line.

In contrast to the 'golden age' school another group of retrospective writers came to depict the Edwardian age as overshadowed by an inescapable commitment to violent dissolution in war. The thesis of one prominent Cambridge political scientist, Goldsworthy Lowes Dickinson (1862–1932), in *The International Anarchy 1904–1914*, published in 1926, was that 'whenever and wherever the anarchy of armed States exists, war does become inevitable'. Unless there was a realization of this effect, leading to the formation of a powerful League of Nations (for which Dickinson was an early campaigner), he was painfully convinced in the nineteen twenties that world war would erupt for a second time. Yet, we may ask, how many Edwardians felt any sense of the first war's inevitability before it began. Even Dickinson himself in 1914 hardly seems to have done so. His friend and biographer E. M. Forster (1879–1970) has described Dickinson's inner surprise at the coming of war: 'that modern Europe, including his own country, should fall into the Devil's trap—that he never believed, however much he may have maintained its possibility in argument'.[2] Others who have recalled their

[1] W. Macqueen-Pope, *Twenty Shillings in the Pound* (1948), esp. 9, 400.
[2] G. Lowes Dickinson, *The International Anarchy 1904–1914* (1926), esp. v, 485; E. M. Forster, *Goldsworthy Lowes Dickinson* (1934), esp. ch. XIII; Virginia Woolf, *Roger Fry* (1940), 200.

Edwardian youth, such as Sir Llewellyn Woodward (1890–1971), a historian writing in the nineteen forties, or Sir Robert Bruce Lockhart (1887–1970), a diplomat and journalist writing in the nineteen fifties, or Harold Macmillan (b. 1894), a former Prime Minister writing in the nineteen sixties, have disclaimed any sense of foreboding. 'Like all my companions,' asserted Lockhart, 'I lived for the moment.' On the other hand, Lord Percy of Newcastle (1887–1958), politician and university administrator also writing in the nineteen fifties, could claim that he remembered no time 'after I began at all to think for myself, when a European war did not seem to me the most probable of prospects'. Yet again, Lord Winterton (1887–1962), another politician, and J. B. Priestley (b. 1894), the man of letters, have offered interpretations of the mood of early summer 1914, in circles as contrasting as London high society and provincial Bradford, which seek to reconcile surface unconcern with subconscious awareness. 'The *jeunesse dorée* danced the fashionable rag-time all through the night', suggested Winterton, 'with a feverish intensity that came subconsciously, perhaps, from a feeling that the boys would never see another English May or June.' 'I believe I did nothing but enjoy what could be enjoyed', confirmed Priestley, 'because we were soon to be at war. Consciously of course we never entertained a thought of it; but deep in the unconsciousness . . . already the war was on.' Clearly, all these surviving Edwardians were deeply affected by exposure to the trauma of war. No evidence can be without bias, but strictly contemporary Edwardian testimony and record is at least free from this additional sad distortion.[1]

With this same aim of minimizing distortion, editorial comment has been kept to a minimum in this volume. Readers will find a full commentary upon Edwardian society and politics in my book *Edwardian England 1901–15* (Harrap, 1972).

[1] E. L. Woodward, *Short Journey* (1942), 38–9; Earl Winterton, *Orders of the Day* (1953), 73–4; Sir R. Bruce Lockhart, *Your England* (1955), 33; E. Percy, *Some Memories* (1958), 11; J. B. Priestley, *Margin Released* (1962), 79; H. Macmillan, *Winds of Change* (1966), 59.

CHAPTER ONE

Optimism and Pessimism

The first of these extracts from *The Times* leading articles (1) was written while Queen Victoria was still alive. Its tone was optimistic, though it recognized that Britain would need firm support from her Empire if she were to retain her world position in the new century. After the death of the Queen, by contrast, *The Times* felt much less buoyant (2). The third extract (3), headed 'The Outlook for 1914', emphasized the need for a balanced assessment of Britain's prospects. The outbreak of war seven months later was not, of course, foreseen.

1) *The Times*, 1 January 1901.

The twentieth century has dawned upon us; and as we float past this quiet landmark on the shores of time feelings of awe and wonder naturally creep over us. . . . To Englishmen, Scotsmen, and Irishmen, the first of all considerations must be —How will the new century affect the moral and material greatness of their country and of their Empire?... The auguries are not unpropitious. We enter upon the new century with a heritage of achievement and of glory older, more continuous, and not less splendid than that of any other nation in the world. Our national character, as the ordeal of the past year has abundantly shown, has lost nothing of its virility and dogged-ness when put to the proof of war. Our Constitution has developed from a personal Monarchy limited by the power of an hereditary aristocracy into a democratic system of the most liberal kind, knit together by a Throne to which all the self-governing communities of the Empire are profoundly attached. This transition has been effected without any of those violent breaks with the past which in less happy lands than ours have robbed the victories of freedom of the blessings and advantages they naturally produce. . . . With such an instrument of government, with our vast accumulations of wealth widely diffused among the community; and, above all, with a people prosperous, contented, manly, intelligent, and self-reliant, we may look forward with good hope to the storms and conflicts that may await us.

But the greatest of all the advantages with which we face the future lies in the fact that our race is not confined to these small islands. This day a daughter-nation sprung from our loins is celebrating in the distant Pacific her birth as a great federated State. Canada has already lived and prospered for a generation under a system not unlike that inaugurated in Australia today, and never has her prosperity advanced by such leaps and bounds as within the last few years. The progress of New Zealand has been not less marked than that of her sister colonies. In South Africa difficulties have confronted us, and yet confront us, which we do not under-estimate. But there, too, our colonists have shown, like their brothers from Australia and from Canada, that they possess in full measure the qualities that have made England great. . . . We have a reasonable trust that England and her sons will emerge triumphant from that ordeal at the end of the Twentieth Century as at the end of the Nineteenth, and that then and for ages to come they will live and prosper, one united and Imperial people, to be 'a bulwark for the cause of men'.

2)   *The Times*, 23 January 1901.

There is much in what we see around us that we may easily and rightly wish to see improved. The *laudator temporis acti* may even contend that we have lost some things that had better have been preserved. But no permissible deductions can obscure the fact that the period in question has been one of intellectual upheaval, of enormous social and economic progress, and, upon the whole, of moral and spiritual improvement. It is also true, unfortunately, that the impetus has to some extent spent itself. At the close of the reign we are finding ourselves somewhat less secure of our position than we could desire, and somewhat less abreast of the problems of the age than we ought to be, considering the initial advantages we secured. The 'condition of England question' does not present itself in so formidable a shape as at the beginning of the reign, but it does arouse the attention of those who try to look a little ahead of our current business. Others have learned our lessons and bettered our instructions while we have been too easily content to rely upon the methods which were effective a generation or two ago. In this way the Victorian age is defined at its end as well as at its beginning. The command of natural forces that made us great and rich has been superseded by newer discoveries and methods, and we have to open what may be called a new chapter.

3)   *The Times,* 1 January 1914.

Nowhere is there greater proneness to self-depreciation than in this country, and the opening of a new year is our multitudinous pessimists' opportunity. England, it has been said, is the only place where a man can always get a living by disparaging his own people. He may have come down in the world; but, no matter how often he has failed otherwise, it is still open to him to pursue a profitable career, and even attain reputation, by constantly and loudly asserting that everything is going to the bad. Never were there so many sermons upon this familiar text as now. We have dropped, or are dropping, behind in everything—even in sport, in which we were once indisputably first. In boxing, so long an exclusively English sport, our flag has been lowered; a negro and a Frenchman are the champions of the world. How often are the supineness of the English merchant and the intelligent enterprise of the German, the idleness of the English clerk and the diligence of the foreign, the technical skill of our industrial rivals and the routine habits of Englishmen, contrasted? The dominant note in a large part of our literature, especially dramatic, is one of laudation of foreign life and habits and depreciation of our own, of our narrowness and insularity. Taking us at our word, strangers are often, and never more often than just now, disposed to say, 'At last, *finis Britanniae*'.

Many of those who join in this perpetual chorus of disparagement know better. . . . We are told, for example, that there is a physical decadence in the race. The signs of it are by no means obvious. The death-rate in our population, far lower than that of most countries, does not speak of diminished vitality. To quote another common charge, our youth are lacking in the splendid and varied enterprise of their valorous fathers. But scores of examples of heroism, the commonplace incidents of the streets, come to mind to contradict and confute the charge. Not to mention the never failing enterprise of explorers, there is not a mining accident or a shipwreck with many lives in jeopardy which does not bring its unequivocal witness that the fibre of the race is unimpaired. To pass to another common charge, our education, it is often said, is not suited to modern conditions; we must copy the ways of other countries if we are not to be left behind. And yet somehow in the higher walks of literature and science, wherever the best quality of brainwork has to be done, the names of Englishmen are as numerous as they ever were. . . .

The case against pessimism is imperfectly stated if it does not take account of at least two facts. The first is that the task of England is more difficult and complex than that of other communities, and that every year those difficulties multiply. The white man's burden lies especially heavy upon our race. . . . The second fact to be remembered in any fair estimate is that we are now applying higher standards to our institutions and social conditions. Evils which once seemed inevitable and irremoveable are being hopefully attacked. Preventive measures, demanding for their success knowledge and patience, are being carried out; and, if there are failures, they are such as necessarily come with greater boldness in conception or accompany new enterprises. There may be a trifle too much 'softness', which is apt to come with a cycle of material prosperity, a little too much slackness, and far too much making of amusement the chief object of the day. But the failures of which we hear so much are in the main due to the presence of aspirations for a higher civilisation than any which we have yet known.

CHAPTER TWO

The Declining Birth-Rate

Despite Sidney Webb's (admittedly insufficient) evidence
(4), fears were widespread about a racial decline in fertility (5).
The semi-official National Birth-rate Commission, appointed
in 1913, dismissed these alarms; but its report was not published
until 1916 (6). Moreover, the prospect remained of a stationary
or even a declining population later in the twentieth century
(7). In such circumstances Edwardians were uneasy about their
high emigration rate, though the outflow to the Empire could
be justified on patriotic grounds (8).

4) S. Webb, *The Decline in the Birth-Rate*, Fabian Tract no. 131
    (Fabian Society, 1907), 8–15.

The falling off in the birth-rate, which has during the last
twenty years deprived England and Wales of some 200,000
babies a year, is the result of deliberate intention on the part
of the parents. The persistence and universality of the fall in
town and country alike; the total absence of any discoverable
relation to unhealthy conditions, mental development, the
strain of education, town life or physical deterioration of any
kind; the remarkable fact that it has been greatest where it is
known to be widely desired; the evidence that it accompanies
not extreme poverty but a variety of conditions (among which
social well-being is only one) leading to a positive wish not to
have a large family; and that it is exceptionally marked where
there is foresight and thrift—all this points in one and the same
direction. . . .
  Common report that such deliberate regulation of the marriage state, either with the object of limitation of the family, or
(which has the same result) with that of regulating the interval

between births, has become widely prevalent during the past quarter of a century—exactly the period of the decline—reaches us from all sides—from doctors and chemists, from the officers of friendly societies and philanthropists working among the poor, and, most significant of all, from those who are engaged in the very extensive business to which this new social practice has given rise. What is needed to complete the demonstration is direct individual evidence that volitional regulation exists. This the sub-committee of the Fabian Society set itself to obtain. . . . What is recorded here is the result of 316 marriages, and concerns 618 parents—not, of course, an adequate sample of the people of Great Britain, but, being drawn from all parts of the country and from every section of the great 'middle' class, sufficient, perhaps, until more adequate testimony can be obtained, to throw some light on all the previous statistics.

If we take the decade 1890–1899, which may be regarded as the typical period, we find that out of 120 marriages 107 are limited and 13 unlimited, whilst of these 13 five and possibly six were childless at the date of the return. *In this decade, therefore, only seven or possibly eight unlimited fertile marriages are reported out of a total of 120.* . . . the offspring of each limited marriage (judging from the period named) is almost precisely one and a half children per marriage. The average number of children to be expected from each marriage, in England and Wales twenty-five years ago, was at least three times as great! . . . out of the 128 marriages in which the cause of limitation is stated, the poverty of the parents in relation to their standard of comfort is a factor in 73 cases, sexual ill-health (that is, generally, the disturbing effect of child-bearing) in 24 and the other ill-health of the parents in 38 cases. In 24 cases the disinclination of the wife is a factor, and the death of a parent has in eight cases terminated the marriage. . . .

It is not, of course, suggested that so tiny a sample of the kingdom affords any valid ground for inference as to the rest of the community. But it does prove, with logically complete demonstration, that the hypothesis suggested by the statistics of the births in the entire population, and of the births among so large a sample as a million and a quarter persons, is a *vera causa*. Volitional regulation of the marriage state is demonstrably at work in many different parts of Great Britain, among all social grades except probably the very poorest. It cannot rightly be inferred from the particulars of so small a number as 316 marriages that it is at work elsewhere *to the same extent* as among them. The statistics indicate, indeed, that (as might have been expected) the voluntary regulation of the marriage state among this tiny sample of (presumably) very deliberate and foreseeing citizens has resulted in a higher degree of restriction of births than among the population at large. This very fact emphasizes the character of the 'selection' that is going on. And to the present writer, at any rate, it is the differential character of the decline in the birth-rate, rather than the actual extent of the decline, which is of the gravest import.

5)   'The Declining Birth-Rate', *The Times*, 31 October 1913.

Is there a general decline in fertility amongst Western civilized nations? Is the declining birth-rate an index of physical deterioration? Or why are our families smaller than they were? The marriage-rate has scarcely varied during the period under survey; the marriageable age has remained fairly constant, although later marriages are becoming the rule, especially among the professional classes, and the population increases, yet our birth-rate declines. All manner of explanations of this singular phenomenon come to mind—the high standard of living and greater love of pleasure, and the consequent shirking of parental responsibility; the higher education of women and their wider entrance into industrial and professional pursuits; even fear of the pains of parturition have been pressed into the argument; our alleged moral degeneration has been frequently upon the lips of preachers, whilst the view that the most worthy desire to give the fewer children a better chance than the many had in earlier days is quoted with applause. Some biologists have come to the rescue with the plausible statement, which strongly appeals to our pride, that a lower birth-rate is a sign of our advance in the scale of civilization, whilst 'over-populationists' triumphantly argue that a lower birth-rate actually increases the productive capacity of the nation. Indeed, the catalogue of explanation is limited only by the ingenuity of the makers. But when it is finally exhausted, the one question the answer to which all must dread comes uppermost: not whether the birth-rate is falling, but whether the fertility of our people is falling.

6) *The Declining Birth-Rate, its Causes and Effects (Being the Report of and the chief evidence taken by the National Birth-Rate Commission, instituted, with official recognition, by the National Council of Public Morals—for the Promotion of Race Regeneration —Spiritual, Moral and Physical)* (Chapman & Hall, 2nd ed., 1917), 21, 37.

We think that it being clear that contraceptive devices or restriction of the occasions of sexual intercourse are widely employed the existence of such customs must be presumed to have played a part in the decline of the birth-rate, and that it is unnecessary to invoke any hypothetical decline of natural fertility, a course adopted by certain witnesses before us. . . .

We consider that the following propositions are definitely established.

1. That the birth-rate has declined to the extent of approximately one-third within the last thirty-five years.

2. That this decline is not, to any important extent, due to alterations in the marriage-rate, to a rise of the mean age at marriage, or to other causes diminishing the proportion of married women of fertile age in the population.

3. That this decline, although general, has not been uniformly distributed over all sections of the community.

4. That on the whole the decline has been more marked in the more prosperous classes.

5. That the greater incidence of infant mortality upon the less prosperous classes does not reduce their effective fertility to the level of that of the wealthier classes.

We consider that the following propositions, although based upon evidence less substantial than that upon which conclusions (1) to (5) rest, are also sufficiently well established.

6. Conscious limitation of fertility is widely practised among the middle and upper classes, and there is good reason to think that, in addition to other means of limitation, the illegal induction of abortion frequently occurs among the industrial population.

7. There is no reason to believe that the higher education of women (whatever its indirect results upon the birth-rate may be) has any important effect in diminishing their physiological aptitude to bear children.

7)   E. M. Forster, *Howards End* (Arnold, 1910), ch. VI.

'Evening, Mr. Bast.'

'Evening, Mr. Cunningham.'

'Very serious thing this decline of the birthrate in Manchester.'

'I beg your pardon?'

'Very serious thing this decline of the birthrate in Manchester,' repeated Mr. Cunningham, tapping the Sunday paper, in which the calamity in question had just been announced to him.

'Ah, yes,' said Leonard, who was not going to let on that he had not bought a Sunday paper.

'If this kind of thing goes on the population of England will be stationary in 1960.'

'You don't say so.'

'I call it a very serious thing, eh?'

'Good evening, Mr. Cunningham.'

'Good evening, Mr. Bast.'

8)   S. C. Johnson, *A History of Emigration* (Routledge, 1913: reprinted Cass, 1966), ch. XIV.

One person out of every hundred and forty is destined to leave the Mother Country and settle within the Colonies or under the flag of a foreign Power. . . . A question of supreme importance is: 'Can the Homeland afford to spare, in ever-growing numbers, these valuable members of its community?'

It needs little argument to affirm that the migration of such people to foreign lands does involve a loss to the parent State unless the individual sets out to take up work in which his native country is directly interested. . . . Touching the outflow of British subjects to the Colonies the question is of a much more complicated nature. At the present time the United Kingdom stands in need of a strong population to face the competitive strength of Germany; Canada is appealing for men not only to open out her industries, but also to guard against commercial and intellectual absorption by the United States, while the thoughts of Australia are turned towards Japan. Thus it is imperative that the great centres of the Empire should either maintain or increase the strength of their numbers.

How can this be done? The only solution seems to lie in a recourse to colonial emigration. Population, we know, increases more freely in the Colonies than at home; therefore, if a number of the inhabitants of the United Kingdom are permitted to emigrate, it is logical to argue that the Empire will benefit numerically and, consequently, in military and commercial strength. But this giving of population by the Mother Country to her Colonies should not be done in a haphazard way, without any understanding or arrangement as at present holds. . . . If we, in Britain, send the pick of our youth to people the dominions beyond the seas, and if, at the same time, we largely bear the burden of the Empire's defence, then the dominions should be ready to give us the assurance that their support will be forthcoming whenever we require it. . . .

The continuous and constant outflow of British subjects to our overseas possessions is a force of greater power than almost any other in the economy of our Empire. . . . Colonial emigration opens up new fields for the investment of capital, and so brings about the potential increase of Imperial riches; this, in turn, induces greater desires for national safety. To be safe to-day a nation must be strong, and its strength eventually depends on its capacity to pay for its armaments. Any new fund from which armaments or men can be derived is a source of national safety. . . .

Emigration has made our interests world-wide: no movement can be undertaken in any quarter of the globe without its reflection being cast, in some manner, upon the British Empire. Our pride of race has also been enhanced by this important movement, for the vigorous communities which are now proud to call themselves British are a tribute to our capabilities for reducing the undeveloped areas of the world to law, order, and prosperity. This has not been done by high-sounding phraseology, but by a steady stream of emigrants who have successfully transplanted the English type in such diverse quarters of the globe as Canada, South Africa, Australia, and New Zealand.

CHAPTER THREE

Rural and Urban Crisis

Too many countrymen and women, unhappy in their villages (9), were migrating to the towns, often only to meet again in their new urban environment similar problems of bad housing, shortage of employment, and poverty. To pessimistic observers rural decline seemed to be reaching the point where all natural balance between town and country was being lost, with disastrous effects for the towns themselves and for national well-being (10). The people of England were now overwhelmingly urban by residence, and increasingly also urban by birth. Rural 'John Bull' had been replaced by the town 'man in the street' (11, 12). The 'rise of the suburbs' had solved some urban problems, but it had created others, such as social segregation and a sprawling monotony of building (13). Though Ebenezer Howard and other 'garden city' enthusiasts failed in their hopes of exerting a dramatic transforming influence upon London and other big cities (14, 15, 16), their ideas and example at Letchworth did influence standards of town planning and housing (17). Only through town (and country) planning could conditions begin to be improved for most of the new urban masses, and Britain's urbanized future be made as congenial as H. G. Wells foresaw it (18).

9) Letter signed 'Ex-Milkmaid' to the *Sheffield Independent*, reprinted in Mrs Cobden Unwin, *The Land Hunger, Life under Monopoly, Descriptive Letters and Other Testimonies from Those Who Have Suffered* (Fisher Unwin, 1913), 68–71.

Sir,—I am pleased to notice that some of our Liberal members are taking note of the fact that by bettering the conditions of our rural workers they will get to the root cause of so much labour unrest. Only those who have actually experienced the struggle that an ordinary farm labourer and his wife have to make to appear anything like respectable can understand how very hard it is.

There is no other trade—and here let me say the average farm labourer, as we call him, is as skilled a workman at his trade as the average man at other trades, and many a farmer owes much of his success to the advice of his men—at which it is impossible for a workman, by working hard, to earn enough to bring up a family moderately comfortable on his own earnings. In most families at certain seasons of the year the wife and children go out into the fields to earn a little to help make ends meet, and as the average farm labourer's family is more numerous than most others, there is quite plenty for the mother to do at home without helping to earn the living outside. What wonder is it then that when the children are old enough they resolve they will find better conditions for themselves in the towns and lands far away. The drudgery and monotony, lack of educative and recreative opportunity, are too great for the young people of either sex who have any ambition at all. In the villages, and towns, too, of Lincolnshire the manservants and maidservants are engaged yearly and receive their wages yearly, and Bank Holidays—apart from Christmas Day and Good Friday—are unknown to them as holidays. They may get a day's holiday occasionally, but that is the exception rather than the rule.

Another burning question in most rural districts is the shocking housing accommodation. Some of the people have to live in houses quite unfit for human habitation, but they must live somewhere, and there is nothing better to be got. Some time ago I went on a visit not far from John Wesley's old home. In the house was what was supposed to be two bedrooms. In the highest part of the one it was impossible for an average upgrown person to stand upright: the only light was from one glass tile let into the roof, and the bed had to be made on the floor. The only water for drinking purposes was to be had from a ditch which ran near by, and I, who had been accustomed to our good Sheffield water, felt parched for the want of a drink either of nice water or tea.

Whilst so much is being said just now about the farmer and his labourers not being able to afford their contributions under the Insurance Act, it is up to us as a nation to see that they are enabled to do so, either by better wages, or land which they may cultivate for their own interests. Owing to exposure to wet and severe weather the agriculturalist is just as much in need of sickness benefits as other workmen.

Country life has certain advantages over town life in so much as it is healthier, there is less rush and turmoil, and a purer food supply. If added to this we can get a more just remuneration for labour, leisure, and facilities for both bodily and mental recreation, there will no longer be the need of the cry 'back to the land'. Yours, etc.,

Ex-Milkmaid.

10)   B. S. Rowntree and May Kendall, *How the Labourer Lives, a Study of the Rural Labour Problem* (Nelson, 1913), 14–15.

The physique of the town population in the past has been maintained to some extent by constant reinforcement of the anæmic town dwellers by countrymen. But the source from which these reinforcements have been obtained is rapidly becoming exhausted. Already the country dwellers have given up their best, and the prospect, from the point of view of the maintenance of the national physique, is not bright. It is doubtful whether the health conditions in the cities are being improved as rapidly as the vitality of the country districts is being exhausted.

But there is another point of view from which the matter should be considered—that of the national character. Work on the land, in constant contact with natural objects and often in comparative isolation, produces a solid strength of character which our English nation can ill afford to lose. Town dwellers may call the countryman slow or stupid. Certainly he thinks slowly, but his opinions when formed are not infrequently shrewd and sensible, and based on personal observation. The town dweller, on the other hand, suffers from living too quickly and living in a crowd. His opinions are the opinions of the crowd—and a crowd is easily swayed, for evil as well as for good. Not only, then, from the point of view of physical deterioration, is it well that at last the British nation has awakened to the importance of recruiting and developing her rural districts.

11) C. F. G. Masterman (ed.), *The Heart of the Empire, Discussions of Problems of Modern City Life in England* (Fisher Unwin, 1902 ed.), 7–9.

MASTERMAN ON 'REALITIES AT HOME'

At the opening of a new era, it is necessary to recognise that we are face to face with a phenomenon unique in the world's history. Turbulent rioting over military successes,[1] Hooliganism,[1] and a certain temper of fickle excitability has revealed to observers during the past few months that a new race, hitherto unreckoned and of incalculable action, is entering the sphere of practical importance—the 'City type' of the coming years; the 'street-bred' people of the twentieth century; the 'new generation knocking at our doors'.

The England of the past has been an England of reserved, silent men, dispersed in small towns, villages, and country homes. The England of the future is an England packed tightly in such gigantic aggregations of population as the world has never before seen. The change has been largely concealed by the perpetual swarm of immigrants from the surrounding districts, which has permeated the whole of such a town as London with a healthy, energetic population reared amidst the fresh air and quieting influences of the life of the fields. But in the past twenty-five years a force has been operating in the raw material of which the city is composed. The texture itself has been transformed as by some subtle alchemy. The second generation of the immigrants has been reared in the courts and crowded ways of the great metropolis, with cramped physical accessories, hot, fretful life, and long hours of sedentary or unhealthy toil. The problem of the coming years is just the problem of this New Town type; upon their development and action depend the future progress of the Anglo-Saxon Race, and for the next half-century at least the policy of the British Empire in the world. . . . Here, then, in London we shall find manifest both the diminishing virulence of the older social

[1] The national hysteria on hearing the news of the relief of Mafeking in May 1900 added the verb 'to maffick' to the language, defined by the *Oxford English Dictionary* as 'to indulge in extravagant demonstrations of exultation'. The same dictionary traces 'hooligan' to the London backstreets of 1898, quoting the *Daily News*, 26 July: 'It is no wonder . . . that Hooligan gangs are bred in these vile, miasmatic byways.' See also E. Partridge, *Dictionary of Slang and Unconventional English* (5th ed., 1961), 403, 1136.

diseases and the steadily deepening gravity of the problem of the coming race.

12)   C. F. G. Masterman (ed.), *The Heart of the Empire, Discussions of Problems of Modern City Life in England* (Fisher Unwin, 1902 ed.), 263–4.

F. W. HEAD ON 'THE CHURCH AND THE PEOPLE'

The background of all this life of course is the home. And this is known to the outside world by the title of 'the Housing Question'. But to the working man it is no question of a discussion of possible solutions on a large scale. There is the immediate, everyday, unending though half-unconscious sense of confinement. Either two or three rooms on the average have to be a home for the father, mother, and a family increasing and growing up. And the weariness of the day's work can seldom look forward to the privacy of quiet which will make up for the strain of toil.

Such is the life of M. or N., labourer. It goes on from the time of early youth until old age makes its continuance impossible. Except for a Bank Holiday four times a year there is no rest, no time off. The prevailing attitude of life is therefore materialistic. The two things that are certain are the satisfaction of eating and drinking and the requirement of propagating the species. Beyond this there is little time for thought, and what there is is not for edification.

Above this class there comes the higher stratum of the skilled artisan, the shop assistant, or the small clerk. With him, of course, the conditions of life are more favourable, for his income will range from thirty shillings to two pounds a week. He will probably begin work at eight instead of six, and will live in four rooms instead of three. But his daily work will be hardly more interesting, and the word 'monotony' might be spelt over his life in just the same way.

Sunday is a great break in the week here too. But the pleasure is a little less materialistic than in the other case. The Sunday dinner is still the culminating point to the day, but the shirt-sleeves element tends rather to become a black-coated one. A new ideal, in fact, begins to appear—the ideal of outward respectability. This in a large degree rests on the fact of the extra room in the home. The sense of confinement gives place to a consciousness of expanse. The father need not always have his children with him. There is a sacred room where the blinds hang down all day and there are antimacassars. It is the parlour. And with the parlour there is less need for the public-house. The head of the house therefore prides himself on drinking at home, nor does he always go out to the bar.

13) 'The Formation of London Suburbs,' *The Times,* 25 June 1904.

London proper—the county of London—increases at the rate of over 300,000 persons every decade; in other words the capital adds to her children a population nearly equal to that of the largest town in the Dominion of Canada. But land within the county is now for the most part occupied, and the growth of London is forced outwards on all sides. Greater London—roughly, the area within 15 miles of Charing Cross—increased by 900,000 souls between 1891 and 1901; thus the increase in the ring of suburbs outside the county was just double that of the county. Since the last census the growth has probably been still more rapid, for the number of new houses built within the last three or four years has largely exceeded any previous average. A visit to any of the outer suburbs will disclose streets barely formed and rows of houses barely finished; and the statistics of the builders' activity confirm the impression thus produced.

The question, then, of the mode in which London is to grow is not a trivial one. . . . It is not necessary that the heart of a town should be overcrowded and insanitary; it is not necessary that the outskirts should be ugly and depressing. Something has been done to prevent the evils of bad drainage and bad water; overcrowding is recognised as a disease to be combated; but no attempt has yet been made to regulate, in the interests of all classes, the formation and development of suburbs.

Formerly, indeed, the manner of suburban extension seemed to affect mainly the middle classes supposed to be able to take care of themselves. But this is no longer the case. The habit of living at a distance from the scene of work has spread from the merchant and the clerk to the artisan, and one has only to observe the substitution of small housés for large in the older suburbs, and the streets of cottages in new extensions, to realize that the suburb is now mainly the residence of the family of small means—say, from £100 to £300 per annum. The man of comfortable income no longer cares for suburban life; a small flat within a cab drive of Charing Cross and a cottage some twenty to forty miles out take the place of the spacious villa with its four or five acres at Clapham or Wimbledon. And not only is the suburb becoming from natural causes the residence of the clerk and the thriving artisan; experiments are on foot to attract thither those for whom Parliament has authorised local authorities to provide dwellings. The London County Council has launched two considerable housing schemes in the suburbs, one on the south, another on the north of the Metropolis; and Mr. Charles Booth has declared that the remedy for congested districts is to be found in cheap means of transit to the fringe of London . . . railways, tramways, omnibuses, all means of cheap transit, multiply and increase exceedingly; and it becomes every day more easy to cover a considerable distance in a short time at small expense. No doubt much may be done to replace slums in central London by sanitary dwellings for the working classes; but every success of this kind means provision for fewer residents than before; and the surplus drifts away to the suburbs. The suburbs become more and more the abode of working London. . . .

The actual process of suburb forming at the present day is but too apparent. The speculative builder descends upon green fields, cuts straight roads through them, and plants as many houses on a given space as he thinks he can let. Formerly detached or semi-detached villas with small gardens were his staple in trade. But the day for these seems to have gone by. Only in more favoured spots are they to be found; elsewhere rows of small houses, either one-storied cottages, or buildings let in two flats, the upper story having a separate entrance, take their place. A tenement of this kind is said to let at about £20 to £25 a year; and there is a certain neatness about its external appointments when new. But the effect of street after street of such houses with an admixture of second-rate shops, lumber yards, and public houses is very dreary. Practically the town is reproduced in its least interesting or stimulating form. The hurry and bustle, the lights and excitement of London are gone; but they are not replaced by the repose of green grass and waving trees, and bright flowers and wide spaces. To land the artisan or the clerk in such surroundings after a hard day's work scarcely repays him for the journey from town; to surround London with acres of such streets is to produce a district of appalling monotony, ugliness and dullness. And every suburban extension makes existing suburbs less desirable. Fifty years ago Brixton and Clapham were on the edge of the country; a walk would take one into lanes and meadows. Now London stretches to Croydon. It is no longer possible to escape from the dull suburbs into unspoiled country. It is the more necessary, if possible, to redeem the suburb from meanness and squalor.

14)   E. Howard, *Garden Cities of Tomorrow* (Sonnenschein, 1902; reprinted Faber, 1965), 42, 45–7, 127, 155–6.

It is wellnigh universally agreed by men of all parties, not only in England, but all over Europe and America and our colonies, that it is deeply to be deplored that the people should continue to stream into the already over-crowded cities, and should thus further deplete the country districts. . . . The question is universally considered as though it were now, and for ever must remain, quite impossible for working people to live in the country and yet be engaged in pursuits other than agricultural; as though crowded, unhealthy cities were the last word of economic science; and as if our present form of industry, in which sharp lines divide agricultural from industrial pursuits, were necessarily an enduring one. This fallacy is the very common one of ignoring altogether the possibility of alternatives other than those presented to the mind. There are in reality not only, as is so constantly assumed, two alternatives —town life and country life—but a third alternative, in which all the advantages of the most energetic and active town life, with all the beauty and delight of the country, may be secured in perfect combination; and the certainty of being able to live this life will be the magnet which will produce the effect for which we are all striving—the spontaneous movement of the people from our crowded cities to the bosom of our kindly mother earth, at once the source of life, of happiness, of wealth, and of power. The town and the country may, therefore, be regarded as two magnets, each striving to draw the people to itself—a rivalry which a new form of life, partaking of the nature of both, comes to take part in. This may be illustrated by a diagram of 'The Three Magnets', in which the chief advantages of the Town and of the Country are set forth with their corresponding drawbacks, while the advantages of the Town-Country are seen to be free from the disadvantages of either. . . .

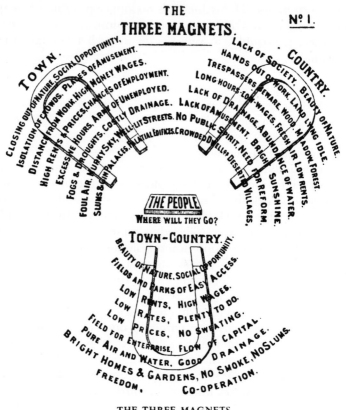

THE THREE MAGNETS

My proposal is that there should be an earnest attempt made to organize a migratory movement of population from our overcrowded centres to sparsely settled rural districts; that the mind of the public should not be confused, or the efforts of organizers wasted in a premature attempt to accomplish this work on a national scale, but that great thought and attention shall be first concentrated on a single movement yet one sufficiently large to be at once attractive and resourceful; that the migrants shall be guaranteed (by the making of suitable arrangements before the movement commences) that the whole increase in land values due to their migration shall be secured to them; that this be done by creating an organization, which, while permitting its members to do those things which are good in their own eyes (provided they infringe not the rights of others) shall receive all 'rate-rents' and expend them in those public works which the migratory movement renders necessary or expedient—thus eliminating rates, or, at least, greatly reducing the necessity for any compulsory levy; and that the golden opportunity afforded by the fact that the land to be settled upon has but few buildings or works upon it, shall be availed of in the fullest manner, by so laying out a Garden City that, as it grows, the free gifts of Nature—fresh air, sunlight, breathing room and playing room—shall be still retained in all needed abundance, and by so employing the resources of modern science that Art may supplement Nature, and life may become an abiding joy and delight. . . .

We may next notice, very briefly, the bearing of this migration of population upon two great problems—the problem of the housing of the people of London, and the problem of finding employment for those who remain. The rents now paid by the working population of London, for accommodation most miserable and insufficient, represents each year a larger and larger proportion of income, while the cost of moving to and from work, continually increasing, often represents in time and money a very considerable tax. But imagine the population of London falling, and falling rapidly; the migrating people establishing themselves where rents are extremely low, and where their work is within easy walking distance of their homes! Obviously, house-property in London will fall in rental value, and fall enormously. Slum property will sink to zero, and the whole working population will move into houses of a class quite above those which they can now afford to occupy. Families which are now compelled to huddle together in one room will be able to rent five or six, and thus will the housing problem temporarily solve itself by the simple process of a diminution in the numbers of the tenants.

But what will become of this slum property? Its power to extort a large proportion of the hard earnings of the London poor gone for ever, will it yet remain an eye-sore and a blot, though no longer a danger to health and an outrage on decency? No. These wretched slums will be pulled down, and their sites occupied by parks, recreation grounds, and allotment gardens. And this change, as well as many others, will be effected, not at the expense of the ratepayers, but almost entirely at the expense of the landlord class: in this sense, at least, that such ground rents as are still paid by the people of London in respect of those classes of property which retain some rental value will have to bear the burden of improving the city. Nor will, I think, the compulsion of any Act of Parliament be necessary to effect this result: it will probably be achieved by the voluntary action of the landowners, compelled, by a Nemesis from whom there is no escape, to make some restitution for the great injustice which they have so long committed.

For observe what must inevitably happen. A vast field of employment being opened outside London, unless a corresponding field of employment is opened within it, London must die—when the landowners will be in a sorry plight. Elsewhere new cities are being built: London then must be transformed.

15)   G. B. Shaw, *John Bull's Other Island* (1904), Act I.

Broadbent.   Have you ever heard of Garden City?

Tim (*doubtfully*).   D'ye mane Heavn?

Broadbent.   Heaven! No: it's near Hitchin. If you can spare half an hour I'll go into it with you.

Tim.   I tell you what. Gimme a prospectus. Lemme take it home and reflect on it.

Broadbent.   Youre quite right. I will. (*He gives him a copy of Mr. Ebenezer Howard's book, and several pamphlets.*) You understand that the map of the city—the circular construction—is only a suggestion.

Tim.   I'll make a careful note o that (*looking dazedly at the map*).

Broadbent.   What I say is, why not start a Garden City in Ireland?

Tim (*with enthusiasm*).   Thats just what was on the tip o me tongue to ask you. Why not? (*Defiantly*) Tell me why not.

16) 'Civilization and Transport,' *The Times*, 17 September 1908.

It is true that the poor now are apt to prefer the excitement of the town to the dullness of the country. But the country has been made dull by the growth of great towns and the concentration of all life into them. If this concentration ceased, if there were more numerous and smaller towns, free from provincial stagnation, the country would lose its dullness and huge cities would lose their attraction. Already there is a conscious effort towards diffusion, helped even now by the most modern improvements in transport, and already the size of our greatest towns is becoming a serious material disadvantage to their inhabitants. The amount of time and energy and money wasted every day in getting about London, and into it and out of it, is so enormous that, if there is much further increase in that waste, it will go far to nullify even the present advantages of concentration. Those advantages are all material. Our spiritual instincts revolt against them, and their revolt grows stronger every day. Every further advance in transport will help that revolt; and perhaps some of us will live to see the decline of London brought about by a great ring of subsidiary towns, each growing daily into greater independence and keener competition with it. Thus it may be that all the conditions of our life will be swiftly altered again, and for the better. But the improvement will be great only if we have learnt the lesson of the past and refuse to be taken by surprise yet again. Little towns can be as squalid as big ones, and even more barbarous, as any one can see in Yorkshire and Lancashire and the Black Country. A mere diffusion of London slums will not help us. We must be ready with our ideal of the small town of the future, and we must have the determination to make that ideal come true.

17) R. Unwin, *Town Planning in Practice, an Introduction to the Art of Designing Cities and Suburbs* (Fisher Unwin, 1909), ch. I.

We have forgotten that endless rows of brick boxes, looking out upon dreary streets and squalid backyards, are not really homes for people, and can never become such, however complete may be the drainage system, however pure the water supply, or however detailed the bye-laws under which they are built. Important as all these provisions for man's material needs and sanitary existence are, they do not suffice. There is needed the vivifying touch of art which would give completeness and increase their value tenfold; there is needed just that imaginative treatment which could transform the whole. . . . It is the lack of beauty, of the amenities of life, more than anything else which obliges us to admit that our work of town building in the past century has not been well done. Not even the poor can live by bread alone; and substantial as are the material boons which may be derived from such powers for the control of town development as we hope our municipalities will soon possess, the force which is behind this movement is derived far more from the desire for something beyond these boons, from the hope that through them something of beauty may be restored to town life. We shall, indeed, need to carry much further the good work begun by our building bye-laws. We shall need to secure still more open ground, air-space, and sunlight for each dwelling; we shall need to make proper provision for parks and playgrounds, to control our streets, to plan their direction, their width, and their character, so that they may in the best possible way minister to the convenience of the community. We shall need power to reserve suitable areas for factories, where they will have every convenience for their work and cause the minimum of nuisance to their neighbours. All these practical advantages, and much more, may be secured by the exercise of powers for town planning; but above all, we need to infuse the spirit of the artist into our work. . . .

Civic art is too often understood to consist in filling our streets with marble fountains, dotting our squares with groups of statuary, twining our lamp-posts with wriggling .acanthus leaves or dolphins' tails, and our buildings with meaningless bunches of fruit and flowers tied up with impossible stone ribbons. William Morris said: 'Beauty, which is what is meant by Art, using the word in its widest sense, is, I contend, no mere accident of human life which people can take or leave as they choose, but a positive necessity of life, if we are to live as Nature meant us to—that is, unless we are content to be less than men.' The art which he meant works from within outward; the beauty which he regarded as necessary to life is not a quality which can be plastered on the outside. . . .

First, let our markets be well built and our cottage areas well laid out; then there will soon grow up such a full civic life, such a joy and pride in the city as will seek expression in adornment. . . . The concentration of industry, the decay of agriculture, the growing contrast in the conditions of life offered in the country and the town, have all had their influence in leading people in such vast numbers to forsake the lonely cottage on the hillside or the sleeping village in the hollow in favour of the dirty street in the slum town. The impulse partly springs from the desire for higher wages and the attraction of varied amusement and flaring gas lamps; but it equally arises from the desire for a greater knowledge, wider experience and fuller life generally which men realize they can only find in closer association with their fellows. But whatever their motives in leaving their villages, the people have broken many old ties of interest and attachment; it should be our aim to secure that in going to the city they find new ties, new interests, new hopes, and that general atmosphere which will create for them new homes and new local patriotism.

18) H. G. Wells, *Anticipations of the Reaction of Mechanical and Scientific Progress upon Human Life and Thought* (Chapman & Hall, 1904 ed.), 25–7.

Enough has been said to demonstrate that old 'town' and 'city' will be, in truth, terms as obsolete as 'mail coach'. For these new areas that will grow out of them we want a term, and the administrative 'urban district' presents itself with a convenient air of suggestion. We may for our present purposes call these coming town provinces 'urban regions'. Practically, by a process of confluence, the whole of Great Britain south of the Highlands seems destined to become such an urban region, laced all together not only by railway and telegraph, but by novel roads such as we forecast in the former chapter, and by a dense network of telephones, parcels delivery tubes, and the like nervous and arterial connections.

It will certainly be a curious and varied region, far less monotonous than our present English world, still in its thinner regions, at any rate, wooded, perhaps rather more abundantly wooded, breaking continually into park and garden, and with everywhere a scattering of houses. These will not, as a rule, I should fancy, follow the fashion of the vulgar ready-built villas of the existing suburb, because the freedom people will be able to exercise in the choice of a site will rob the 'building estate' promoter of his local advantage; in many cases the houses may very probably be personal homes, built for themselves as much as the Tudor manor-houses were, and even, in some cases, as æsthetically right. Each district, I am inclined to think, will develop its own differences of type and style. As one travels through the urban region, one will traverse open, breezy, 'horsey' suburbs, smart white gates and palings everywhere, good turf, a Grand Stand shining pleasantly; gardening districts all set with gables and roses, holly hedges, and emerald lawns; pleasant homes among heathery moorlands and golf links, and river districts with gaily painted boat-houses peeping from the osiers. Then presently a gathering of houses closer together, and a promenade and a whiff of band and dresses, and then, perhaps, a little island of agriculture, hops, or straw-berry gardens, fields of grey-plumed artichokes, white-painted orchard, or brightly neat poultry farm. Through the varied country the new wide roads will run, here cutting through a crest and there running like some colossal aqueduct across a valley, swarming always with a multitudinous traffic of bright, swift (and not necessarily ugly) mechanisms; and everywhere amidst the fields and trees linking wires will stretch from pole to pole. Ever and again there will appear a cluster of cottages —cottages into which we shall presently look more closely— about some works or workings, works, it may be, with the smoky chimney of to-day replaced by a gaily painted wind-wheel or waterwheel to gather and store the force for the machinery; and ever and again will come a little town, with its cherished ancient church or cathedral, its school buildings and museums, its railway-station, perhaps its fire-station, its inns and restaurants, and with all the wires of the countryside converging to its offices. All that is pleasant and fair of our present countryside may conceivably still be there among the other things. There is no reason why the essential charm of the country should disappear; the new roads will not supersede the present high roads, which will still be necessary for horses and subsidiary traffic; and the lanes and hedges, the field paths and wild flowers, will still have their ample justification. A certain lack of solitude there may be perhaps. . . .

And as for the world beyond our urban regions? The same line of reasoning that leads to the expectation that the city will diffuse itself until it has taken up considerable areas and many of the characteristics, the greenness, the fresh air, of what is now country, leads us to suppose also that the country will take to itself many of the qualities of the city. The old antithesis will indeed cease, the boundary lines will altogether disappear; it will become, indeed, merely a question of more or less populous.

CHAPTER FOUR

Class and Behaviour

Mass production, mass communication and mass education, on the one hand, plus heavy taxation of the rich, on the other, have significantly reduced class differences during the course of the twentieth century—differences in styles of life, manners, clothes, possessions, interests and accent. One 1912 writer was already claiming that it was becoming 'more and more difficult to tell from their appearance to what class persons accidentally encountered belong—until they open their mouths' (*What the Worker Wants*, 158). But in the Edwardian years, before the impact of two world wars, before the rise of the BBC and the coming of the 'affluent society', this process of standardization was only in its early stages (19, 20), as Gissing's story of social aspiration collapsing under social inadequacy made plain (21). The Edwardians revelled in distinctions between and within classes, not least round and within the middle class (22). Middle-class emphasis upon status, social observances and material possessions was persistently attacked by such leading Edwardian writers as Bennett (23), Galsworthy (24), and Shaw (25). Yet many of the Edwardian middle classes continued to practice the Victorian virtues of industry, sobriety, foresight, and love of family and home, people such as 'Robert Thorne', the London clerk, raising a family on little more than £100 a year (26). Admittedly, the practice of these virtues could bring with it smugness and narrowness in social and political attitudes, including a strong belief in the fecklessness of the working classes. But dangerous rot in the Edwardian social fabric was only to be found nearer the top. While middle-class suburbia's 'keeping up with the Joneses' was relatively innocent, the 'conspicuous consumption' of the plutocrats was gross and decadent; and many social critics drew the moral from the grim fate of the *Titanic*, though left-wing writers noted how even in this disaster the rich remained privileged (27, 28). Socialist Chiozza Money challengingly measured the wealth gap in precise statistical terms, presenting his conclusions with striking visual simplicity (29). Liberal Winston Churchill, while President of the Board of Trade in 1909, convinced himself (erroneously) that the rich were actually getting richer, and also (correctly) that the wages of the workers were stationary (30). Working men themselves, now increasingly seeing and reading about the wealthy, were encouraged thereby not so much to demand the destruction of the rich as to be given the means in some modest degree to live more like them (31). Working-class drunkenness remained a serious problem, but a reducing one, more an effect than a cause of poverty, notwithstanding uninformed middle-class opinion to the contrary (32). Widening popular interest in sport—especially in watching football—was providing one alternative to heavy drinking, a benefit unrecognized by *Punch* (33). Active religion attracted only a minority of the working classes (34, 35, 36), but relatively few followed Blatchford into militant atheism (37).

19)   F. G. D'Aeth, 'Present Tendencies of Class Differentiation', *Sociological Review*, III (Sherratt & Hughes, 1910), 270–1.

There may be said to be in theory two standards of life—the standard of simple necessities, and the standard of refined and educated necessities. The former can be secured for an average family on about 25/- a week; the latter on about £600 a year.

People do not, however, fall exactly into these two groups, receiving these two sets of wages and living at these two theoretic standards. Instead we find a considerable degree of variation. These varying standards tend to fall into seven groups, a brief description of which may be given. Such brevity is obviously unsatisfactory. A few salient features, indicative of the general character of the class, alone can be stated. Exceptions can be made to each statement.

A.   The Loafer. *Standard*—18/- a week; *Housing*—slum, cellar dwelling or single room, no proper furniture; *Occupation* —irregular labour, or drinks a higher wage.

B.   Low-skilled labour. *Standard*—25/- a week; *Housing*— four-roomed house: scanty but sufficient furniture; *Occupation* —low-skilled labour: lowest type clerk, shop assistant, etc.;

Social customs—some change clothes and put on collar in evening; *Ability*—general intelligence rather low; need to be told.

C.   Artizan. *Standard*—45/-; *Housing*—five-roomed house, with parlour: homely but comfortable furniture; *Occupations*— very varied: skilled labourers, foremen, petty officers, clerks, smaller officials, etc.; *Social customs*—table set for meals: married children visit parents on Sundays; *Ability*—technical skill; a very fair general intelligence; shrewd at times; a simple mind, not following a connected argument; laborious procedure at business meetings.

D.   Smaller Shopkeeper and clerk. *Standard*—£3 a week; *Housing*—above shop or £25 to £30 a year; *Occupation*—very varied; clerks, shopkeepers and tradesmen, commercial travellers, printers, engineers, etc., elementary school teachers, a few ministers; *Social customs*—furnish their houses; entertain visitors; some have a young servant: *Ability*—varied; either a high degree of technical skill; or a little capital and managing a business; shrewd in small matters; read magazines; express superficial opinions freely upon all subjects: *Education*—elementary school; in some cases a technical career.

E.   Smaller Business Class. *Standard*—£300 a year: *House* —£48: *Occupation*—various forms of business; the smaller manufacturer and professional man: *Social customs*—visiting; cards; some dine late: *Ability*—business management or clerical skill, with steadiness and trustworthiness and some conscious refinement of manner; readers; interested popularly in scientific and public affairs: *Education*—grammar school.

F.   Professional and Administrative Class. *Standard*—£600 a year: *House*—£60–£80: *Occupation*—heads of business firms, professional men, administrative posts: *Education*—secondary or public school, university generally.

G.   The Rich. *Standard*—£2,000 and upwards: *Occupation* —heads of firms, manufacturers, a few salaried posts: *Education* —public school, university.

Of these groups, the first three (A, B, C) represent the development of the old working class and tend to centre round the simpler of the two theoretic standards. A represents the refuse of a race; C is a solid, independent and valuable class in society. Groups E, F, G represent the fluctuation round the second theoretic standard. E possesses the elements of refinement; provincialisms in speech are avoided, its sons are selected as clerks, etc., in good class businesses, *e.g.*, banking, insurance. F enables the expression of the full degree of cultured life. G enables the satisfaction of luxurious habits.

The only available figures bearing upon the numerical extent of these different classes seem to be those of Mr. Chiozza Money. These are given below and relate to the year 1903–4:—

Persons with incomes of less than £160 a year
  and their families - - - - - - 38,000,000

Persons with incomes of between -			
	-	£160 and £400	3,035,000
,,		£400 and £500	265,000
,,		£500 and £600	145,000
,,		£600 and £700	65,000
Unplaced -	-	- - - -	240,000
			3,750,000
Persons with incomes of £700 and over		- -	1,250,000
			43,000,000

Classes A, B, C, D represent therefore the great bulk of the population.

20) S. Reynolds, *Seems So! A Working-Class View of Politics* (Macmillan, 1911), xviii–ix.

In a country where, being poor, one may not even sleep under the sky without money in one's pocket, the economic difference tells most in the long run. Between master and man, ruler and ruled, top-dog and under-dog; the man who has something to start on and something to fall back on, and the man who has neither; the man who looks forward to a competency at the end of his working days, and the man who can only look forward to a bare subsistence at best; the man to whom failure means bankruptcy and diminished ease, and the man to whom it means starvation for himself and for his wife and children; between the man of one tradition and of another, of one education and of another, of one domestic habit and of another, of one class-feeling and of another class-feeling—that is where the line of cleavage runs through town and country alike. Compared with that wide cleavage, the political cleft is narrow and artificial. It serves to obscure the issue, and is used for that purpose. Whatever else he may be, a working man is first and foremost a working man. One recognizes it, feels it, without further inquiry. He betrays it as indefinably and as certainly as a man betrays himself who has been accustomed to authority. It is the common opinion and point of view, the underlying feeling of working men in general, that we have tried to set forth.

Several times we have been asked, 'Why be so down on the likes o' they? Most of them mean very well, and are very decent people. Do you hate the likes o' they?' On the contrary, we have many good friends among the likes o' they, and often great pleasure in their company. But it is impossible to attack a system—the class system or any other—without attacking those who carry it out and are made what they are by it; those who, collectively, are the system. Dives may have been a kindly old boy, and Lazarus a lazy sponger, but the point of the parable remains just the same. Class antagonism is a very powerful force, growing rather than diminishing, acting in all sorts of unsuspected ways, cropping up in all sorts of unexpected places. Let things go wrong, make a false step, and in a moment it flashes out: 'Ignorant fellow!'—'Bloody gen'leman!' It was there, beneath, all the time. Each side wrongs the other; but neither side seems fully to realize how unconsciously most of the wrong is done, how much it is a matter of upbringing.

21)   G. Gissing, *The Private Papers of Henry Ryecroft* (Constable, 1903), 122–4.

I was taking a meal once at a London restaurant—not one of the great eating-places to which men most resort, but a small establishment on the same model in a quiet neighbour-hood—when there entered, and sat down at the next table, a young man of the working class, whose dress betokened holiday. A glance told me that he felt anything but at ease; his mind misgave him as he looked about the long room and at the table before him; and when a waiter came to offer him the card, he stared blankly in sheepish confusion. Some strange windfall, no doubt, had emboldened him to enter for the first time such a place as this, and now that he was here, he heartily wished himself out in the street again. However, aided by the waiter's suggestions, he gave an order for a beef-steak and vegetables. When the dish was served, the poor fellow simply could not make a start upon it; he was embarrassed by the display of knives and forks, by the arrangement of the dishes, by the sauce bottles and the cruet-stand, above all, no doubt, by the assembly of people not of his class, and the unwonted experience of being waited upon by a man with a long shirt-front. He grew red; he made the clumsiest and most futile efforts to transport the meat to his plate; food was there before him, but, like a very Tantalus, he was forbidden to enjoy it. Observing with all discretion, I at length saw him pull out his pocket handkerchief, spread it on the table, and, with a sudden effort, fork the meat off the dish into this receptacle. The waiter, aware by this time of the customer's difficulty, came up and spoke a word to him. Abashed into anger, the young man roughly asked what he had to pay. It ended in the waiter's bringing a newspaper, wherein he helped to wrap up meat and vegetables. Money was flung down, and the victim of a mistaken ambition hurriedly departed, to satisfy his hunger amid less unfamiliar surroundings.

It was a striking and unpleasant illustration of social differences. Could such a thing happen in any country but England? I doubt it. The sufferer was of decent appearance, and, with ordinary self-command, might have taken his meal in the restaurant like any one else, quite unnoticed. But he belonged to a class which, among all classes in the world, is distinguished by native clownishness and by unpliability to novel circumstance. The English lower ranks had need be marked by certain peculiar virtues to atone for their deficiencies in other respects.

22)   G. S. Street, 'English Classes', in *Books and Things* (Duckworth, 1905), 161–7.

I have been reading an account of a play in which the situations arose (the writer said) out of the marriage of an 'upper-middle-class' man to a 'lower-middle-class' woman. Not pretty phrases, are they? How far they imply, as in the case of the play they were meant to imply, genuine and useful distinctions of culture and taste, how far their rather rough and unsympathetic tone of the social drill-sergeant is really practical, are questions to which in my casual way I shall return. But the unlovely phrases set me thinking first of all of the extraordinary complexity and involution of this class business in England. I wish that some philosopher with a strictly scientific habit of mind but a trivial taste would set himself to a thorough classification, with tables and diagrams, of our classes. He would have to determine first the several grades in so far as they can be distinguished, and next (of course keeping to the average) how each grade respects or despises the grades above or below it. Thus, if the classes were A, B, and C, and so on, they would be arranged in several tables in accordance with the ideas of precedence held by each of these classes, A, B, and C, etc., with regard to itself and the others. So if you are a wholesale bootmaker you could find out at a glance how a peer, a barrister, or a boot-black ranked you in the social scale. There might also be a table expressing what distinctions, if any, are made by intelligent people who try to see men as they are. All this would be the merest ground plan of the work, of course. A multitude of excursuses and appendices would be needed, and something colossal in the way of prolegomena. Such a work, when completed, would be of immense value to the foreigner, to whom the present confusion must be bewildering. And incidentally it would enable me when my friend Jones, an ordinary barrister, speaks contemptuously of 'the middle classes', to know (a) what he means by the middle classes; (b) if he thinks he belongs to them; and (c) if he thinks I belong to them. . . .

The distinction between trade and professions is still pushed to an incredibly puerile minuteness. A and B are next-door shopkeepers; A makes a parson of his son, B takes his into the business; A's grandson despises B's grandson on the score of his inferior birth. And that sort of imbecility in varying degrees runs through English life, and plays havoc (among fools, of course) with freedom and courtesy.

A man is ranked altogether differently by different people. Mr. Levantheim, whose father was a Frankfort money-lender, who owns three large houses and consorts with dukes, regards himself—or certainly Mrs. Levantheim regards herself—as definitely of the aristocracy, the natural superior of Jones and me, but Jones regards Levantheim as unfit to black his (Jones's) boots. Some people, again, still regard players as persons of no account, others as somewhere in precedence between earls and marquises, 'actor-managers' between royal and ordinary dukes, and so forth. An exhaustive tabulation would make these obscure things plain.

As for the intelligent Englishman who respects himself for what he may be and tries to see other men as they are, his position is probably something as follows. One class he admits to be apart. So long as the institution of monarchy remains with us he admits it is a logical and convenient corollary that royalty is socially a definitely superior class, entitled to a deference not given to others. Americans, if I may say so, proud of their own equality, are inclined to attribute to him a sort of servility towards royalty from which he is free; in some past reigns his criticism has been of the freest, and he is happy in this and the last that it has not been stimulated. For the aristocracy, if he belongs to it, it is quite possible that he has still a feeling of caste he would not confess—that is merely human; if he does not, he grants it no social privileges outside the House of Lords, or in such trifles as precedence at formal dinners. Save for the legislative privilege—a political question not for these pages—he regards it as a pleasantly picturesque survival. There, again, Americans sometimes misjudge him, sometimes take (I have been told) when they join our aristocracy a view of their position he does not share. If I may put in a word for myself, I confess to rather a liking for your genuine old families, people who represent the direct line of a knightly house for eight or nine hundred years; but they are very few, and are hardly to be found among our titles. The intelligent Englishman (to go back to him) takes little account indeed of all the minor distinctions which have their absurd value only in the small radius about them. For it is a curious fact, which they who talk of classes and masses quite forget, that the lower you go in the social scale the keener are the differences.

The philosophy of the matter I take to be roughly that our system of classes is in essence an inconvenient survival from a caste system that had its meaning and uses. Inconvenient, if not worse, I say, for this reason; unintelligent Englishmen—and most people everywhere are unintelligent—who admit that A, B, and C classes are superior to themselves, thereby weaken that sense of possession in the country which a citizen should feel with no qualification. So much, I think, is true, but

I believe the inconvenience to be passing away. The usefulness of those terms we started withal, your upper-middle and your lower-middle? Infinitesimal, I do believe. They may still roughly express real differences in culture and taste, but in my own experience the exceptions are so many, we are being so rapidly mixed up, we are growing so rapidly in a rough way alike—save always the really cultivated, who must always be few and for whose qualities class is no sort of guarantee—that I think it hardly worth while to keep them up. Hardly worth their ugliness.

23)   A. Bennett, 'Middle Class' (1909), in *Books and Persons* (Chatto & Windus, 1920), 67–70.

Three hundred and seventy-five thousand persons paid income-tax last year, under protest: they stand for the existence of perhaps a million souls, and this million is a handful floating more or less easily on the surface of the forty millions of the population. The great majority of my readers must be somewhere in this million. There can be few hirers of books who neither pay income-tax nor live on terms of dependent equality with those who pay it. I see at the counters people on whose foreheads it is written that they know themselves to be the salt of the earth. Their assured, curt voices, their proud carriage, their clothes, the similarity of their manners, all show that they belong to a caste and that the caste has been successful in the struggle for life. It is called the middle-class, but it ought to be called the upper-class, for nearly everything is below it. I go to the Stores, to Harrod's Stores, to Barker's, to Rumpelmeyer's, to the Royal Academy, and to a dozen clubs in Albemarle Street and Dover Street, and I see again just the same crowd, well-fed, well-dressed, completely free from the cares which beset at least five-sixths of the English race. They have worries; they take taxis because they must not indulge in motor-cars, hansoms because taxis are an extravagance, and omnibuses because they really must economize. But they never look twice at twopence. They curse the injustice of fate, but secretly they are aware of their luck. When they have nothing to do, they say, in effect: 'Let's go out and spend something.' And they go out. They spend their lives in spending. They deliberately gaze into shop windows in order to discover an outlet for their money. You can catch them at it any day. . . .

Chief among its characteristics—after its sincere religious worship of money and financial success—I should put its intense self-consciousness as a class. The world is a steamer in which it is travelling saloon. Occasionally it goes to look over from the promenade deck at the steerage. Its feelings towards the steerage are kindly. But the tone in which it says 'the steerage' cuts the steerage off from it more effectually than many bulkheads. You perceive also from that tone that it could never be surprised by anything that the steerage might do. Curious social phenomenon, the steerage! In the saloon there runs a code, the only possible code, the final code; and it is observed. If it is not observed, the infraction causes pain, distress. Another marked characteristic is its gigantic temperamental dullness, unresponsiveness to external suggestion, a lack of humour—in short, a heavy and half-honest stupidity: ultimate product of gross prosperity, too much exercise, too much sleep. Then I notice a grim passion for the *status quo*. This is natural. Let these people exclaim as they will against the structure of society, the last thing they desire is to alter it. This passion shows itself in a naïve admiration for everything that has survived its original usefulness. . . . The passion for the *status quo* also shows itself in a general defensive, sullen hatred of all ideas whatever. You cannot argue with these people. 'Do you really think so?' they will politely murmur, when you have asserted your belief that the earth is round, or something like that. And their tone says: 'Would you mind very much if we leave this painful subject? My feelings on it are too deep for utterance.' Lastly, I am impressed by their attitude towards the artist, which is mediæval, or perhaps Roman. Blind to nearly every form of beauty, they scorn art, and scorning art they scorn artists. It was this class which, at inaugurations of public edifices, invented the terrible toast-formula, 'The architect *and contractor*.' And if epics were inaugurated by banquet, this class would certainly propose the health of the poet and printer, after the King and the publishers. Only sheer ennui sometimes drives it to seek distraction in the artist's work. It prefers the novelist among artists because the novel gives the longest surcease from ennui at the least expenditure of money and effort.

24)   J. Galsworthy, 'Fashion', in *A Commentary* (Grant
Richards, 1908: reprinted Heinemann, 1923), 81–4.

I have watched you this ten minutes, while your carriage
has been standing still, and have seen your smiling face change
twice, as though you were about to say: 'I am not accustomed
to be stopped like this'; but what I have chiefly noticed is that
you have not looked at anything except the persons sitting
opposite and the backs of your flunkeys on the box. Clearly
nothing has distracted you from following your thought: 'There
is pleasure before me.' Yours is the three-hundredth carriage
in this row that blocks the road for half a mile. In the two
hundred and ninety-nine that come before it, and the four
hundred that come after, you are sitting too—with your face
before you, and your unseeing eyes.

Resented while you gathered being; brought into the world
with the most distinguished skill; remembered by your mother
when the whim came to her; taught to believe that life consists
in caring for your clean, well-nourished body, and your manner
that nothing usual can disturb; taught to regard Society as the
little ring of men and women that you see, and to feel your
only business is to know the next thing that you want and get it
given you——*You have never had a chance!*

You take commands from no other creature; your heart
gives you your commands, forms your desires, your wishes,
your opinions, and passes them between your lips. From your
heart well-up the springs that feed the river of your conduct;
but your heart is a stagnant pool that has never seen the sun.
Each year when April comes, and the earth smells new, you
have an odd aching underneath your corsets. What is it for?
You have a husband, or a lover, or both, or neither, whichever
suits you best; you have children, or could have them if you
wished for them; you are fed at stated intervals with food and
wine; you have all you want of country life and country sports;
you have the theatre and the opera, books, music, and religion!
From the top of the plume, torn from a dying bird, or the
flowers, made at an insufficient wage, that decorate your head,
to the sole of the shoe that cramps your foot, you are decked
out with solemn care; a year of labour has been sewn into
your garments and forged into your rings—you are a breathing
triumph!

You live in the centre of the centre of the world; if you wish

you can have access to everything that has been thought since thought began; if you wish you can see everything that has ever been produced, for you can travel where you like; you are within reach of Nature's grandest forms and the most perfect works of art. You can hear the last word that is said on everything, if you wish. When you do wish, the latest tastes are servants of your palate, the latest scents attend your nose——
You have never had a chance!

For, sitting there in your seven hundred carriages, you are blind—in heart, and soul, and voice, and walk; the blindest creature in the world. Never for one minute of your little life have you thought, or done, or spoken for yourself. You have been prevented; and so wonderful is this plot to keep you blind that you have not a notion it exists.

25)   G. B. Shaw, *Fanny's First Play* (1911), Act III.

[Out of the mouth of Mrs. Knox I have delivered on them the judgement of her God (preface).]

Mrs. Knox. . . . . I've noticed it all my life: we're ignorant. We don't really know what's right and what's wrong. We're all right as long as things go on the way they always did. We bring our children up just as we were brought up; and we say what everybody says; and it goes on all right until something out of the way happens: there's a family quarrel, or one of the children goes wrong, or a father takes to drink, or an aunt goes mad, or one of us finds ourselves doing something we never thought we'd want to do. And then you know what happens: complaints and quarrels and huff and offence and bad language and bad temper and regular bewilderment as if Satan possessed us all. We find out then that with all our respectability and piety, we've no real religion and no way of telling right from wrong. We've nothing but our habits; and when they're upset, where are we? Just like Peter in the storm trying to walk on the water and finding he couldn't.

26)   S. F. Bullock, *Robert Thorne, the Story of a London Clerk* (Werner Laurie, 1907), 247–50.

Life was not easy. The years brought fresh burdens. To Himself came a brother and sister, no burdens these by any means: still they cost. There were doctor's bills. In course of time we found it necessary to remove into a small house, and that, besides increased rent, meant expenses of various kinds, rates and taxes, the wages of a girl to help Nell, another long credit account with the Little man. It took a long time, even with Bertie's assistance, to repay Mr Hope his loan. During the first ten years of our married life we were always in debt. Only by exercising the greatest care, were we able, at the best of times, to get both ends within a penny of meeting; and often enough Nell and I have looked up from our work on the Budget with something like hopelessness in our eyes. It was so hard. Neither of us cared for money in itself. We wanted only enough, or nearly enough, to maintain life decently. We recognised that not for us, not yet, were amusements and holidays, luxuries in the shape of food and raiment. It cost us no pang to replace the labels on our matchboxes with others marked: *Rates and Taxes—Debts—Sundry Calls*: and every time we dropped a coin, the larger the better, through a slit, we knew that we were doing simply our little duty in the world. But the trouble was to find coins, either large or small, for the slits. Walking home saved a penny and wore out twopenn'orth of shoe leather. Substituting cocoa for beer did not appreciably swell the contents of our *Sundry Calls* box. Wearing an overcoat or a jacket for another winter meant economy, but nothing tangible for Mr Hope and the Little man. We tried many ways of making a little extra money. Nell lost rather than gained in attempting to satisfy the taste of certain advertising parties who, in return for cash, sent her the material for artistic and fancy work. I, amongst other adventures, corrected students' papers for a Coach, addressed circulars for a firm of drapers, laboured exceedingly over the prize schemes of weekly journals, spent many hours in composing tales and articles that succeeded only in wasting postage stamps. At last, by a happy chance, I, under an assumed name, got occasional night work on the books of a local firm, thereby easing several accounts in the family Budget. . . .

We had the gift of hope. We saw more sunshine than gloom in the world. We knew, we saw, that around us were thousands in worse condition than ourselves. We felt that for many things we had cause for thankfulness. Health was ours, and youth, and content. Yes, content. The worst was past. The future held promise. Here in the living present was our home, our own, the children in it and ourselves. We were quite happy there. To see and hear us, you might have thought we had never a care, hardly a want. Like most others in our neighbourhood, in every neighbourhood perhaps, we hid much and made a show. In the main, what is life but heroic pretence? Our houses are jerry-built, our clothes shoddy, our food adulterated, ourselves not what we are. It is the penalty of civilisation. There seems no other way.

Ours was a pleasant enough home, if humble—one of a row of six-roomed cottages in a quiet neighbourhood near Denmark Hill. In front was a privet hedge behind an oak fence, and a tiny flower bed under the parlour bay window; at the back, within brick walls, was a small garden having a grass plot, two beds with a sub-soil of sardine tins and brickbats, a poplar at the bottom, and a lilac-tree near the scullery window. The hall door had its brass knocker and letter-box. The rooms were small but comfortable: downstairs a dining-room, draw-ing-room, kitchen and scullery, upstairs two bedrooms and a little back room containing a chair, a table, and a shelf of books which it pleased us to call the Study. You will see that, despite circumstances, we were finding our feet in the social world, making the best show we could. The brass knocker, the bay window, the dining and drawing rooms, establish the fact; whilst the Study gives evidence that already we had in view the great suburban ideal of being superior to the people next door. I can see nothing petty in all this. When a man attains to the privileges of a voter and ratepayer, when his wife reaches the servant standard, when it comes to living in a dining-room and receiving in a drawing-room, I think pre-tensions are excusable. They are harmless. They give tone. They relieve monotony and supply diversion. I know that it gave Nell great satisfaction to discuss the vices and virtues of her servant (she was of the kind called Daily and cost us half-a-crown a week, exclusive of food, breakages and thefts) with the neighbouring ladies, and to dispense afternoon teas in the drawing-room; I am sure that it was wholesome pride which stirred me as I clipped our privet hedge or talked gardening and politics with Mr Robinson across the garden wall. Doubt-less he knew all about me, and more, as Mr Judkins would say; and doubtless he and Mrs Robinson at the supper-table often put us in our proper place; but what of that? Nell and I could do the same with Mr and Mrs Robinson. We knew that

Mr Robinson was only a traveller in hardware; that Mrs Robinson dyed her hair, dealt at the Colonial meat store, whitened her own doorstep, and did her own washing; and when the riot of Miss Robinson's feats on the piano became unendurable was it not possible for me to get close to the partition wall and retaliate on Bertie's banjo. Also when Mr Robinson swelled big on his grass plot, talked Bank balances, Family history, and Jingoism, was it not in me to give him back something about Devon and the North-West passage, and to douche him gently with a little Radical sentiment?

27)   H. G. Wells in *What the Worker Wants* (Hodder & Stoughton, 1912), 12.

It was one of those accidents that happen with a precision of time and circumstance that outdoes art; not an incident in it all that was not supremely typical. It was the penetrating comment of chance upon our entire social situation. Beneath a surface of magnificent efficiency was—slapdash. The ship was not even equipped to save its third-class passengers; they had placed themselves on board with an infinite confidence in the care that was to be taken of them, and they went down, and most of their women and children went down with the cry of those who find themselves cheated out of life.

In the unfolding record of behaviour it is the stewardesses and bandsmen and engineers—persons of the trade-union class —who shine as brightly as any. And by the supreme artistry of Chance it fell to the lot of that tragic and unhappy gentleman Mr. Bruce Ismay to be aboard and to be caught by the urgent vacancy in the boat and the snare of the moment. No untried man dare say that he would have behaved better in his place. But for capitalism and for our existing social system his escape —with five and fifty third-class children waiting below to drown—was the abandonment of every noble pretension. It is not the man I would criticise but the manifest absence of any such sense of the supreme dignity of his position as would have sustained him in that crisis. He was a rich man and a ruling man, but in the test he was not a proud man. In the common man's realisation that such is indeed the case with most of those who dominate our world lies the true cause and danger of our social indiscipline. And the remedy in the first place lies not in social legislation and so forth, but in the consciences of the wealthy. Heroism and a generous devotion to the common good are the only effective answer to distrust.

28)   *Daily Herald,* 22 April 1912.

FIRST-CLASS FIRST

Class Discrimination on the 'Titanic'

The various representatives of the capitalist Press have taken Mr. Ben Tillett sharply to task for declaring, in a printed statement, that obvious discrimination was apparent in favour of the cabin passengers when the 'Titanic's' lifeboats were being manned. Mr. Tillett probably overstated himself when he spoke of 'the vicious class antagonism shown in the practical forbidding of the saving of the lives of the third-class passengers'.

That the facts in the long run justify Mr. Tillett, however, is shown in the proportions of those rescued in each class to their several totals, which the *Daily Herald* here prints for the first time. They are as follows:

	Per cent
Proportion of 1st Class saved	61
Proportion of 2nd Class saved	36
Proportion of 3rd Class saved	23
Proportion of Crew saved	22
Proportion of whole Ship's Company	29

29)   L. G. Chiozza Money, *Riches and Poverty* (Methuen, 1905),
frontispiece.

BRITISH INCOMES IN 1904

RICH 1,250,000 persons £585,000,000	COMFORTABLE 3,750,000 persons £245,000,000

P O O R

38,000,000 PERSONS

£880,000,000

*The Aggregate Income of the 43,000,000
people of the United Kingdom is approximately
£1,710,000.
1¼ million persons take £585,000,000;
3¾ million persons take £245,000,000;
38 million persons take £880,000,000.
(See Chapters 2 and 3.)*

30) R. S. Churchill, *Winston S. Churchill*, volume II, companion part 2 (1969), 924–6.

WSC to Lord Morley

27 November 1909   Board of Trade

Confidential

Milner's statement that 'the accumulated wealth of the nation is not remarkably progressive. It is alarmingly stationary', is altogether contrary to the facts. Sir Robert Giffen estimated some years ago that the addition to the capital wealth of the nation was at least between two and three millions a year. The paid-up capital of registered companies alone, which was 1,013 millions sterling in 1893, had grown naturally up to 2,123 millions sterling in 1908. The gross amount of income which comes under the view of the Income Tax Commissioners was 762 millions in the year 1898–9, and it had risen to 980 millions in the year 1908–9. That is to say by 218 millions in 10 years. No doubt a substantial deduction must be made from this for more efficient methods of collection. Even if this were taken to be a half (which the Treasury tell me would be a handsome allowance) the increased annual income of the classes paying income tax (only 1,100,000 all told) is therefore 109 millions in rents, dividends, interest and profits. It is true that the valuation of estates paying estate duty does not keep step with this, the increase being only 6% as against rather more than 12% net increase of income assessable to income tax. The increase in the number of estates liable to estate duty has, however, increased by nearly 9%. There can be no doubt about the income tax figures; and the fact that the death duty figures do not fully sustain them, or go all the way with them, is probably due to an increase of gifts *inter vivos* and to other methods of evading what is unquestionably, in many cases, an onerous tax.

It is melancholy to turn from these gigantic accumulations and augmentations of the wealth of the income tax-paying & propertied classes to the condition of the wage earners. The wages of 10 million persons (the aristocracy of labour) are comprised in the annual Board of Trade Returns. In the last 10 years the increased annual wage has only been about 10 millions, and nearly the whole of that has only been attained during the last four years. A steady increase in rents, and latterly an unfavourable movement in food prices, must be set against this. When we consider that the alternatives before us for raising the money required by the State are to draw upon the overflowing fund of wealth or upon the almost stationary wages of labour, the general policy and substantial justice of the Budget are alike conclusively vindicated.

All the facts set out in this letter came either from the Treasury or the Board of Trade, and are I believe unimpeachable.

31)   C. Watney and J. A. Little, *Industrial Warfare, the Aims and Claims of Capital and Labour* (Murray, 1912), 2–3.

To them London is the Mecca. They come up from time to time in their thousands, by very cheap excursion trains and otherwise; they wander or drive round the City and the West End, and they see much of the opulence and glory that London offers to the eyes of every visitor. They go home impressed by what they have seen, and depressed by what they are going to see when they return and resume their drab, daily round. And then they read about it all in the papers, not on one day, but on every day. Take up any journal you like on any day of the week you like, and see how much of what appears refers, directly or indirectly, to wealth or to the possessors of it. Read the unconscious unctuousness with which ownership is extolled, and the greater glory which enhaloes the owners. These men from our poorer cities read glowing accounts of the displays of wealth, not necessarily ostentatious, but of everyday occurrence. They know it exists, for they have often caught a fleeting glimpse of it themselves, and in their ignorance interpreted ordinary everyday methods of life as vulgar show. They read of costly menus, and they know their own outlay on bread and dripping—if that—for their children. They see the pictures in the papers, which love, both from interest and inclination, to chronicle the doings of the financially famous. They even witness the actual portrayal of it all in the cinematograph shows which are springing up—indeed, have sprung up—in legions. People do not always rightly appreciate the influence of these two factors in moulding popular thought. As there are thousands who still believe that the veracity of the written word is always above suspicion, so there are an almost equally large number who place unquestioning reliance on the accuracy of the photographic representation. These are the days of popular prices for entertainments idealising wealth or displaying it attractively; of free libraries, in which the daily press is much more studied than serious literary matter; of cheap travelling facilities. These, too, are the days when to alter our fiscal system the worker is vehemently and earnestly urged to believe that he fares so badly because of his adhesion to a certain school of economic thought. Perhaps he may hesitate about crediting the suggested reason, and about applying the remedy; but why should he disbelieve the fact, which is so much dinned into his ears, that he is doing badly, might do better, and ought to do well under altered conditions?

32) J. Rowntree and A. Sherwell, *The Temperance Problem and Social Reform* (Hodder & Stoughton, 9th ed., 1901), xv–vi, xviii–ix, 22–3, 598–601.

The agencies which make for Temperance fall into two main divisions—those which are of a restrictive or controlling character, and those which seek to dry up the springs from which intemperance flows. For the sake of convenience they may be spoken of as the 'restrictive' and the 'constructive' agencies. To the former class belong such measures as a reduction by statute in the number of licensed houses, and a shortening of the hours of sale. The importance of proposals of this kind has received general acceptance. But far less thought has hitherto been given to the provision of constructive agencies. It is true that the Temperance value of all elevating influences, such as education, has been recognised, and there have been both personal and associated efforts to provide better recreation than that which the public-house offers. But the question in its wider aspects has not yet been taken up as a matter of high national concern, too vast and too important to be left to private enterprise.

In making proposals for Temperance legislation, it would be foolish to ignore the enormous strength of the liquor trade, the magnitude of its vested interests, and the degree in which these interests permeate British society. Were it not that moral forces are ultimately stronger than selfish interests, one might despair of success. . . . the urgent need of the present time is to secure legislation which will give full opportunity for the progressive application of Temperance sentiment to the varied needs of localities in accordance with local public opinion. If communities possessed this power, reforms which are now long delayed and difficult of realization would be accomplished with comparative ease. Progress is almost indefinitely retarded when the most forward places have to wait for the most backward. 'Birmingham and Dorset should not be made to walk abreast.'

There can be little doubt that if Temperance reform is to advance upon the ordinary lines of social progress in this country, it must do so by giving the localities a large measure of self-government in relation to the drink traffic, and, subject to the observance of a few conditions to be laid down by Parliament, everything is to be gained by the grant of such liberty. The public opinion of the large towns, with their intelligence and municipal spirit quickened by the possession of power to deal effectively with intemperance, will shape itself in definite forms. But there must be a real liberation of the local forces. . . .

INTEMPERANCE AND POVERTY

Now it would be foolish to suggest that intemperance is the sole, or even—to speak for the moment of *direct* causes only—the preponderating cause of poverty. On the contrary, it is unquestionable that to a large extent poverty is to be regarded as an industrial disease—the result of conditions and forces over which the workers have little control; while it is hardly less certain that of the intemperance that is found in intimate conjunction with poverty, a not inconsiderable proportion must be assumed to be the effect rather than the cause of the poverty.[1]

[1] It must not, however, be overlooked that while intemperance is sometimes an effect, as well as a cause, of poverty, it is a *reproductive* effect, which by demoralizing the worker still further destroys his industrial efficiency, and, as a necessary consequence, seriously aggravates the problem to be solved. The helpless despair of a sober poverty is unutterably sad, but it is not hopeless; but a poverty that deadens despair in drink creates for the statesman an almost insoluble problem.

1. *Summary of leading propositions on which legislation should be based.*

The propositions which we have attempted to establish are chiefly these:—

(a) That the present consumption of intoxicants in this country is not only excessive, but also seriously subversive of the economic and moral progress of the nation.

(b) That the enormous political influence wielded, directly and indirectly, by those interested in the drink traffic, threatens to introduce 'an era of demoralisation in British politics,' and that this menace to the independence of Parliament and to the purity of municipal life can only be removed by taking the retail drink trade out of private hands.

(c) That when the retail trade is taken out of private hands, regulations for its conduct can be quickly adapted to the special needs of each locality, and reforms now difficult to attain, such as Sunday closing, reduction in the number of licensed houses, the shortening of the hours of sale, the non-serving of children and of recognised inebriates, will then become easy of accomplishment.

(d) That in the present state of public opinion the adoption of prohibition *in the large towns* is to be regarded as impracticable, although it is possible that local veto might be successfully exercised in a suburb, or ward, of a town.

(e) That in no English-speaking country has the problem of the intemperance of large towns been solved.

(f) That an examination of the causes of alcoholic intemperance shows us that, while some of these are beyond our reach, others that are of the utmost importance are distinctly within the sphere of legislative influence.

(g) That we must recognise as among the chief causes of intemperance the monotony and dullness—too often the actual misery—of many lives, coupled with the absence of adequate provision for social intercourse and healthful recreation.

(h) That it is unreasonable to expect to withdraw men from the public-house unless other facilities for cheerful social intercourse are afforded. Such counteracting agencies, to be effective, will cost a great sum—estimated by the present writers at £4,000,000 per annum.

(*i*)   That this sum can be easily obtained if the retail trade is taken out of private hands, but that it is not likely that the necessary funds will be furnished either from municipal taxation or the national revenue. . . .

These proposals provide for a system of local restriction and control from which all that is commonly objected to in schemes for public management has been effectually and of set purpose excluded.

It is provided:—

(*a*)   That localities shall have permissive powers to organise and control the retail traffic in liquor either directly through the municipal council or through a company (as in Norway), but always under the direct supervision of the central government and only within clearly defined statutory limits.

(*b*)   That the *whole* of the profits shall be handed over to a central state authority for disbursement: the first charge upon such profits to be the provision and maintenance of adequate counter-attractions to the public-house; the balance of the profits being paid into the national exchequer.[1]

(*c*)   That the *sole* benefit which a locality shall receive from the profits of the traffic shall be an annual grant from the State authority for the establishment and maintenance of recreative centres, the primary object of which shall be to counteract the influence of the drink traffic. Such grant to be a fixed sum *in ratio to population, and not in ratio to profits earned.*

(*d*)   That similar grants shall be made to prohibition areas, all inducement to continue the traffic for the sake of the grants being thus effectually destroyed.

(*e*)   That where municipal councils adopt the system and elect to control the traffic, they shall, as in the case of the present technical education committees, invite the active co-operation of a fixed number of influential citizens, other than members of the council, in the work of local management.

(*f*)   Finally, the right of prohibiting the traffic is placed within the power of every locality.

---

[1] In any scheme for the disbursement of profits regard would of course be had to necessary appropriations for sinking funds, etc.

33)   *Punch*, 15 July 1914.

TOO MUCH CHAMPIONSHIP

Once life was an easy thing.

Yorkshire or Surrey or Kent were cricket champions. RANJI or W. G. headed the batting averages; RHODES or RICHARDSON the bowling. The office boy who knew these details plus the Boat Race winner and the English Cup-holders could keep his end up in conversation. He even found time to do a little work.

But now! That poor brain must know that McGinty of Fulham fetched £4,000 when put up for auction, that the front line of Blackburn Rovers represents an expense of £11,321 13s. 4d., and that Chelsea have played before 71,935 spectators. He must know the champions of the First, Second, Southern, Midland, and Scottish Leagues, and the teams that gained promotion.

Then there is cricket—all worked out to 'those damned dots,' as Lord RANDOLPH said in an inspired moment. Think of the strain of remembering that Middlesex stands at 78·66 and Surrey at 72·94. And the sporting papers are publishing lists of catches made; and lists of catches missed are sure to follow. Think of it—you may have to name the Champion Butter-fingers in 1915!

Come to tennis. You must know the names of the Australian Terror, the New Zealand Cyclone, the American Whirlwind. You must at a glance be able to pronounce on the nationality of Mavrogordato or Froitzheim. You have the strain of proving that the victory of a New Zealander over a German proves the vitality of the dear old country.

Or boxing. How can an ordinary mind retain the names of all the White Hopes or Black Despairs. At any moment some Terrible Magyar may wrest the bantam championship from us. You must learn to distinguish between WELLS, the re-constructor of the universe, and Knock-out WELLS. You must be acquainted with the doings and prospects of Dreadnought Brown and Mulekick Jones. You must know the F. E. Smithian repartees of JACK JOHNSON.

Let us talk of golf. No, on second thoughts, let us notably refrain from talking about golf. Only if you don't know who defeated TRAVERS (*plus* lumbago) and who eclipsed America's Bright Boy, you must hide your head in shame.

We come to rowing. Once one could say, 'Ah, Leander,' and with an easy shrug of the shoulders pass from the subject. But when international issues are involved, and the win of a Canadian or American or German crew may cause *The Daily Mail* to declare (for the hundredth time) that England is played out, a man simply has to keep abreast of the results.

There are a score of other things. Name for me, if you can, the Great American Four, the hydro-aeroplane champion, the M.P. champion pigeon-flyer, and the motor-bike hill-climbing champion.

And the Olympic games are coming! Who are England's hopes in the discus-throwing and the fancy diving? What Britisher must we rely on in the javelin hop-skip-and-jump?

Your brain reels at the prospect. We must decide to ignore all future championships. We must decline to be aggravated if a Japanese Badminton champion appears. We must cease to be interested if Britain's Hope beats the Horrible Peruvian at Tiddly-winks.

There are three admirable reasons for this.

The first is that we must play some games ourselves.

The second, that, unless a check be put to championships, the Parliamentary news will be crowded out of the papers and we shall find ourselves in an unnatural state of peace and goodwill.

The third, which one puts forward with diffidence, is that somebody, somewhere, somehow, sometime must do a little work.

34)   G. K. A. Bell, *Randall Davidson, Archbishop of Canterbury* (Oxford University Press, 1935), I, 488–9.

The ARCHBISHOP OF CANTERBURY *to the* REV. F. L. DONALDSON

Lambeth Palace. June 8, 1905.

I have today received your letter of yesterday. I yield to no one in my appreciation of the difficulties of present industrial conditions in many parts of England, and I have from early days done my best to understand the practical questions which have from time to time arisen. But such study as I am able to give to these questions tends to deepen my sense of their difficulty, and of the danger which is incurred by attempting rough and ready solutions of far reaching and complicated economic problems. Few things would give me more satisfaction than to be able so to devote myself to a deeper study of economics as to learn how to co-operate more adequately in promoting the amendment of present hardships where such exist. But a man who, like myself, has to work for 16 or 17 hours a day in discharging his own more immediate responsibilities cannot hope to be able to give to these studies so much time as many others can.

I need hardly tell you how deeply I sympathise with those whom you represent in their present lack of employment. But I am bound to say that I fail at present to see what good I could hope to effect by receiving such a Deputation as you suggest, and I cannot help fearing that I might really do harm by raising hopes and expectations which I should have no power whatever of satisfying. If what is desired is merely that I should be in possession of a statement of facts respecting the scarcity of employment in certain midland towns, I honestly believe that I should master those facts better were I to study them in writing than I should by listening to an oral statement. You think that I might, by receiving such a Deputation, shew that the Church (I quote your words) 'seals the cause as in itself sacred and noble'. I have no wish to throw any doubt upon what you describe as the sacredness and nobility of the cause. But in the ceaseless stress of other duties I must admit that I have not at present given to the details of this particular controversy such study as would justify me in making myself responsible for thus endorsing the representation of those who are coming to London to plead their cause, nor dare I hope to be able speedily to master the intricacies of the problem.

It is honestly because I am afraid of causing misunderstanding, and probably of even harming the cause I am invited to help, that I feel compelled to ask that anything which you want me to consider should be put before me in writing rather than by word of mouth.

It pains me even to seem to be unsympathetic. Nothing could be further from the facts. But it would be cowardly on my part were I, for fear of seeming unsympathetic, to do what might prejudice the very cause which you have taken in hand.

35)   Keir Hardie in the *Labour Leader*, 23 June 1905, quoted
       in G. Haw (ed.), *Christianity and the Working Classes*
       (Macmillan, 1906), 4–5.

The Archbishop of Canterbury, writing the other day, said
he had to devote seventeen hours a day to his work, and had
no time left in which to form opinions on how to solve the
unemployed question. The religion which demands seventeen
hours a day for organisation, and leaves no time for a single
thought about starving and despairing men, women, and
children, has no message for this age.

36)   R. Tressell, *The Ragged Trousered Philanthropists* (Lawrence
       & Wishart, complete edition, 1965), 153–4.

'Religion is a thing that don't trouble *me* much,' remarked
Newman; 'and as for what happens to you after death, it's a
thing I believes in leavin' till you comes to it—there's no sense
in meetin' trouble 'arfway. All the things they tells us may be
true or they may not, but it takes me all my time to look after
this world. I don't believe I've been to church more than arf a
dozen times since I've been married—that's over fifteen years
ago now—and then it's been when the kids 'ave been
christened. The old woman goes sometimes and of course the
young 'uns goes; you've got to tell 'em something or other,
and they might as well learn what they teaches at the Sunday
School as anything else.'
    A general murmur of approval greeted this. It seemed to be
the almost unanimous opinion, that, whether it were true or
not, 'religion' was a nice thing to teach children.
    'I've not been even once since I was married,' said Harlow,
'and I sometimes wish to Christ I 'adn't gorn then.'
    'I don't see as it matters a dam wot a man believes,' said
Philpot, 'so long as you don't do no 'arm to nobody. If you see
a poor b——r wot's down on 'is luck, give 'im a 'elpin' 'and.
Even if you ain't got no money you can say a kind word.'

37)   R. Blatchford, *God and My Neighbour* (Clarion Press,
       1903), ix, 192–3.

If to praise Christ in words, and deny Him in deeds, be
Christianity, ther. London is a Christian city, and England is

a Christian nation. For it is very evident that our common English ideals are anti-Christian, and that our commercial, foreign, and social affairs are run on anti-Christian lines. . . .

Here is a cultured, educated, earnest man rhapsodising about holiness and the glory of a God no mortal eye has ever seen, and of whom no word has ever reached us across the gulf of death. And while he rhapsodised, with a congregation of honest bread-and-butter citizens under him, trying hard with their blinkered eyes and blunted souls to glimpse that imaginary glamour of ecstatic 'holiness,' there surged and rolled around them the stunted, poisoned, and emaciated life of London.

Holiness!—Holiness in the Strand, in Piccadilly, in Houndsditch, in Whitechapel, in Park Lane, in Somerstown, and the Mint.

Holiness!—In Westminster, and in Fleet Street, and on 'Change.

Holiness!—In a world given over to robbery, to conquest, to vanity, to ignorance, to humbug, to the worship of the golden calf.

Holiness!—With twelve millions of our workers on the verge of famine, with rich fools and richer rogues lording it over nations of untaught and half-fed dupes and drudges.

Holiness!—With a recognised establishment of manufactured paupers, cripples, criminals, idlers, dunces, and harlots.

Holiness!—In a garden of weeds, a hotbed of lies, where hypnotised saints sing psalms and worship ghosts, while dogs and horses are pampered and groomed, and children are left to rot, to hunger, and to sink into crime, or shame, or the grave.

Holiness! For shame. The word is obnoxious. It has stood so long for craven fear, for exotistical inebriation, for selfish retirement from the trials and buffets and dirty work of the world.

What have we to do with such dreamy, self-centred, emotional holiness, here and now, in London?

What we want is citizenship, human sympathy, public spirit, daring agitators, stern reformers, drains, houses, schoolmasters, clean water, truth-speaking, soap—and Socialism.

CHAPTER FIVE

Mass Communication and Mass Entertainment

Harmsworth's *Daily Mail* led the way in Edwardian daily journalism, and his 1905 article (38), written in *Mail*-style short paragraphs, showed how he liked to regard his achievement. He believed that the *Mail* had raised the standards both of journalists and of newspaper readers. This claim was not without some substance, though it ignored the heightened prominence given to trivia in his publications. But through such trivia Harmsworth was able to keep in touch with the lower middle-class mind, contact which the subsidized radical intellectual weekly *Nation* affected to despise (39). A writer who contrived both to entertain and to influence a popular audience, while also impressing the intellectuals, was H. G. Wells. His best novels remain major Edwardian social documents, not least because (in his own words) 'they have a power of veracity quite beyond that of actual records' (40). Did the social involvement of Wells and other leading Edwardian writers mean then that they were more journalists than men of letters? (41) Was even Rupert Brooke's 'Sonnet Reversed' journalized by its realistic tone and everyday language? (42) Surviving Victorians might despairingly think so, but younger readers welcomed literature's new freedom.

Popular entertainment was undergoing its own transformation. The music hall reached its peak of popularity (43), but already by the later Edwardian years the cinema was gaining ground (44). The gramophone too was rapidly improving its quality of reproduction, though still treated with disdain, even hostility, by older people (45).

38) Sir Alfred Harmsworth, 'The Daily Newspaper of To-Day' in *Mitchell's Newspaper Press Directory* (Mitchell, 1905), 8–9.

The general contents of the Daily Press years ago would greatly surprise the present day reader of newspapers. Only thirty years ago some newspapers were accustomed to print topics now unmentionable. . . . How many years is it since a leading morning newspaper reported a prize fight, round by round, to the extent of a page? Fifty? Twenty? Less than ten years.

The modern newspaper has many faults, but it is at least decent, and it does not give the rest of the world the impression that English life largely centres round the Divorce Court and the prize ring. . . .

The daily newspaper to-day appears to me to be less a personal organ than a news gathering machine. Foreign news in the old journals was limited in volume and very slow in transmission. Long after the telegraph was invented the bulk of the news still came by post and only occasionally a message by wire, while the home news was obtained not apparently by a special staff of reporters as is the case now, but by a class of writer now disappearing, known as the 'penny-a-liner'. . . . I came into the business at the end of the Bohemian era. To-day, alcoholism is as rare in Fleet Street as it is in any other professional quarter. No person who spends his leisure in a pothouse could maintain his place amidst the strain and stress of the production of a daily newspaper.

The journalist to-day is as often as not a journalist *tout court*. He is not an unsuccessful barrister, and he has not adopted journalism as a means to some other occupation. The prizes may not be as great as they are in one or two instances at the Bar, but they are infinitely more numerous. The social position is as good as that of any other working profession. The brain equipment must needs be as complete. . . .

Each person has his own ideal of the perfect newspaper, and none has yet attained it. Mine is the quick, accurate presentation of the world's news in the form of a careful digest. I regard the newspaper primarily as a news recording machine. When I open a newspaper I like to see that trained minds have carefully arranged the news in order that I may be saved time in the perusal of it. Formerly the news was arranged by the

master printer to suit the exigencies of his mechanical needs. I
like to feel that when I have paid my small contribution
towards the great co-operative fund that goes to produce the
newspaper each day, I have at my call the services of careful
inquirers in all parts of the world who ascertain for me that
which is requisite I should know in order that I may be able
to form a judgement on the ways of the world.

All that is provided, more or less inadequately I admit, by
the modern news gathering machine. To editorial opinions I
do not personally attach much importance unless they are the
work of experts. In the modern newspaper, fortunately, they
very often are authoritative in the highest sense.

39)   *The Nation*, 18 May 1912.

[Harmsworth's] supple courtship of the mass, fortified as it is
by a power of directing and stimulating its passion for amusement, gives him an easy hold on a community like our own.
Yet it is money, not power, which the *Daily Mail* wants and
gets. When London was in earnest about civic reform, or when
Britain grew tired of *laissez faire* Toryism and fearful of Protection, a dozen *Daily Mails* would not have availed to stem
the tide. It is, indeed, on the slighter Southern half of England,
clinging tight to London, itself the great parasite of the Empire,
that the *Daily Mail* and its satellites maintain their chief hold.
But the part of the caterer is to watch and feed the caprices of
the great goddess Usus, not to control them, to make the
motley world of buyers and sellers, gossips, entertainers, artists,
athletes, professionals, adventurers, charlatans, sportsmen,
servants, and average souls feel that the Harmsworth press is
something that can turn the current of money and fashion a
little their way. Thus its thought is always timid and conventional like their thought, changeable like theirs, senti-
mental like theirs, sham-romantic, beneath the clever calculation of its real aims, as theirs is often genuinely romantic.
Occasionally it tries something like an adventure. It aims at
catching out a Radical leader like the Chancellor at the
moment when it thinks he has gone too far, or made too heavy
a call on the easily slackened energies of the nation. But the
conditions of the life of such a press forbid any prolonged or
serious intellectual effort.

40)   H. G. Wells, 'The Contemporary Novel', in *An English-man Looks at the World* (Cassell, 1914), 167–9.

The novel has neither the intense self-consciousness of autobiography nor the paralysing responsibilities of the biographer. It is by comparison irresponsible and free. Because its characters are figments and phantoms, they can be made entirely transparent. Because they are fictions, and you know they are fictions, so that they cannot hold you for an instant so soon as they cease to be true, they have a power of veracity quite beyond that of actual records. Every novel carries its own justification and its own condemnation in its success or failure to convince you that *the thing was so*. Now history, biography, blue-book, and so forth, can hardly ever get beyond the statement that the superficial fact was so.

You see now the scope of the claim I am making for the novel; it is to be the social mediator, the vehicle of understanding, the instrument of self-examination, the parade of morals and the exchange of manners, the factory of customs, the criticism of laws and institutions and of social dogmas and ideas. It is to be the home confessional, the initiator of knowledge, the seed of fruitful self-questioning. Let me be very clear here. I do not mean for a moment that the novelist is going to set up as a teacher, as a sort of priest with a pen, who will make men and women believe and do this and that. The novel is not a new sort of pulpit; humanity is passing out of the phase when men *sit under* preachers and dogmatic influences. But the novelist is going to be the most potent of artists, because he is going to present conduct, devise beautiful conduct, discuss conduct, analyse conduct, suggest conduct, illuminate it through and through. He will not teach, but discuss, point out, plead, and display. And this being my view you will be prepared for the demand I am now about to make for an absolutely free hand for the novelist in his choice of topic and incident and in his method of treatment; or rather, if I may presume to speak for other novelists, I would say it is not so much a demand we make as an intention we proclaim. We are going to write, subject only to our limitations, about the whole of human life. We are going to deal with political questions and religious questions and social questions. We cannot present people unless we have this free hand, this unrestricted field. What is the good of telling stories about people's lives if one may not deal freely with the religious beliefs and organisations that have controlled or failed to control them? What is the good of pretending to write about love, and the loyalties and treacheries and quarrels of men and women, if one must not glance at those varieties of physical temperament and organic quality, those deeply passionate needs and distresses from which half the storms of human life are brewed? We mean to deal with all these things, and it will need very much more than the disapproval of provincial librarians, the hostility of a few influential people in London, the scurrility of one paper, and the deep and obstinate silences of another, to stop the incoming tide of aggressive novel-writing. We are going to write about it all. We are going to write about business and finance and politics and precedence and pretentiousness and decorum and indecorum, until a thousand pretences and ten thousand impostures shrivel in the cold, clear air of our elucidations. We are going to write of wasted opportunities and latent beauties until a thousand new ways of living open to men and women. We are going to appeal to the young and the hopeful and the curious, against the established, the dignified, and defensive. Before we have done, we will have all life within the scope of the novel.

41)   A. Compton-Rickett, *A History of English Literature* (Jack, 1918), 664–5.

Mr. Bernard Shaw has expressed the view that good journalism is much rarer and more important than good literature. This is probably only his extravagant and provocative way of drawing attention to the importance of dealing with the concrete actualities of one's own age; examining its particular problems; of being vital and, in the best sense of the word, topical. And, in so far as Mr. Shaw seeks to discourage the purely academic view of literature as a by-product—a scholar's game—we may sympathise with his aims.

Great literature, however, as Mr. Shaw knows perfectly well, is great only so far as it is a living, organic thing, intimately related to life and related in two ways. Its tap-root lies in the soil from which it draws its sustenance; the soil of a particular age, with its limitations and characteristics; but its flower is blown upon by the breezes of heaven and fed by the rain and the sun—in this respect it is related to the universal, and is an expression not of an age but of the ages.

And the difference between great journalism and great literature is this, that great journalism deals with the application of general ideas to particular and transient problems, great literature to universal problems; great journalism has an immediate and localised aim in view; it is in a sense literature in a hurry. Its form and method, therefore, necessarily differ from the form and method of literature, inasmuch as it is essentially controversial and deliberately one-sided, and the qualities it needs are not beauty, subtlety, or symmetry, but clarity, conciseness, and sincerity. To speak of journalism as slipshod literature is quite as absurd as it would be to maintain seriously that journalism was more important than literature.

Journalism is as emphatically an art as literature; but it is a different art, and is governed by different rules—the one conforms to the poster, the other to an etching; and it is scarcely necessary to point out to-day what excellent art there may be in a first-class poster. No sensible man would maintain that a poster is more *important* than an etching, just because the poster aims at a more immediate effect upon practical life. It would be as sensible to say that a policeman was more important than the Lord Chancellor, because his immediate influence could be traced more easily.

So long as the distinction between journalism and literature is recognised, there is no reason why journalism should not exercise a wholesome influence upon letters. Each has an important work to do in focussing and reflecting contemporary life; but while journalism is concerned primarily with the stuff of life, for the sake of its content, literature seeks to enshrine that content in some permanent art-form.

The great value of journalism lies in its close correspondence with actual life; and thus it should tend to preserve literature from becoming conventional and unreal. That it is doing this to a considerable extent may be admitted, but at the present time, journalism is a much more vigorous thing than literature, and consequently in place of being merely a useful ally it is a somewhat tyrannous autocrat. The literature of to-day is like the young lady of Riga who went for a ride on a tiger. Journalism is the tiger, and the two should ever prove good friends; the young lady's refining influence proving beneficial to the tiger, and the activity of the tiger proving a perambulating blessing to the young lady. But unhappily, as we are reminded in the verse, 'They returned from the ride with the lady inside, and a smile on the face of the tiger.' In other words, journalism has practically swallowed up literature. Our ablest men to-day are, with few exceptions, able as journalists, not as men of letters. They have deliberately chosen journalistic methods by which to appeal to their generation; their verse is journalistic, their fiction is journalistic, their drama is journalistic, but the methods of the journalist are even more notorious when we come to the essay.

We need lament no lack of brains; we have among our writers men as vigorous in intellect as in any age of letters; but in common with their brainless comrades they are moved by the restlessness, the mutability and hurry of the day. They do not talk over their ideas with us as did the elder writers; there is no genial button-holing; no mellow discursiveness. They think it better to spring at our throats, and hurl their ideas at us with a catapultic violence that is often disconcerting and daring. This is the peculiarity of such men as Shaw, Chesterton, Bennett, and Hilaire Belloc, who throw many of their best ideas into essay form. The essays are live enough, provocative, stimulating, but they are essentially journalistic in form.

Nor is this by any means due to contrariness or pose. Let it be frankly admitted that life as it is lived to-day is not favourable to literature. The still small voice of the artist will not be heard in the babel of sound. The journalist has better lungs, and knows he must shout in order to be heard at all; and that if the imagination of the great crowd is to be arrested, he must achieve the capture by vigorous methods.

It is improbable that the writers in question are not fully alive to this; that they do not deliberately sacrifice the more permanent value of artistic form to the more transient methods of the journalistic touch. Both Mr. Shaw and Mr. Chesterton would doubtless defend their methods by saying that they did not write for future generations, but for the present; that they were concerned with the live questions of the hour, and wished to present these with an instant urgency that would effect their ends. The attitude is not a new one. Browning, when particularly interested in some point of psychology or philosophy, frankly disregarded his manner of speech, intent only upon the thing he wished to say. The attitude is quite a reasonable one from the point of view of the reformer and dialectician; but it removes the work of such writers *to that extent* out of the domain of pure literature, and out of the domain of fine art.

42)   Rupert Brooke, 'Sonnet Reversed' (1911).

> Hand trembling towards hand; the amazing lights
> Of heart and eye. They stood on supreme heights.
>
> Ah, the delirious weeks of honeymoon!
>   Soon they returned, and, after strange adventures,
> Settled at Balham by the end of June.
>   Their money was in Can. Pacs. B. Debentures,
> And in Antofagastas. Still he went
>   Cityward daily; still she did abide
> At home. And both were really quite content
>   With work and social pleasures. Then they died.
> They left three children (besides George, who drank):
>   The eldest Jane, who married Mr. Bell,
> William, the head-clerk in the County Bank,
>   And Henry, a stock-broker, doing well.

43)   C. Booth, *Life and Labour of the People in London*, final volume (Macmillan, 1902), 53–5.

There has been a great development and improvement upon the usual public-house sing-song, as to the low character and bad influence of which there are not two opinions. The story of progress in this respect may be traced in many of the existing places which, from a bar parlour and a piano, to an accompaniment on which friends 'obliged with a song,' have passed through every stage to that of music hall; the presiding chairman being still occasionally, and the call for drinks in almost every case, retained. But the character of the songs on the whole is better, and other things are offered: it becomes a 'variety' entertainment. The audiences are prevailingly youthful. They seek amusement and are easily pleased. No encouragement to vice can be attributed to these local music halls. The increase in the number, as well as size of these halls, has been rapid. The profits made by the proprietors have been great, and the favourite performers, being able to appear before a succession of audiences, passing rapidly with their repertoire from hall to hall, can be and are very highly remunerated. The performances also can be continually varied, for the supply of artistes is without end. The taste becomes a habit, and new halls are opened every year; soon no district will be without one. Then theatres follow. But meanwhile, and especially in poor neighbourhoods, the old-fashioned style of sing-song still continues in force.

In the central districts all places of amusement are very largely supported by the rich or by strangers visiting London. People from the outskirts come occasionally, but it is the music hall or theatre of their own neighbourhood that they frequent, and of which the influence has mainly to be considered. It is, perhaps, too much to ask that the influence of music halls and theatres should be positively and entirely good; at any rate no one claims that it is so. If it is not directly, or on the whole, evil, or if one can hope that it takes the place of something worse, a measure of improvement may be indicated. This can, I think, be claimed. It is not very much. A tendency in the direction of the drama, which is certainly an advance, may be noticed in music-hall performances, and it is to be regretted that questions arising from the separate licensing of play-houses should check the freedom of development in this direction amongst the halls. Excluding the dramatic pieces or 'sketches', the production of which is hampered in this way, the attractions most usually offered are those of a low form of art or of blatant national sentiment, neither of which can be carried further without becoming worse; or of displays of physical strength and skill on the part of acrobats and gymnasts, or of performing animals; all representing, indeed, a background of patient and unwearied effort, but involving, it cannot but be supposed, not a little cruelty in the training of children and animals necessary to secure the rewards of popularity. But the 'variety' of the entertainments increases. In addition to conjuring and ventriloquism, which are old fashioned, we have now, for instance, the cinematograph and various forms of the phonograph, and there has been much development in the forms of stage dancing.

Limitations in the form of entertainment apply less to the halls in Central London, where, for instance, beautiful and elaborate ballets are produced. These fashionable resorts have the best of everything that can be offered, and the per-formances, consequently, reach a perfection which silences criticism in that respect, though in some cases there may remain ground for attack on the score of encouraging vice. In these palaces of amusement even music is not neglected. The orchestra at the Alhambra is very famous, whilst those at the Empire and the Palace are also excellent. But in the minor halls, development is never in the direction of music. Strange as it may sound, anything that can rightly be called music is seldom produced at a local music hall. The only exceptions I call to mind are a performance of Lancashire bell ringers and the vagaries of a musical clown on his violin. In this respect, the efforts of negro minstrelsy have been far superior. Perhaps music might some day find its way in through operatic sketches, if these were encouraged.

44)   Lady Bell, *At the Works, a Study of a Manufacturing Town* (Nelson, 1911 ed.), 185–6.

At the moment of writing there are ten music-halls in full swing, at all of which Moving Pictures are shown on the Cinematograph, and at seven of which a variety entertainment is given as well. These pictures have made an extraordinary difference to the leisure hours of the working class, adults as well as children, to whom they seem to give untiring delight. The price in most of the halls ranges from 6d. to 2d., children being half price: in two of them the best places are 2s. and 1s. respectively. The seating capacity of the biggest of these halls is about 2,000; of the smallest, 350. It may appear to many of us that if a wisely tolerant supervision could be exercised over the selection of the pictures, excluding the actually harmful, but not always insisting on the improving, it would be an innocuous and not undesirable form of amusement. The front row of the gallery generally consists of children, mostly little boys between seven and ten, eagerly following every detail of the entertainment. Each of them there must have paid for his place—how he did it who can tell? perhaps either by begging or by playing pitch and toss in the street. One may sometimes see a queue of women waiting to go to the cheap seats, often with their husbands accompanying them. These women, many of whom have their babies in their arms, come out of the place looking pleased and brightened up. The kind of variety entertainment usually offered does not to the critical onlooker seem either particularly harmful or especially ennobling. The curious fact that, in almost any social circle, it makes people laugh convulsively to see any one tumble down, is kept well in view, and utilized to frequent effect. Six of these halls show their moving pictures on a Sunday, an incalculable boon.

45)   L. P. Jacks, *Life and Letters of Stopford Brooke* (Murray, 1917), II, 503.

DIARY ENTRY FOR 18 JANUARY 1899

Called in at Pillischer's, and heard the gramophone—a vile concoction of the scientific people. Cannot they let us alone? Why will they reproduce the human voice, and if they do it, why should they choose music hall songs for reproduction? It is a revolting thing to listen to. I had far sooner hear a Papuan sing his battle song to the accompaniment of a cannibal feast than listen to this instrument; but Pillischer's son or nephew treated it as if it were a baby of his own, handled it with fascinated love, devoted himself to it, and longed for me to admire it. It is an ingenious piece of work, but the voice that came out of it was like the voice of a skeleton—a weird, vile, uncanny, monstrous thing! I hate it even more than I hate the telephone, and all its ramified iniquities. To put by and reproduce the voice of the dead, can the meanest imagination conceive anything more insolent, more insulting to the dead than that? The folk that are beyond are silent, let them keep silence. It is not their living voice we hear; it is the voice of a thin ghost, squeaking like a rat behind the arras. To hear it is to violate the sacred silence of the dead.

CHAPTER SIX

Constitutional Change

Edwardian court life reached new levels of splendour (46), even while democratizing influences were forcing important constitutional changes. The King retained some influence but little real power. He could make difficulties over promising a mass creation of peers for the purpose of submerging the Conservative majority in the House of Lords (47); but in the end a Prime Minister at the head of a Liberal-Labour majority in the Commons could insist upon royal compliance (48). It was the strength of the British system that even such a major change as the 1911 Parliament Act (49) could be enacted peacefully even if noisily, a revolutionary reform secured without revolution (50, 51). Another important reform introduced in the same year was payment of Members of Parliament, an innovation which helped to assimilate the new Labour Members into Parliamentary politics (52). But the importance of individual Members of Parliament was declining in proportion as the rigidity of the party system and the power of party leaders, of the Cabinet and of the Prime Minister was increasing (53). Leading Ministers now conducted a dialogue directly with the electorate, rather strained in the case of patrician personalities such as Balfour or Asquith, much warmer in the case of popularly admired (or hated) figures such as Joseph Chamberlain or Lloyd George (54). At the local government level 'municipal socialism' was spreading widely, provoking alarm from Victorian individualists such as Lord Avebury (1834–1913) (55), satisfaction from Bernard Shaw and other Fabians (56), and enquiries about methods of improved administration from Winston Churchill (57).

46)   B. J. Hendrick, *Life and Letters of Walter H. Page* (Heinemann, 1925), III, 51–9.

American Embassy, London,
9 June, 1914.

DEAR MR. PRESIDENT:

. . . Just now it has been Their Majesties' 'Courts', two of them on two successive evenings. Since this is the last such splendid mediæval thing left in the world, it has an historical interest in addition to being a first-class show; and I'm glad to find myself young and simple enough really to enjoy it. It's the crowning act of the royal social system—most admirably staged and managed. You walk a mile along halls and across picture galleries and drawing rooms and through the throne room till you come to your waiting place, the diplomatic corps in one room and the common herd (of hundreds of ladies) in another, passing on your way gaudy pikemen of pre-Elizabethan England by every door and stairway, and greeted by gentlemen-and-ladies-in-waiting at every turn— beautiful women and inexpressibly gaudy men in white silk stockings and breeches and gold-laced coats. The King and Queen are so punctual that you might set your watch by them. The Lancers and the Indian bodyguard take their places in front; at exactly 9.30 you hear the fanfare, the orchestra plays 'God Save the King,' and their royalties enter, the gold-stick, the silver-stick, and the rest backing before them. A dozen of the royal family follow, all taking their places on the raised dais, a gold-embroidered and gold-fringed rug on it, and the great canopy over them that was brought from the Durbar. When all the attendants have taken their places, the ladies of the diplomatic corps go in, one by one, the ambassadorial ladies first. The mediæval attendants straighten out their trains, and with feathers in their hair,—the North American Indians wore Eagle feathers, these ladies, ostrich feathers, allee samee at the bottom!—they march in, in due order, of course, according to the period of their service.

It made no matter last night that Mrs. Page and the German ambassadress were discussing the proper bringing-up of babies. When the bugles sounded they had to fall into line and to sit with the Spanish ambassadress between them to the postponement of baby-lore. Each curtseys to the King, then to the Queen, and goes to her proper place. Then follow the Ambassadors, each with a secretary (once a year with his full staff), each bows to the King and to the Queen and marches to his place. The diplomatic corps all in, their royalties sit and the great ladies all sit—the diplomatic ladies on one side the throne in rows according to rank and the duchesses on the other side. All the men and the ladies of no high rank stand for two mortal hours while the stream of presentees flows by— in trains and with feathers and jewels, every one making her obeisance. The King and the Queen nod—that's all. But everyone has been admitted to the royal presence; that's the game, you see, and when you've done that you've won—won over the 38,000,000 other persons who are not on that evening so admitted. The orchestra plays softly. The uniforms and the jewels make any opera-scene pale into sheer make-believe; the tiaras and the coronets sparkle everywhere, and the 'creations' of all the great frock-makers flow along—'The liquefaction of her clothes.' The Ambassadors, all gaudier than gold and colours ever before made men—all but me in my distinguished waiter-black—stand a little to the left of the throne and carry on whispered conversations with one another and the gentle-men-in-attendance and the princes. The long procession goes on for nearly two hours. Meantime you can pick up a lot of knowledge that, but for this experience, you would have died without gaining. For instance, no two women curtsey alike, and most of them do it very badly. And you couldn't ever know how many pounds of silver and gold and pearls and diamonds a woman can carry till you have seen these. Now and then one trips. Now and then the lady behind steps on the train of the one before her—three and a half yards long, you know. . . .

Presently a comely woman in the line kneels before the King and with outstretched hands begins her suffragette plea: 'Your Majesty, for God's sake——' She got no further for two of the gentlemen-in-waiting grasped her, one on either side, and marched her out. The King gave no sign of even having seen her, but the Queen became very red. But the procession moved on without interruption. There were people in the room who didn't know that anything had happened. This show is perhaps the best managed, best mannered show in the whole world . . .

There's no organization ever devised by man for its own perpetuity so admirably unless it be the Roman Church. The

King works hard for more than half the year—amazingly hard; he leads a regular life. He grinds away at his job with an appearance of toil. The Conservatives openly accuse the Liberals of such an ultimate purpose as the abolition of royalty. Everybody agrees that an indiscreet or openly dissolute King would come to grief. The Bishops know that the State Church will one day pass. Hence they fight like tigers to keep it in Wales. But all these things yet rest on a pretty solid foundation, so long as everything goes well—namely the vanity of women and the haughtiness of privileged men.

47)   J. A. Spender and C. Asquith, *Life of Herbert Henry Asquith, Lord Oxford and Asquith* (Hutchinson, 1932), I, 261–2.

MEMORANDUM BY VAUGHAN NASH,
ASQUITH'S PRIVATE SECRETARY

10 DOWNING STREET,
WHITEHALL, S.W.
Dec. 15, 1909.

Lord Knollys asked me to see him this afternoon and he began by saying that the King had come to the conclusion that he would not be justified in creating new peers (say 300) until after a second general election and that he, Lord K., thought you should know of this now, though, for the present he would suggest that what he was telling me should be for your ear only. The King regards the policy of the Government as tantamount to the destruction of the House of Lords and he thinks that before a large creation of Peers is embarked upon or threatened the country should be acquainted with the particular project for accomplishing such destruction as well as with the general line of action as to which the country will be consulted at the forthcoming Elections.

When it came to discussing this more in detail the following points emerged:

1.   That if the plan adopted for dealing with the Veto follows the general lines of the House of Commons resolution coupled with shorter Parliaments (the King prefers four years to five) the King would concur, though apparently he would still hesitate to create Peers.

2. That his objection to the creation of Peers would be 'considerably diminished' if Life Peers could be created. (I pointed out to Lord Knollys that this would involve legislation to which the House of Lords might object.)

As to the first point I said that your speech at the Albert Hall indicated that the plan to be adopted would follow the general lines of the C.-B. plan.

Lord Knollys went on to say that it was in view of the objections which the King was likely to raise that he had advocated the introduction of legislation dealing with the Lords before supplies were dealt with by the new Parliament as by this means a lever might be brought to bear which would obviate the necessity of creating Peers. I replied that whatever the merits of such a procedure might be, the practical difficulties were, as I understood, serious, the gravest being the short time available for getting the Finance Bill through. Moreover the onus as regards a financial deadlock would, in the circumstances, be held to rest not on the Lords but on the Government. And he quite saw the force of this.

Lord Knollys was very anxious that some alternative method of coercion should be devised. For instance was there anything in the idea of summoning only such Peers as would give a majority to the Finance Bill? I said I would ask your opinion, but I thought you would regard such a scheme as fantastic and impracticable, apart from its bearing on the Monarch.

Before coming away I thought I had better ask Lord Knollys whether the King realised that at the next General Election the whole question of the Lords would be fully before the country, and that the electors would know that they were being invited to pronounce, not indeed on the details, but on the broad principles which were involved in the Government's policy. I also asked what he thought would be the position as regarded the creation of peers if it turned out that the House of Lords refused to accept legislation forbidding them to touch finance. From the vague answers he gave I came away with the impression that the King's mind is not firmly settled and that it might be useful if you saw him some time before the Elections, possibly on the 8th, the day of the Dissolution Council.

V.N.

48)   J. A. Spender and C. Asquith, *Life of Herbert Henry Asquith,
Lord Oxford and Asquith* (Hutchinson, 1932), I, 305–6.

MEMORANDUM BY ASQUITH FOR THE KING

10 DOWNING STREET,
WHITEHALL, S.W.
December 1910.

The part to be played by the Crown, in such a situation as
now exists, has happily been settled by the accumulated traditions and the unbroken practice of more than 70 years. It is
to act upon the advice of the Ministers who for the time being
possess the confidence of the House of Commons, whether that
advice does or does not conform to the private and personal
judgment of the Sovereign. Ministers will always pay the
utmost deference, and give the most serious consideration, to
any criticism or objection that the Monarch may offer to their
policy; but the ultimate decision rests with them; for they,
and not the Crown, are responsible to Parliament. It is only
by a scrupulous adherence to this well-established Constitutional doctrine that the Crown can be kept out of the arena
of party politics.

It follows that it is not the function of a Constitutional
Sovereign to act as arbiter or mediator between rival parties
and policies; still less to take advice from the leaders on both
sides, with the view to forming a conclusion of his own.
George III in the early years of his reign tried to rule after this
fashion, with the worst results, and with the accession of Mr.
Pitt to power he practically abandoned the attempt. The
growth and development of our representative system, and the
clear establishment at the core and centre of our Constitution
of the doctrine of Ministerial responsibility, have since placed
the position of the Sovereign beyond the region of doubt or
controversy.

It is technically possible for the Sovereign to dismiss
Ministers who tender to him unpalatable advice. The last
instance of such a proceeding was in 1834, when William IV
compelled the resignation of Lord Melbourne and his colleagues. The result was, from the King's point of view,
singularly unsatisfactory. The dismissed Ministers found an
adequate majority in the new House of Commons. The King
was compelled to take them back again, and they remained

in power for another 6 years. During the long reign of Queen Victoria, though she was often in disagreement with the Ministry of the day, she never resorted to this part of the prerogative. She recognised that, so long as a Ministry possessed the confidence of the House of Commons, she had no alternative but to act on its advice. The reason is plain. The House of Commons, by reason of its power over Supply, has every Ministry at its mercy. The King cannot act without Ministers, and Ministers are impotent to carry on the government of the country without a majority in the House of Commons.

The position becomes exceptionally clear and simple, when —as the case is now—a ministry has appealed to the country upon the specific and dominating issue of the day, and upon that issue commands a majority of more than 100 in the House of Commons.

49) *The Public General Acts passed in the First and Second Years of the Reign of His Majesty King George the Fifth* (HMSO, 1911), 38–40.

An Act to make provision with respect to the powers of the House of Lords in relation to those of the House of Commons, and to limit the duration of Parliament.

[18th August 1911.]

Whereas it is expedient that provision should be made for regulating the relations between the two Houses of Parliament:

And whereas it is intended to substitute for the House of Lords as it at present exists a Second Chamber constituted on a popular instead of hereditary basis, but such substitution cannot be immediately brought into operation:

And whereas provision will require hereafter to be made by Parliament in a measure effecting such substitution for limiting and defining the powers of the new Second Chamber, but it is expedient to make such provision as in this Act appears for restricting the existing powers of the House of Lords:

Be it therefore enacted by the King's most Excellent Majesty, by and with the advice and consent of the Lords Spiritual and Temporal, and Commons, in this present Parliament assembled, and by the authority of the same, as follows:

1.—*(1)* If a Money Bill, having been passed by the House of Commons, and sent up to the House of Lords at least one month before the end of the session, is not passed by the House of Lords without amendment within one month after it is so sent up to that House, the Bill shall, unless the House of Commons direct to the contrary, be presented to His Majesty and become an Act of Parliament on the Royal Assent being signified, notwithstanding that the House of Lords have not consented to the Bill.

(2) A Money Bill means a Public Bill which in the opinion of the Speaker of the House of Commons contains only provisions dealing with all or any of the following subjects, namely, the imposition, repeal, remission, alteration, or regulation of taxation; the imposition for the payment of debt or other financial purposes of charges on the Consolidated Fund, or on money provided by Parliament, or the variation or repeal of any such charges; supply; the appropriation, receipt, custody, issue or audit of accounts of public money; the raising or guarantee of any loan or the repayment thereof; or subordinate matters incidental to those subjects or any of them. In this subsection the expressions 'taxation', 'public money', and 'loan' respectively do not include any taxation, money, or loan raised by local authorities or bodies for local purposes.

(3) There shall be endorsed on every Money Bill when it is sent up to the House of Lords and when it is presented to His Majesty for assent the certificate of the Speaker of the House of Commons signed by him that it is a Money Bill. Before giving his certificate, the Speaker shall consult, if practicable, two members to be appointed from the Chairmen's Panel at the beginning of each Session by the Committee of Selection.

2.—*(1)* If any Public Bill (other than a Money Bill or a Bill containing any provision to extend the maximum duration of Parliament beyond five years) is passed by the House of Commons in three successive sessions (whether of the same Parliament or not), and, having been sent up to the House of Lords at least one month before the end of the session, is rejected by the House of Lords in each of those sessions, that Bill shall, on its rejection for the third time by the House of Lords, unless the House of Commons direct to the contrary, be presented to His Majesty and become an Act of Parliament on the Royal Assent being signified thereto, notwithstanding that the House of Lords have not consented to the Bill: Provided that this provision shall not take effect unless two years have elapsed between the date of the second reading in the first of those sessions of the Bill in the House of Commons and the date on which it passes the House of Commons in the third of those sessions.

(2) When a Bill is presented to His Majesty for assent in pursuance of the provisions of this section, there shall be endorsed on the Bill the certificate of the Speaker of the House of Commons signed by him that the provisions of this section have been duly complied with.

(3) A Bill shall be deemed to be rejected by the House of Lords if it is not passed by the House of Lords either without amendment or with such amendments only as may be agreed to by both Houses.

(4) A Bill shall be deemed to be the same Bill as a former Bill sent up to the House of Lords in the preceding session if, when it is sent up to the House of Lords, it is identical with the former Bill or contains only such alterations as are certified by the Speaker of the House of Commons to be necessary owing to the time which has elapsed since the date of the former Bill, or to represent any amendments which have been made by the House of Lords in the former Bill in the preceding session, and any amendments which are certified by the Speaker to have been made by the House of Lords in the third session and agreed to by the House of Commons shall be inserted in the Bill as presented for Royal Assent in pursuance of this section:

Provided that the House of Commons may, if they think fit, on the passage of such a Bill through the House in the second or third session, suggest any further amendments without inserting the amendments in the Bill, and any such suggested amendments shall be considered by the House of Lords, and, if agreed to by that House, shall be treated as amendments made by the House of Lords and agreed to by the House of Commons; but the exercise of this power by the House of Commons shall not affect the operation of this section in the event of the Bill being rejected by the House of Lords.

3. Any certificate of the Speaker of the House of Commons given under this Act shall be conclusive for all purposes, and shall not be questioned in any court of law.

4.—*(1)* In every Bill presented to His Majesty under the preceding provisions of this Act, the words of enactment shall be as follows, that is to say:—

'Be it enacted by the King's most Excellent Majesty, by and with the advice and consent of the Commons in this present Parliament assembled, in accordance with the provisions of the Parliament Act, 1911, and by authority of the same, as follows.'

(2) Any alteration of a Bill necessary to give effect to this section shall not be deemed to be an amendment of the Bill.

5.   In this Act the expression 'Public Bill' does not include any Bill for confirming a Provisional Order.

6.   Nothing in this Act shall diminish or qualify the existing rights and privileges of the House of Commons.

7.   Five years shall be substituted for seven years as the time fixed for the maximum duration of Parliament under the Septennial Act, 1715.

8.   This Act may be cited as the Parliament Act, 1911.

50)   A. V. Dicey, *Lectures on the Relation between Law and Public Opinion in England* (Macmillan, 2nd ed., 1914), 57–9.

Democracy in modern England has shown a singular tolerance, not to say admiration, for the kind of social inequalities involved in the existence of the Crown and of an hereditary and titled peerage; a cynic might even suggest that the easy working of modern English constitutionalism proves how beneficial may be in practice the result of democracy tempered by snobbishness. The people of England have certainly shown no hostility to the existence either of large fortunes or of large estates, and during the nineteenth century have betrayed no ardent desire for that creation of a large body of peasant proprietors, or yeomen, which enlightened Liberals have thought would confer untold benefits on the country. In truth, the equal division of a man's property among his descendants or his nearest relatives at his death, though almost essential to the maintenance of small estates, is thoroughly opposed to that absolute freedom of testamentary disposition to which Englishmen have so long been accustomed that they have come to look upon it as a kind of natural right. The English ecclesiastical establishment, opposed as it is to many democratic ideas or principles, has not been the object of much popular attack. The Established Church is more influential and more popular in 1904, than it was in 1830, and the influence of Non-conformists is, under the democratic constitution of to-day, apparently less considerable than was the influence some sixty or seventy years ago of what was then called the Dissenting interest. English democracy, in short, whilst caring somewhat for religious freedom, exhibits indifference to religious equality. From another point of view the position of the English democracy is peculiar. Almost alone among popular governments of the world, it has hitherto supported complete freedom of trade, and has on the whole, though on this matter one must speak with less certainty, favoured everything that promotes freedom of contract. Now the point to be specially noted is that the attitude of the English people (and this holds true of the attitude and legislative action of the people of every great country) is determined much less by the mere advance of democracy than by historical, and, even what one may fairly term, accidental circumstances. Democracy in England has to a great extent inherited the traditions of the aristocratic government, of which it is the heir. The relation of the judiciary to the executive, to the Parliament, and to the people, remains now much what it was at the beginning of the century, and no man dreams of maintaining that the government and the administration, are not subject to the legal control and interference of the judges. Our whole system of government, lastly, is, as it has been since 1689, essentially parliamentary. And the supremacy of Parliament involves in England constant modification of the law of the land. The English Parliament is now a legislative machine which, whatever the party in office, is kept constantly in action.

51) A. L. Lowell, *The Government of England* (Macmillan, 1912 ed.), II, 536–8.

The fact that the government is in the hands of a small upper class, while the electorate is mainly composed of workingmen, has also a noteworthy effect. Although the men who sit in Parliament and in the cabinet are constrained to follow the wishes of the mass of the voters, and even to bid against one another for popular support, they cannot divest themselves altogether of the opinions derived from their education and environment. They are for the most part men of social position and wealth, who cannot lead a class war or a general assault on property; and in fact the Socialist-Labour organisations complain bitterly that both of the great parties are capitalist at heart. The parliamentary leaders may go a long way in socialistic legislation, but they cannot move very fast, and there is a limit to the distance they will go. To entrust a man of conservative traditions with the execution of a radical programme is a safe and sometimes a wise proceeding. Such a condition does not obviate pressure for democratic class legislation, or prevent it from being effective, but it does act as a moderating force.

This may be put in another way. All government involves compulsion, and is therefore based ultimately on power. But power among men has many sources, of which numbers is only one. Another is wealth, another the capacity for organisation, another intelligence, and in fact it would be easy to mention many more without exhausting the possible list. Taking all the various sources of power together and ascribing to each its real weight, we could find what might be called the actual centre of gravity of a community. . . . The political centre of gravity is quite a different thing. Nominally it depends upon the distribution of political power, or in a popular government upon the extension of the franchise. Practically it may be determined in other ways. Now these two centres of gravity can never long remain very far apart. What we have called the actual centre of power will assert itself, peacefully if it can, forcibly if it must. A government that is seriously out of accord with it will provoke resistance, unless it yields. When numbers are insufficiently represented there may be violent outbreaks. With other forces the pressure is more commonly exerted steadily, silently and often without attracting attention. This has been true in all ages of the world, and not least in recent years. We live in a period of democracy where every man's vote has equal weight, but in spite of the great force that organisation has placed in the hands of masses of men, numbers are still not the only source of power. Education and wealth are still strong and they make themselves felt, sometimes by a natural leadership with the voters, sometimes unfortunately by corrupt means. In England the balance between numbers and the other forces in the state would seem to be brought about largely by the fact that the electorate comprises almost the whole community, while the immediate direction of affairs is still mainly in the hands of a smaller governing class.

52) Lord Elton, *Life of James Ramsay MacDonald 1866–1919* (Collins, 1939), 152–3.

SPEECH AS RETIRING ILP CHAIRMAN, 1909

How are we to regard the House of Commons? I sometimes receive resolutions beginning in this way: 'Seeing that the unemployed are of more importance than the rules of the House of Commons'—you know the rest. If I said that I see nothing of the kind, I would of course be misunderstood. So I shall put it in this way—The opposition between Parliamentary procedure and the question of how to deal with the unemployed is purely a fictitious one. The unemployed can never be treated by any Parliament except by one which has rules of procedure and these rules must prescribe majority responsibility. Every facility given to a minority to impose its will upon the majority is a facility which any minority can use, and not merely a Labour or a Socialist minority. To protect the conditions and existence of democratic government is just as essential to the building up of the Socialist State as is the solution of the problem of unemployment. The latter is our aim, the former is the only condition under which our aim can be secured. The Party which proposes to strike at the heart of democratic government in order to make a show of earnestness about unemployment will not only not be tolerated by the country, but does not deserve to be.

53) *Parliamentary Debates,* fourth series, CXXXVII (1904), 358–9.

House of Commons, 1 July 1904, speech by Lawson Walton (1852–1908) [Liberal Attorney General 1905–8] on a Conservative Government proposal to introduce 'guillotine' procedure to accelerate passage of the Licensing Bill.

Here they had a Bill, not unduly long, and not unduly complicated, but highly controversial. There seemed to be no ground for putting this measure into an exceptional category, except that it excited strong feeling in the country, which was reflected on these Benches of the House of Commons. There had been no waste of time involved in its discussion during the few hours devoted to it; and if, under the circumstances, they were to come to the conclusion that the machinery of the House of Commons was to be acknowledged to be unequal to the strain of framing the measure, then there was no highly contentious Bill to which, in the future, the same argument might not be applied with equal force. He would ask the House for one moment to look at the practical result of this Motion. Were they, or were they not, prepared to declare that, as a body, the House was unfitted to frame its measures? He agreed that that did not involve the declaration that they were unable to define the principles of these measures, because to some extent these were settled by the debate on the Second Reading of the Bills. But the Motion declared when a Bill passed into Committee, if time was short, or if the measure was controversial, or if any elements of complication arose, it was to be taken, not in the form in which Parliament had settled it, but in the form in which the Government draftsman had framed it, and in which the Cabinet had chosen to adopt it? The Constitution had undergone a serious change. It was said that it had ceased to be government by Parliament. It had become government by Cabinet, and an even later development, they were told, had taken place, and it was now government by Prime Minister in Cabinet, little distinguishable from the autocracies into which the democracies of the past had degenerated.

But the present point was not so much the authority of the Cabinet or the Prime Minister in the Cabinet. The question was one which was very near to every one of them, whether they were the enemies of this Government, or any other Government. It was a question for every individual Member of Parliament who was proud of the institution to which he belonged, whether or not the House was to surrender the function of giving its impress, after debate and deliberation, on the form of the measures which it passed.

54)   M. Ostrogorski, *Democracy and the Organization of Political Parties* (Macmillan, 1902), I, 304–5.

Parliamentary government reposes on a division of labour and an apportionment of powers between public opinion and the leaders, the rulers,—an apportionment prescribed by the very nature of both. While public opinion by a sort of volcanic process upheaves and hurls forth one problem after another, the party leaders who alternately come into office, the rulers, fasten on those problems the solution of which appears to them necessary and possible; they are not to meddle with the others, and it is a crime on their part to play with them. Taking up questions which await solution on their own responsibility, they must not shirk it or let their hand be forced, no more than they may arrest or damn the current of opinion which fertilizes the soil of every free political community. It is this which constitutes the real separation of power on which Parliamentary government rests, rather than that mechanical separation which Montesquieu fancied he had discovered in English constitutionalism, and which has since been naïvely copied in various countries.

55)   Lord Avebury, *On Municipal and National Trading* (Macmillan, 1906), 174–6.

In the preceding chapters it has, I think, been clearly shown—
  1.   That local expenditure is increasing more rapidly than rateable property.
  2.   That local indebtedness is increasing more rapidly than rateable property.
  3.   That municipal trading cannot fail to give rise to awkward labour problems.
  4.   That profits are only made, if at all, when municipalities have a monopoly; they are confined to businesses such as the manufacture of gas, which has long been established and reduced to regular rules; that even in such cases the accounts have been so kept as to make it impossible to determine what the real result has been; that the profit, if any, has been but small; and that much more satisfactory and remunerative results might have been obtained if the works had

been leased to private companies or firms.

5.   That municipal trading has seriously interfered with private enterprise and our foreign commerce.

6.   That the State management of railways is open to similar objections; that on State railways the fares are higher, the trains slower, fewer, and less convenient, and that to introduce questions of railway management into the domain of politics is open to serious objections.

7.   That it is unwise to give votes to those who pay no rates, and unjust to withhold them from those who do.

8.   That by reducing the demand for labour, while increasing prices and raising rates, it has not only injured the ratepayers generally, but especially the working classes; and that if carried to its logical conclusion, it will involve the loss of their freedom. . . .

Having been Chairman of the London County Council, I fully recognise, and ungrudgingly admit, the great public services which the members of that body have rendered and are rendering to the country; their industry, integrity, and devotion to their public duties. It is not inconsistent with the sincere admiration I feel for them that I should differ as regards one portion of the policy of our municipalities. Nor is it in indiscriminate opposition to Socialism. Free Libraries are a part of the Socialist programme, and I have always done what I could to support them. The acquisition of open spaces, street improvements, the construction of baths and washhouses, must, I agree, in each case, be judged on their own merits. Probably, in most cases, the expenditure has been wise and justifiable. The fact that the duties of Government and of the municipalities are so numerous, so difficult, and so important, is one of the strongest reasons why they would be wise to devote their whole energies to duties which necessarily devolve upon them.

56)   G. B. Shaw, *The Commonsense of Municipal Trading* (Cape, for the Fabian Society, 2nd ed., 1908), 1–5.

Municipal Trading seems a very simple matter of business. Yet it is conceivable by a sensible man that the political struggle over it may come nearer to a civil war than any issue raised in England since the Reform Bill of 1832. It will certainly not be decided by argument alone. Private property will not yield its most fertile provinces to the logic of Socialism; nor will the sweated laborer or the rackrented and rackrated city shopkeeper or professional man refrain, on abstract Individualist grounds, from an obvious way of lightening his burden. The situation is as yet so little developed that until the other day few quarter columns in the newspaper attracted less attention than the occasional one headed Municipal Trading; but the heading has lately changed in the *Times* to Municipal Socialism; and this, in fact, is what is really on foot among us under the name of Progressivism.

At first sight the case in favor of Municipal Trading seems overwhelming. Take the case of a shopkeeper consuming a great deal of gas or electric light for the attractive display of his wares, or a factory owner with hundreds of work benches to illuminate. For all this light he has to pay the cost of production plus interest on capital at the rate necessary to induce private investors to form ordinary commercial gas or electric light companies, which are managed with the object of keeping the rate of interest up instead of down: all improvement in the service and reductions in price (if any) being introduced with the sole aim of making the excess of revenue over cost as large as possible.

Now the shopkeeper in his corporate capacity as citizen-constituent of the local governing body can raise as much capital as he likes at less than four per cent. It is much easier to stagger consols than to discredit municipal stock. Take the case of the London County Council. For ten years past the whole weight of the Government and the newspapers which support it has been thrown against the credit of the Council. A late prime minister denounced it in such terms that, to save his face, his party was forced to turn all the vestries into rival councils on the 'divide and govern' principle. The name of the London County Council has been made a hissing among all who take their politics from the Court and the Conservative papers. To such a torrent of denunciation a private company would have succumbed helplessly: the results of an attempt to issue fresh stock would not have paid the printer's bill. But the County Council has only to hold up its finger to have millions heaped on it at less than four per cent. It has to make special arrangements to allow small investors a chance. The very people who have been denouncing its capital as 'municipal indebtedness' struggle for the stock without the slightest regard to their paper demonstrations of the approaching collapse of all our municipal corporations under a mountain of debt, and of the inevitable bankruptcy of New Zealand and the Australasian colonies generally through industrial democracy. The investor prefers the corporation with the largest municipal debt exactly as he prefers the insurance company with the largest capital. And he is quite right. Municipal expenditure in trading is productive expenditure: its debts are only the capital with which it operates. And that is why it never has any difficulty in raising that capital. Sultans and South American Republics may beg round the world in vain; chancellors may have to issue national stock at a discount; but a Borough Treasurer simply names a figure and gets it at par.

This is the central commercial fact of the whole question. The shopkeeper, by municipal trading, can get his light for the current cost of production plus a rate of interest which includes no insurance against risk of loss, because the security, in spite of all theoretical demonstrations to the contrary, is treated by the investing public and by the law of trusteeship as practically perfect. Any profit that may arise through accidental overcharge returns to the ratepayer in relief of rates or in public service of some kind.

The moment this economic situation is grasped, the successes of municipal trading become intelligible; and the entreaties of commercial joint stock organization to be protected against the competition of municipal joint stock organization become as negligible as the plea of the small shopkeeper to be protected against the competition of the Civil Service or Army and Navy Stores. Shew the most bitterly Moderate ratepayer a municipal lighting bill at sixpence a thousand feet or a penny a unit cheaper than the private company charges him, and he is a converted man as far as gas or electric light is concerned. And until commercial companies can raise capital at lower rates than the City Accountant or the Borough Treasurer, and can find shareholders either offering their dividends to relieve the rates or jealously determining to reduce the price of light to a minimum lest they should be paying a share of their neighbors' rates in their lighting bills, it will always be possible for a municipality of average capacity to underbid a commercial company.

Here, then, is the explanation of the popularity and antiquity of municipal trading. As far as their legal powers have gone, municipalities have always traded, and will always trade, to the utmost limits of the business capacity and public spirit of their members.

57) R. S. Churchill, *Winston S. Churchill*, volume II, companion, part 2 (Heinemann, 1969), 761–2.

WSC to Thomas Horsfall

13 February 1908   Colonial Office

[Copy]

Dear Mr Horsfall,
    Many thanks for sending me your papers on town planning. I will read them with the interest which I always derive from your disquisitions on social subjects.
    I should like to know more about the proposal to have skilled professional mayors on the German plan instead of our present happy-go-lucky amateur system.
    How could you interweave the German plan with the habits of our life in England so as to cause the least possible alteration in the appearance and form of things, the least possible break with the past, and the minimum of disappointment to individuals who may have nourished hopes of civic honour?
    What is to happen to a burgomaster appointed, let us say, for seven or eight years, no longer in my opinion under any circumstances, who in his third or fourth year gives general dissatisfaction? Has the town got to stand him until his full term is up? What disciplinary machinery is there for removing such a person even before their new term of office will occur?
    What effective method of control have they got over the whole policy of the system? How far can they act in opposition to the will of their council? What proportion do you think right between paid and unpaid members? How much real power have the elected unpaid members against their paid colleagues and the professional mayor?
    What do you think is the best system to apply to Manchester as a concrete instance?
    Another point occurs to my mind. Would it be a good thing

to try to form the municipal and local civil service in the country into one large body of similar character, though necessarily of a somewhat lower standard, to the existing civil service of the crown?

Would it not enhance the dignity and efficiency of surveyors, electricians, boro' architects, poor law officers, sanitary inspectors, and all the body of minor officials indispensable to modern local government, if they found themselves all members of one great organization animated by a high spirit of corporate honour?

Would not the institution of such a service as this have the effect of affording more skilled advice to town councillors and provincial mayors who under the present system come into office, in the same way that ministers of the Crown who are new to the work of their new departments are aided by the great body of civil servants?

On any of those points I should be delighted to have your opinion, for I believe the times are now coming when active and increasing social construction and reconstruction will be the order of the day.

[WINSTON S. CHURCHILL]

CHAPTER SEVEN

The Individual and the State

Inspired by T. H. Green, Edwardian Idealist philosophers sought to define the relationship between individuals and the state not (as many Victorians had done) in terms of separation but in terms of connection (58, 59). The Idealists took pains, however, not to seem to be advocating socialist egalitarianism and nationalization (60). H. G. Wells wanted both, but he learnt to set conciliatory limits to his 'constructive socialism' (61). He knew that the masses remained apathetic (62), and that social reform therefore depended upon cultivating the social conscience of the propertied middle and upper classes (63). Socialist ultras attacked the 'astonishing spectacle' of Wells's pleas for restraint (64). Though few of them advocated the use of force, they did demand an uncompromising 'class war' programme of unlimited state intervention on behalf of the underprivileged (65). The language of the ILP constitution was more restrained but equally committed to socialism (66), as was the Fabian Society 'basis' (67). Shaw's presentation of the Fabian case was characteristically lively (68). The Labour Representation Committee, renamed the Labour Party in 1906, was formed not as an explicitly socialist body but as an organization to secure the election of representatives of the working class to Parliament (69). The pressure of socialist theory and Labour practice greatly stimulated radical thinking within the Liberal Party (70, 71). From the Conservative side it provoked much negative alarmism (72), but it also exerted a positive influence, forcing some studiedly moderate response (73).

58) J. H. Muirhead, *The Service of the State, Four Lectures on the Political Teaching of T. H. Green* (Murray, 1908), 90–1, 101–3.

There is an old-world air about the whole controversy as to

the right, and even as to the limits of State interference with any of the actions of individuals. There is a general admission that liberty is no fixed quantity which necessarily diminishes as corporate control increases, but that it is a growing function to which wisely-directed legislation may continually contribute. The idea, we may say, of a fixed liberty-fund has gone the way of the wage-fund, the work-fund and other similar metaphysical and mischievous theories. The centre of political interest at the present day has shifted to the different and more definite issue of the general type of social and industrial order that is most favourable to social liberty in the new and positive meaning of the word; more specifically to the question of the consonance of the control of land and of capital by individuals or private associations with the material and moral well-being of the people as a whole. The question that the philosophic student of politics is more likely to ask is the bearing of the ideas with which we have been occupied on the meaning and prospects of the growing movement that is founded on the belief in the fundamental inconsistency between private ownership of capital and social liberty. . . .

Green would probably have directed his main efforts as a politician, had he lived, to securing a concentration of progressive purpose, inspired by the ideal of more fully-developed human capacity. . . . With such a union in view I can conceive of him addressing at the present crisis a concordat to all classes of active reformers, liberal and radical, moderate and progressive, religious and secular, and more particularly to individualists and socialists. To the individualist it would say: 'By all means hold to the moral individualism which is the counterpart of the moral socialism we have spoken of. Individual character is the bed-rock—the one thing that is needful. But remember, too, that character, particularly in its early formations, is a sensitive and delicately responsive thing. Environment exercises an enormous influence upon it. Environment, moreover, is itself enormously controllable, and in these days we have made enormous strides in learning how to control it. See, therefore, that no individualistic shibboleths, or the ghosts of shibboleths, frighten you out of the courageous and consistent use of the most effective means of moulding it to your purpose that civilisation has put into your hands—the modern state and municipality.'

To the socialist it would say: 'By all means preach the

influence of circumstance and the power and duty of the organised community to mould it to the highest ends. If you like, and you understand what it means, teach as a part of this the collective control of the means of production. But never forget that the highest and only real end or good is a form of will and character, and that this is something that can never in strict sense be given from without. The community may open up to each the way to achieving it for himself. It is pledged by the Grace and the human effort in the past that have brought it into being to nothing less on behalf of each and all in the time to come. But if its gifts are such as to fail to call out the energy needed to turn them to truly human ends, they will serve merely to hinder the object it has in view. Socialism, or as much of it as you deserve and as is good for you, will come sure enough with the spread of the social will. When it tries to outrun the available supply of enlightened public spirit it only courts disaster like a column in battle that outruns its base.'

To both it would say: 'Remember withal that in politics as in life, where the end, as here it would seem, is the same, common-sense and common charity can carry people a long way together. Remember that your opponent is more than in his war-paint you take him to be—the individualist more than a capitalist, or the friend of the capitalist; the socialist more than an agitator, or the dupe of agitators. This is not to say merely that he is a good fellow, though he is likely enough to be that, too; but to say that, wanting at bottom to do right, he knows in his heart that life at the best is a complicated business, and that he is in mortal doubt as to what in particular it is right to do. And this means that underneath your differences, whether in inherited instinct or in formed opinion, there is working a principle (perhaps a Will like the best part of your own) leading you by ways that you do not clearly understand to a good that is greater than you know.'

59)   H. Jones, 'The Coming of Socialism', in *The Working Faith of the Social Reformer* (Macmillan, 1910), 104–5, 107–14, 278–80.

The contention that 'Socialism is already upon us' is true, if by that is meant that the method of organised communal enterprise is more in use; but it is not true if it means that the individual's sphere of action, or his power to extract utilities, that is, wealth, out of his material environment has been limited. It is being overlooked that the displacement of the individual is but the first step in his re-instalment; and that what is represented as the 'Coming of Socialism' may, with equal truth, be called the 'Coming of Individualism.' *The functions of the State and City on the one side and those of the individual on the other, have grown together.* Both private and communal enterprise have enormously increased during the last century, and, account for it as we may, they are both still increasing. Hence it is possible that here, once more, the principle is illustrated according to which the realisation of the self, whether on the part of the individual or of the State, is at the same time the realisation of the self's opposite. It is possible that the State as a single organism grows in power, even as its citizens acquire freedom; and that the more free and enterprising the citizens, the more sure the order and the more extensive the operations of the State. The antagonism of the State and the citizen is one of those things, taken for granted without being examined, which have done most mischief in social matters. It is possible, at least, that by its regulation of industries the State while limiting caprice has enlarged freedom; that in appropriating industrial enterprises it has liberated the economic power of its citizens—nay, that it has multiplied owners, and increased for them the utilities of wealth, which is to increase wealth itself. . . .

What the legislature has done, on the whole, is to limit the will to do what is wrong and stupid. It is only the pseudo-freedom of irrational caprice which has been limited. Nor has the State invaded any rights in such action; for the liberty to do wrong is not a right, but the perversion of a right and its negation; and the elimination of caprice is no loss to any one: it is one of the ends of all moral and social development.

But there is much more than this negation and limitation of the individual's caprice involved in his organisation into society. A good law, or social institution, is, at bottom, not negative but positive. It apportions rights, and gives the individual a more effective personality. In taking from the individual the right to be judge of his own cause, and avenger of his own wrongs, it re-instates it on a better basis. . . .

The organisation of modern activities, of which the State is only the supreme instance, has placed in the hands of private persons the means of conceiving and carrying out enterprises that were beyond the dreams of the richest of capitalists in the past. The merchant in his office, the employer in his yard, can command far wider and more varied services, and make their will felt to the ends of the earth. The imperial post, the telegraphic system, the civic lighting and cleansing of the streets—what are they except most powerful instruments of the individual will? The State and the city have appropriated these undertakings and many more, but it makes over their utilities to the citizen, liberates his will for other purposes, and multiplies its power a thousandfold. More men can now say 'Mine' of more things. Citizens have been drawn into the activities of the State, for their good has been identified with it in new ways; and enterprises which in previous times were outside the range of their lives are now within it. We can say '*Ours*' of parks, tramways, bridges, art-galleries, public libraries and museums; and if we are worthy of membership in this organism of many functions, we would as soon impair or destroy these common goods as squander our 'private' wealth. No doubt in all these cases we must say '*Thine*' as well as '*Mine*', for the utilities are common. The negative aspect of property is becoming more contracted, but that is no loss to anyone, not even to the jealous and unsocialised unit, if he would only believe it. . . .

As they grow in strength—that is, in the power to conceive wider ends and to carry them out—State and citizen enter more deeply the one into the other. If the State owns the citizen the citizen also owns the State; each finds in the other the means of its power and the defence of its rights. So that the Individualist might well desire more 'State interference' and the socialist more 'private rights'; for the best means of producing strong men is a highly organised State, and the only way of producing a strong State is to make the citizens own so much, care for so much, be responsible for so much, that each can say, without injury to his neighbour, 'The State is mine'. . . .

But, it will be asked, does this mean that we are to welcome any and every municipal or State activity? Is all increase of corporate enterprise a liberation of the individual's force? By no means, I would answer. There are many reasons why every new departure should be carefully scrutinised, and tried by every test. The dislocation of private enterprises is not to be lightly entered upon: probably never, if the good results which accrue terminate in a class and do not raise the State as a whole, or if private combination can serve the purpose with equal efficiency. The entrance of a municipality or State into the competitive field is not in all respects on a par with the entrance of a private competitor. And, above all, the range of the activities of the State or municipality varies with its intellectual capacity and moral strength. There is hardly too narrow a limit to the functions of a weak State or a corrupt city, or too wide a limit for the intelligent and strong.

The essential point, however, is this—that the limits are not to be fixed by any conception of the abstract antagonism of society and the individual: for each of these is true to itself precisely in the degree to which it is faithful to its opposite. The criterion of the action of the State is the effective freedom of its citizens. There remains in the moral life of the citizens an intensely individual element which the State must never over-ride. The rights of personality can be wisely sacrificed to nothing, nor its good postponed to either city or State or humanity. But, on the other hand, the sovereignty of the individual's will and all its sacredness come from its identification with a wider will. His rights are rooted in the rights of others; and all the rights alike draw their life-sap from the moral law, the universal good, the *objective* rightness, of which no jot or tittle can pass away. Hence, the individual can resist the will of the community or the extension of the functions of his city or State only when he has identified his own will with a will that is more universal, more concrete, and the source of higher imperatives than either. And this means that he can resist the State only for the good of the State, and never *merely* for his own profit. The content of the authoritative will must always be the common good, and the common good must always assume a personal form. . . .

Now, what follows from all this? Manifestly, it seems to me, that the indifference of the individual to his social obligations is in no sense justifiable. His duties towards society are only comparable to the duties of the child to the mother who has carried him under her heart; for he is born, nourished, developed into individuality within the social matrix. He owes to his city and the State a service that never grows weary, a loyalty that never fails, a love that forgets all faults, or rather, remembers them only to endeavour to remove them. Nay, he owes everything to them except the bare potentiality of becoming a rational being, which potentiality would never be realized without his city and the State.

Is there, then, any means of paying back obligations which are so vast, and so obvious? There are many, I would answer; and they have this unique characteristic that in paying them back man enriches himself. The first, the greatest service he can render his city and State, is that of fulfilling the duties of the station in life in which he is placed. For social life is articulated through and through into limited spheres of activity, more or less suitable to the powers of its particular organs. No public activity will make up for the neglect of these more private duties. But in performing these honestly and well the individual is also serving the State. In an ideal condition of society, I am sometimes tempted to believe, no other service can be required of a man except that which his peculiar station, his profession, trade, or craft may bring. But we are far, very far, from that ideal state when everyone, being virtuous and wise, bears his own share of the burden of the general good—which, by the bye, is not only a burden but a privilege. In the meantime, the man who either by his wisdom or his riches, by his happy temperament, his virtuous will, his ready sympathy, his wide intellectual outlook, his social status, or by any other form of wealth within him or without, is endowed beyond his neighbours, is called upon to undertake many a task outside his narrower sphere. I do not deny that even if he confines himself within his immediate personal or family concerns, and wraps himself up in his more private virtues his value to the community is great. But by doing so he will deprive himself of the opportunities of a larger growth: for the wider atmosphere of the city and of the state is to that of the family as the open air is to a closed room—colder and less kindly and sometimes rude, but also bracing. Virtue was never meant to be cloistered, my friends, and the world of human society needs all we possess of it. We have a right to call upon each other to be good citizens, and to endeavour as best we may to pay the debts of honour to the great municipality and the greater empire within which it is our privilege to lead and to spend our little lives.

60)   R. C. K. Ensor (ed.), *Modern Socialism* (Harper, 2nd ed.,
       1907), xxvii–ix.

The reader of this volume will not require here a long
account of Socialistic theory. Summarily we may describe it
as the doctrine, that whereas the means of production (capital,
with land and raw materials) are as indispensable to every
man's existence as his own body, society should secure for all
its members an equally free access to them, by disallowing
private property in them (just as it has secured for all the
equally free disposition of their bodies, by disallowing slavery).
Private property, as it exists, exists solely in virtue of social
action, and the motive for that action is social utility. Its aim
is to secure for the producer the means of production, so that
he who will work may work out his own salvation. Socialists
believe this aim to be unrealized by it, owing to the tendency
of capital to concentration.[1] This tendency divides society into
two classes—a diminishing class who have capital and can
work on their own account, and an increasing class who have
not, but must sell their services—'capitalists' and 'proletarians.'
If the right of private property in capital is secured in its
absolute form (the form taught to Europe by Roman law), the
proletarians are absolutely at the capitalists' mercy. They *must*
work for the capitalists, for otherwise they cannot work at all,
and would starve. The capitalists can make them do what
work they please, under what conditions they please, and need
only give even a subsistence wage so far as they fear a shortage
of labour.

Socialism then asserts, that unless the capitalists' right of
property is limited, the proletarian's degradation will be unlimited. Even Roman law, when it forbade the creditor to
enslave his debtor, acknowledged that the State must fix some
minimum, below which the capitalist cannot bargain for the
proletarian to go. When Socialism advocates, *e.g.,* a com-

---

[1] This tendency, or law, which seems valid for all industry except possibly farming, is that in adding capitals $2+2$ do not $= 4$, but $4+x$, the
x representing a special advantage of concentration. Thus £200 capital
will enable a man to do more than twice as much as £100 would, or
£200,000 more than twice as much as £100,000. x will not always be
realized, but will always tend to be. Its value was enormously raised by
the Industrial Revolution, and seems to be still rising. It operates inside
society as a continual handicap, increasing the amounts of capital owned,
and diminishing the relative number of owners.

pulsory eight hours' day, it proceeds on exactly parallel lines; a capitalist shall not force a proletarian to work nine hours, any more than he can force him to become a slave. Broadly this process may be termed the 'expropriation' of capital. The employers have been quite logical in protesting that 'a man can do what he likes with his own.' As soon as the State says, 'You shall not do this or that with your capital,' expropriation has begun.

We should note here, though, that expropriation may take one of two forms—the State may abolish the owner, or it may abolish ownership. It does the former, whenever a railway system is nationalized or a tramway system is municipalized. It does the latter, partially, when it regulates the hours or conditions of labour, and more completely, when (as by compulsory arbitration) it fixes labour's wage. The two methods sometimes compete. Land nationalization illustrates the former,—the State becomes landlord; while a policy of land registry combines with a heavy progressive land-tax, restraints on leasing, prohibition of mortgages, and regulation of landed inheritance, illustrates the latter,—the State abolishes land-lordism. Doubts will arise as to which method is the best in particular cases; but as a rule the former only protects the proletarian as consumer, and the latter only as producer. Each, therefore, needs to be supplemented by the other. A State railway may benefit the consuming community in any case; but it only benefits railwaymen if it adopts a good standard wage policy (which, *e.g.*, the Prussian State Railways do not). A standard wage system benefits proletarian producers in any case; but they can only realize its value in consumption, if the State protects them against monopolies by intelligently nationalizing and municipalizing them.

The moral claim from which Socialism starts is that for equality of opportunity. This may be made clearer by a single illustration. Elementary education in England is Socialistic; secondary is not. Observe that neither is possible without capital—that is, proletarian children (say 90 per cent. of those reared) must in default of State action or charity go without education. The State has stepped in, and has said to every proletarian child: 'You shall have elementary education; you shall have at least the "three R's" to help you in working and in bargaining for the means to work.' Socialism demands an identical policy for further education. It asks that every child shall have an equal chance of it, and that his capacity shall decide how far he shall go. But under a strict operation of private property the proletarian children must have no chance at all, and the amount of education which each gets be proportioned not to his own capacity so much as to his father's capital.

61)   H. G. Wells, *New Worlds for Old* (Constable, 1908), 303–7.

First, then, the Constructive Socialist has to do whatever lies in his power towards *the enrichment of the Socialist idea*. He has to give whatever gifts he has as artist, as writer, as maker of any sort to increasing and refining the conception of civilized life. He has to embody and make real the State and the City. And the Socialist idea, constantly restated, refreshed and elaborated, has to be made a part of the common circle of ideas; has to be grasped and felt and assimilated by the whole mass of mankind, has to be made the basis of each individual's private morality. That mental work is the primary, most essential function of Constructive Socialism.

And next, Constructive Socialism has in every country to direct its energies and attention to *political reform*, to the scientific reconstruction of our representative and administrative machinery so as to give power and real expression to the developing collective mind of the community, and to remove the obstructions to Socialization that are inevitable where institutions stand for 'interests' or have fallen under the sway of aggressive private property or of narrowly organized classes. Governing and representative bodies, advisory and investigatory organizations of a liberal and responsive type have to be built up, bodies that shall be really capable of the immense administrative duties the secular abolition of the great bulk of private ownership will devolve upon them.

Thirdly, the constructive Socialist sets himself to forward *the resumption of the land by the community*, by increased control, by taxation, by death duties, by purchase and by partially compensated confiscation as circumstances may render advisable, and so to make the municipality the sole landlord in the reorganized world.

And meanwhile the constructive Socialist goes on also with the work of *socializing the main public services*, by transferring them steadily from private enterprise to municipal and State control, by working steadily for such transfers and by opposing every party and every organization that does not set its face resolutely against the private exploitation of new needs and services.

There are four distinct systems of public service which could very conveniently be organized under collective ownership and control now, and each can be attacked independently of the others. There is first the need of public educational machinery, and by education I mean not simply elementary education, but the equally vital need for great colleges not only to teach and study technical arts and useful sciences, but also to enlarge learning and sustain philosophical and literary work. A civilized community is impossible without great public libraries, public museums, public art schools, without public honour and support for contemporary thought and literature, and all these things the constructive Socialist may forward at a hundred points.

Then next there is the need and opportunity of organizing the whole community in relation to health, the collective development of hospitals, medical aid, public sanitation, child welfare, into one great loyal and efficient public service. This, too, may be pushed forward either as part of the general Socialist movement or independently as a thing in itself by those who may find the whole Socialist proposition unacceptable or inconvenient.

A third system of interests upon which practical work may be done at the present time lies in the complex interdependent developments of transit and housing, questions that lock up inextricably with the problem of replanning our local government areas. Here, too, the whole world is beginning to realize more and more clearly that private enterprise is wasteful and socially disastrous, that collective control, collective management, and so on to collective enterprise and ownership of building-land, houses, railways, tramways and omnibuses, give the only way of escape from an endless drifting entanglement and congestion of our mobile modern population.

The fourth department of economic activity in which collectivism is developing, and in which the constructive Socialist will find enormous scope for work, is in connection with the more generalized forms of public trading, and especially with the production, handling and supply of food and minerals.

When the lagging enterprise of agriculture needs to be supplemented by endowed educational machinery, agricultural colleges and the like; when the feeble intellectual initiative of the private adventure miner and manufacturer necessitates a London 'Charlottenburg,' it must be manifest that State initiative has altogether out-distanced the possibilities of private effort, and that the next step to the public authority instructing men how to farm, prepare food, run dairies, manage mines and distribute minerals, is to cut out the pedagogic middleman and undertake the work itself. The State education of the expert for private consumption (such as we see at the Royal School of Mines) is surely too ridiculous a sacrifice of the community to private property to continue at that. The further inevitable line of advance is the transfer from private to public hands by purchase, by competing organizations or what not, of all those great services, just as rapidly as the increasing capacity and experience of the public authority permits.

This briefly is the work and method of Constructive Socialism to-day. Under one or other head it can utilize almost every sort of capacity and every type of opportunity. It refuses no one who will serve it. It is no narrow doctrinaire cult. It does not seek the best of an argument, but the best of a world. Its worst enemies are those foolish and litigious advocates who antagonize and estrange every development of human Good Will that does not pay tribute to their vanity in open acquiescence. Its most loyal servants, its most effectual helpers on the side of art, invention and public organization and political reconstruction, may be men who will never adopt the Socialist name.

62)   H. du Parcq, *Life of David Lloyd George* (Caxton, 1913), IV, 637.

LLOYD GEORGE SPEECH AT MANCHESTER, 1908

After all, this is a rich country. It is the richest country under the sun; and yet in this rich country you have hundreds and thousands of people living under conditions of poverty, destitution, and squalor that would, in the words of an old Welsh poet, make the rocks weep. This is the stain upon the flag. And it ought to be the duty of every man in this country, for the honour of his native land, to put an end to it. There are men in this country, of course, who are in such easy circumstances that they need not apprehend anything from the dread spectre of unemployment. The wolves of hunger may not be awaiting winter to prey upon their child. But still, I am one of those who believe that human sympathy is in the end capable of a deeper and more potent appeal to the human heart than even interest.

If these poor people are to be redeemed they must be redeemed not by themselves, because nothing strikes you more than the stupor of despair in which they have sunk—they must be redeemed by others outside, and the appeal ought to be to every class of the community to see that in this great land all this misery and wretchedness should be put an end to. I cannot boast, like Mr. Hyndman, the Socialist, that I belong to a different class from the audience I address. I am a man of the people, bred amongst them, and it has been the greatest joy of my life to have had some part in fighting the battles of the class from whom I am proud to have sprung.

The task is great and it is difficult. The task of every reformer is heart-breaking. There are sympathies to arouse, there are suspicions to allay. There are hopes to excite, there are fears to calm. There are faint hearts to sustain, there are hot heads to restrain. There is the dormant interest in right to wake up, there is many a vested interest in wrong to be beaten down.

63)   A. V. Dicey, *Lectures on the Relation between Law and Public Opinion in England* (Macmillan, 2nd ed., 1914), lxii–iii.

An Englishman of the middle classes who is freed from the necessity for all-absorbing toil in order to obtain the means necessary for acquiring the independence or the comforts of his life, is more often than not a man of kindly disposition. His own happiness is diminished by the known and felt miseries of his less wealthy neighbours. Now, for the last sixty years and more, the needs and sufferings of the poor have been thrust upon the knowledge of middle-class Englishmen. There are persons still living who can recall the time when about sixty years ago the *Morning Chronicle* in letters on London

Labour and the London Poor revealed to the readers of high-class, and then dear, newspapers the miserable condition of the poorer wage-earners of London. These letters at once aroused the sympathy and called forth the aid of Maurice and the Christian Socialists. For sixty years novelists, newspaper writers, and philanthropists have alike brought the condition of the poor constantly before the eyes of their readers or disciples. The desire to ease the sufferings, to increase the pleasures, and to satisfy the best aspirations of the mass of wage-earners has become a marked characteristic of the wealthy classes of Englishmen. This sentiment of active good-will, stimulated no doubt by ministers of religion, has spread far and wide among laymen, *e.g.* lawyers, merchants, and others not specially connected with any one religious, theo-logical, or political party. There is nothing in all this to excite surprise, though there is much to kindle hope. It may be expected that, as has happened again and again during the history of England, the power of opinion may, without any immense revolution in the institutions of the country, modify and reform their working. No doubt there is something also in the present condition of public sentiment to arouse fear. The years which immediately preceded the French Revolution witnessed the rapid development of benevolence and philan-thropy in France and throughout the civilised countries of Europe. These feelings were not unreal though coloured, under the influence of Rousseau, with too much of rhetoric to suit the taste of the twentieth century, and were connected with speculative doctrines which, in common with modern collec-tivism, combine some important truths with some at least equally important delusions. No criticism, in any case, of public opinion in England is worth anything which fails to take into account the goodwill of the richer classes of English-men towards their less prosperous neighbours.

64)   G. R. S. Taylor, *Leaders of Socialism Past and Present* (New Age Press, 1908), 16–17.

We know what Socialism is; the question is: How can we most quickly bring it to pass? It is a question about which there is practically no dispute on the Continent; where every great nation has its Socialist Party in Parliament, as a declaration that Socialism can only come by the parliamentary action of an independent political body. In Great Britain the case is by no means beyond the stage of argument; we have the astonishing spectacle, for example, of Mr. H. G. Wells pleading for the hope in constructive Liberalism and Toryism. Such a thing could scarcely happen in France or Germany, where they long ago settled that they must have their own party of Socialists. England is waiting for its Jean Jaurès who will gather together into one unified parliamentary party all the elements of Socialist attack.

We are waiting in this country for a great leader who will overthrow this popular delusion that Socialism is social reform, that Englishmen are gentle evolutionaries. When a social reformer in England is afraid of his own demands, when he wonders whether he is not getting in the firing line, with danger of a bullet, then he discreetly retires, with the comforting reflection that, after all, it is foolish to try to push the English people into great revolutions, for it is the natural law of their race to go forward very slowly: slow but sure, is the motto of reform in these islands, and it is useless to kick against the pricks. There is more than a doubt whether this soothing theory is based on historical fact or on the nervous imaginations of timid leaders. It is all very well for the permeating Fabians to say that their peculiar creeping method alone suits the genius of the British people; they, at least, overlook such pertinent facts as the quick change from a despotic monarchy to Oliver Cromwell, with the illuminating spectacle of a headless king to drive home the moral of the incident. Another forty years saw the hurried departure of Scottish James because his people had taken up arms on riotous behalf of Dutch William. And there have been Wat Tylers and Chartists and other popular demonstrators who do not, strictly speaking, come under the head of peaceful evolution. In short, it is doubtful whether this 'peaceful Englishman' is not as mythical a being as the Englishman who is a 'born sailor.' The day for physical rebellion is perhaps past; the day of political revolt has at last come. And the symbol and practice of revolt must take the shape of a Socialist Party that will challenge all other species of reform.

65)   R. C. K. Ensor (ed.), *Modern Socialism* (Harper, 2nd ed., 1907), 351–5.

PROGRAMME OF THE SOCIAL DEMOCRATIC FEDERATION, 1906

In order to ensure greater material and moral facilities for the working-class to organize itself and to carry on the class war, the following reforms must immediately be carried through:—

IMMEDIATE REFORMS

Political

Abolition of the Monarchy.

Democratization of the Governmental machinery, viz. abolition of the House of Lords, payment of members of legislative and administrative bodies, payment of official expenses of elections out of the public funds, adult suffrage, proportional representation, triennial parliaments, second ballot, initiative and referendum. Foreigners to be granted rights of citizenship after two years' residence in the country, without any fees. Canvassing to be made illegal. All elections to take place on one day, such day to be made a legal holiday, and all premises licensed for the sale of intoxicating liquors to be closed.

Legislation by the people in such wise that no legislative proposal shall become law until ratified by the majority of the people.

Legislative and administrative independence for all parts of the Empire.

Financial and Fiscal

Repudiation of the National Debt.

Abolition of all indirect taxation and the institution of a cumulative tax on all incomes and inheritance exceeding £300.

Administrative

Extension of the principle of local self-government.

Systematization and co-ordination of the local administrative bodies.

Election of all administrators and administrative bodies by equal direct adult suffrage.

Educational

Elementary education to be free, secular, industrial, and compulsory for all classes. The age of obligatory school attendance to be raised to 16.

Unification and systematization of intermediate and higher education, both general and technical, and all such education to be free.

State maintenance for all attending State schools.

Abolition of school rates; the cost of education in all State schools to be borne by the National Exchequer.

Public Monopolies and Services

Nationalization of the land and the organization of labour in agriculture and industry under public ownership and control on co-operative principles.

Nationalization of the trusts.

Nationalization of railways, docks, and canals, and all great means of transit.

Public ownership and control of gas, electric light, and water supplies, as well as of tramway, omnibus, and other locomotive services.

Public ownership and control of the food and coal supply.

The establishment of State and municipal banks and pawn-shops and public restaurants.

Public ownership and control of the lifeboat service.

Public ownership and control of hospitals, dispensaries, cemeteries, and crematoria.

Public ownership and control of the drink traffic.

Labour

A legislative eight-hour working-day, or 48 hours per week, to be the maximum for all trades and industries. Imprisonment to be inflicted on employers for any infringement of the law.

Absolute freedom of combination for all workers, with legal guarantee against any action, private or public, which tends to curtail or infringe it.

No child to be employed in any trade or occupation until 16 years of age, and imprisonment to be inflicted on employers, parents, and guardians who infringe this law.

Public provision of useful work at not less than trade-union rates of wages for the unemployed.

Free State insurance against sickness and accident, and free and adequate State pensions or provision for aged and disabled workers. Public assistance not to entail any forfeiture of political rights.

The legislative enactment of a minimum wage of 30s. for all workers. Equal pay for both sexes for the performance of equal work.

Social

Abolition of the present workhouse system, and reformed administration of the Poor Law on a basis of national co-operation.

Compulsory construction by public bodies of healthy dwellings for the people; such dwellings to be let at rents to cover the cost of construction and maintenance alone, and not to cover the cost of the land.

The administration of justice and legal advice to be free to all; justice to be administered by judges chosen by the people; appeal in criminal cases; compensation for those innocently accused, condemned, and imprisoned; abolition of imprisonment for contempt of court in relation to non-payment of debt in the case of workers earning less than £2 per week; abolition of capital punishment.

Miscellaneous

The disestablishment and disendowment of all State churches.

The abolition of standing armies, and the establishment of national citizen forces. The people to decide on peace and war.

The establishment of international courts of arbitration.

The abolition of courts-martial; all offences against discipline to be transferred to the jurisdiction of civil courts.

66) R. C. K. Ensor (ed.), *Modern Socialism* (Harper, 2nd ed., 1907), 357–8.

PROGRAMME OF THE INDEPENDENT LABOUR PARTY, 1906–7

Name.—'The Independent Labour Party.'
Object.—An industrial commonwealth founded upon the Socialization of land and capital.
Methods.—The education of the community in the principles of Socialism.

The industrial and political organization of the workers.

The independent representation of Socialist principles on all elective bodies.

Programme

The true object of industry being the production of the requirements of life, the responsibility should rest with the community collectively, therefore—

The land, being the storehouse of all the necessaries of life, should be declared and treated as public property.

The capital necessary for industrial operations should be owned and used collectively.

Work, and wealth resulting therefrom, should be equitably distributed over the population.

As a means to this end, we demand the enactment of the following measures:—

1. A maximum forty-eight hours' working-week, with the retention of all existing holidays, and Labour Day, May 1, secured by law.

2. The provision of work to all capable adult applicants at recognized trade-union rates, with a statutory minimum of sixpence per hour.

In order to remuneratively employ the applicants, parish, district, borough, and county councils to be invested with powers to—

(*a*) Organize and undertake such industries as they may consider desirable.

(*b*) Compulsorily acquire land; purchase, erect, or manufacture, buildings, stock, or other articles for carrying on such industries.

(*c*) Levy rates on the rental values of the district, and

borrow money on the security of such rates for any of the above purposes.

3.   State pensions for every person over fifty years of age, and adequate provision for all widows, orphans, sick and disabled workers.

4.   Free, secular, moral, primary, secondary and university education, with free maintenance while at school or university.

5.   The raising of the age of child labour, with a view of its ultimate extinction.

6.   Municipalization and public control of the drink traffic.

7.   Municipalization and public control of all hospitals and infirmaries.

8.   Abolition of indirect taxation, and the gradual transference of all public burdens on to unearned incomes, with a view to their ultimate extinction.

The Independent Labour party is in favour of adult suffrage, with full political rights and privileges for women, and the immediate extension of the franchise to women on the same terms as granted to men; also triennial parliaments and second ballot.

67)   R. C. K. Ensor (ed.), *Modern Socialism* (Harper, 2nd ed., 1907), 359–60.

Basis of the Fabian Society

The Fabian Society consists of Socialists.

It therefore aims at the reorganization of society by the emancipation of land and industrial capital from individual and class ownership, and the vesting of them in the community for the general benefit. In this way only can the natural and acquired advantages of the country be equitably shared by the whole people.

The Society accordingly works for the extinction of private property in land and of the consequent individual appropriation, in the form of rent, of the price paid for permission to use the earth, as well as for the advantages of superior soils and sites.

The Society, further, works for the transfer to the community of the administration of such industrial capital as can conveniently be managed socially. For, owing to the monopoly of the means of production in the past, industrial inventions and the transformation of surplus income into capital have mainly enriched the proprietary class, the worker being now dependent on that class for leave to earn a living.

If these measures be carried out, without compensation (though not without such relief to expropriated individuals as may seem fit to the community), rent and interest will be added to the reward of labour, the idle class now living on the labour of others will necessarily disappear, and practical equality of opportunity will be maintained by the spontaneous action of economic forces with much less interference with personal liberty than the present system entails.

For the attainment of these ends the Fabian Society looks to the spread of Socialist opinions, and the social and political changes consequent thereon. It seeks to promote these by the general dissemination of knowledge as to the relation between the individual and society in its economic, ethical and political aspects.

68)   D. H. Laurence (ed.), *Platform and Pulpit, Bernard Shaw* (Hart-Davis, 1962), 93–6.

   Speech delivered at the War Against Poverty Demonstration, under the joint auspices of the Independent Labour Party and the Fabian Society, in the Albert Hall, London, 11 October 1912.

I have received many letters during the last few days from gentlemen who, seeing that I was advertized to take part in a meeting for the abolition of poverty, suggested that I might make a modest beginning in the form of pecuniary accommodation to themselves privately. But all these gentlemen made the mistake of representing themselves as being miserably poor. I am present at this meeting because there is nothing in the world I hate more than a poor man. I should be a Conservative if I had sympathy for the poor.

It happened that when I was a small child my nurse used to take me out for exercise in the open air. She did not exercise me in the open air; she took me to visit her friends. Her friends were mostly poor people. I thought them most horrible people. I simply detested them, and I still detest them. I think such people ought not to exist.

I am perfectly determined not to be poor if I can help it. I don't want to be rich. I would be content with, say, four or five thousand pounds a year. But I am not content to have four or five thousand a year and to be surrounded by dirty, ignorant people who have only a pound a week.

I am not content to have a nice house myself. I want everybody else to have a nice house; I have got to look at those houses. The only reason why I like my drawing room to be nice is that I have to look at it. I don't eat it. For the same reason I want other people's houses to look nice—on the outside, at any rate. If I thought your houses were beautiful inside, you might have the opportunity to enjoy the inestimable favor of hearing my brilliant conversation, which is celebrated throughout Europe.

I want to cure poverty as an abominable disease and as a very horrible crime. I never had any sort of enthusiasm for the ordinary movements for the suppression of crime. If a man is by disposition a murderer you cannot make him a philanthropist. You cannot turn a real, genuine, congenital thief into an honest man. He may be a very pleasant man—I have known many charming thieves—but you cannot change him fundamentally. We are always clamoring to do the impossible.

You can, however, take a dirty man and you can clean him. You can take an ignorant man and you can teach him. You can take a poor man and you can give him money. Then he wont be a poor man any longer.

Therefore, in standing on this platform I claim to be standing upon the only practical platform that exists in England. All the other parties are setting out to do something which cannot be done. That is how the governing classes occupy themselves. They imagine it will keep the people quiet.

Our method of proceeding by demanding a minimum is really the method by which all civilizations have advanced. The law imposes upon everyone in this hall a minimum of clothes. I am sorry the law does not go further and impose a minimum as to the quality of the clothes. I strongly object to the quality of clothes worn in London today. It is foolish to say that everyone should be dressed if you do not say that they shall be well dressed.

In the same way we must insist on a minimum of honesty. We allow a man to be a large shareholder, but we prevent him from being a pickpocket. We insist on that minimum of honesty even for millionaires. But a pickpocket is nowhere nearly so harmful to the community as the poor man. The poor man breeds disease and casts a blight over the people. The first thing to do, therefore, is to insist upon a minimum of money in everyone's pockets.

We have gone so far in this direction as to give a man five shillings a week when he is seventy years of age. I defy you to give one reason for giving a man of seventy five shillings a week, which is not a far better reason for giving a man of twentyseven £500 a year. The thing can be done. There is no difficulty in producing a higher standard of life. You are stupid enough to waste your opportunities. With the exception of a few ladies and gentlemen, everyone who is working is producing more than he consumes. Roughly, he is producing twice as much. What should we, if we were reasonable beings (which I know you are not), expect to follow as a consequence of that extraordinary fact? Would you not expect this country to be getting richer and richer from one generation to another? Would you not expect the children to be healthier and heavier, the men and women stronger and more beautiful? Would you not expect its slums to be disappearing by magic, its disease to be passing away, the necessity for working long hours to be ceasing? Would you not be expecting this earth to be fulfilling its real destiny, to be transforming itself into the Kingdom of Heaven?

What are we actually doing with this enormous surplus of wealth? We are throwing it into the pockets of people who use it, not for the improvement of the country, but for its degradation. When are you going to stop it?

Some enthusiasts tonight have asked, 'When are you going to turn out the Government?' They know very well that we have not the heart nor the power to turn out even the people who interrupt us in this audience. Turn out the Government? We have not the strength in the House of Commons to turn anybody out; it is as much as we can do to keep ourselves in.

The task before us is to turn out a whole epoch of civilization, to turn out a generation which has become entirely corrupt by worn-out traditions and prejudices, to inaugurate and bring in a new epoch. It can only be done by the spreading of a great conception among the people, of a higher conception of life. You, who are here, are a picked and chosen few. I wish you would go amongst those who think they are money-making, and who are really grinding each other down, and break their windows. Other movements besides the Suffrage movement need to be militant. We want a conviction of sin and of salvation, a wave of intense shame at existing conditions which shall make them intolerable to those who imagine that they profit by it.

The hammer of public opinion is needed and, I repeat, a genuine conviction of sin. The greatest curse of poverty is that it destroys the will power of the poor until they become the most ardent supporters of their own poverty. We have to talk to these people, and, if possible, talk sense.

I am not sure that the interrupters tonight have not set us a good example. I suggest that you go to other political meetings, and when someone says, 'Bulgaria,' or 'Ireland,' or 'Land Reform,' you say, 'What about Poverty?' Such action will begin by you being turned out. I hope it will end in a bad epoch being turned out.

69)   R. C. K. Ensor (ed.), *Modern Socialism* (Harper, 2nd ed., 1907) 364–8.

CONSTITUTION OF THE LABOUR PARTY, 1906

ORGANIZATION

I.—Affiliation

1.   The Labour Party is a Federation consisting of Trade-Unions, Trades-Councils, Socialist Societies, and Local Labour Associations.

2.   A Local Labour Association in any constituency is eligible for affiliation, provided it accepts the constitution and policy of the party, and that there is no affiliated Trades Council covering the constituency, or that, if there be such council, it has been consulted in the first instance.

3.   Co-operative Societies are also eligible.

II.—Object

1.   To organize and maintain a Parliamentary Labour Party, with its own whips and policy.

2. To secure the election of candidates for whose candidatures an affiliated society has made itself financially responsible, and who have been selected by a regularly convened conference in the constituency.

III.—Candidates and Members

1. Candidates and members must accept this constitution; agree to abide by the decisions of the Parliamentary party in carrying out the aims of this constitution; appear before their constituencies under the title of Labour candidates only; abstain strictly from identifying themselves with or promoting the interests of any party not eligible for affiliation; and they must not oppose any candidate recognized by the Executive Committee of the party.

2. Candidates must undertake to join the Parliamentary Labour party, if elected.

IV.—The Executive

The executive shall consist of thirteen members, nine representing the Trade-Unions, one the Trades-Council and Local Labour Associations, and three the Socialist Societies, and shall be elected by ballot at the annual conference by their respective sections.

V.—Duties of the Executive

The Executive Committee shall—

1. Appoint a chairman, vice-chairman, and treasurer, and shall transact the general business of the party;

2. Issue a list of its candidates from time to time, and recommend them for the support of the electors;

3. Report to the affiliated organization concerned any Labour member, candidate, or chief official who opposes a candidate of the party, or who acts contrary to the spirit of this constitution;

4. And its members shall strictly abstain from identifying themselves with or promoting the interests of any party not eligible for affiliation.

VI.—The Secretary

The secretary shall be elected by the annual conference, and shall be under the direction of the Executive Committee.

VII.—*Affiliation Fees and Delegates*

1.   Trade-Unions and Socialist Societies shall pay 15*s*. per annum for every 1,000 members or fraction thereof, and may send to the annual conference one delegate for each thousand members.

2.   Trades-Councils and Local Labour Associations shall pay £1 10*s*. per annum, irrespective of membership, and shall be entitled to send one delegate to the annual conference, but they may send one additional delegate for every additional 10*s*. paid as affiliation fee.

3.   In addition to these payments a delegate's fee to the annual conference may be charged.

VIII.—*Annual Conference*

The Executive Committee shall convene a conference of its affiliated societies in the month of January each year.

Notice of resolutions for the conference and all amendments to the constitution shall be sent to the secretary by November 20th, and shall be forthwith forwarded to all affiliated organizations.

Notice of amendments and nominations for secretary and executive shall be sent to the secretary by December 15th, and shall be printed on the agenda.

IX.—*Voting at Annual Conference*

There shall be issued to affiliated societies represented at the annual conference voting cards as follows:—

1.   Trade-Unions and Socialist Societies shall receive one voting card for each thousand members, or fraction thereof paid for.

2.   Trades-Councils and Local Labour Associations shall receive one card for each delegate they are entitled to send.

Any delegate may claim to have a vote taken by card.

PARLIAMENTARY FUND

I.—*Object*

To assist in paying the election expenses of Labour candidates and in maintaining members of the Parliamentary Labour party.

II.—Amount of Contribution

Affiliated societies, except Trades-Councils and Local Labour Associations, shall pay a contribution to this fund at the rate of 1*d.* per member per annum, not later than the last day of each financial year.

III.—Trustees

The Executive Committee of the party shall, from its number, select three to act as trustees, any two of whom, with the secretary, shall sign cheques.

IV.—Expenditure

1. *Maintenance.*—All members elected under the auspices of the Labour party shall be paid from the fund an equal sum not to exceed £200 per annum, provided that this payment shall only be made to members whose candidatures have been promoted by Societies which have contributed to this fund: provided further that no payment from this fund shall be made to a member or candidate of any society which has not contributed to this fund for one year, and that any society over three months in arrears shall forfeit all claim to the fund on behalf of its members or candidates, for twelve months from the date of payment.

2. *Returning Officers' Expenses.*—Twenty-five per cent. of the returning officers' net expenses shall be paid to the candidates, subject to the provisions of the preceding clause, so long as the total sum so expended does not exceed twenty-five per cent. of the fund.

3. *Administration.*—Five per cent. of the annual income of the fund shall be transferred to the general funds of the party to pay for working expenses of the fund.

70)   L. T. Hobhouse, *Liberalism* (Williams & Norgate, 1911), 146–7, 158–62.

The function of State coercion is to override individual coercion, and, of course, coercion exercised by any association of individuals within the State. It is by this means that it

maintains liberty of expression, security of person and property, genuine freedom of contract, the rights of public
meeting and association, and finally its own power to carry out
common objects undefeated by the recalcitrance of individual
members. Undoubtedly it endows both individuals and associations with powers as well as with rights. But over these powers
it must exercise supervision in the interests of equal justice.
Just as compulsion failed in the sphere of liberty, the sphere of
spiritual growth, so liberty fails in the external order wherever,
by the mere absence of supervisory restriction, men are able
directly or indirectly to put constraint on one another. This is
why there is no intrinsic and inevitable conflict between
liberty and compulsion, but at bottom a mutual need. The
object of compulsion is to secure the most favourable external
conditions of inward growth and happiness so far as these
conditions depend on combined action and uniform observance. The sphere of liberty is the sphere of growth itself. There
is no true opposition between liberty as such and control as
such, for every liberty rests on a corresponding act of control.
The true opposition is between the control that cramps the
personal life and the spiritual order, and the control that is
aimed at securing the external and material conditions of their
free and unimpeded development. . . .

It is for the State to take care that the economic conditions
are such that the normal man who is not defective in mind or
body or will can by useful labour feed, house, and clothe
himself and his family. The 'right to work' and the right to a
'living wage' are just as valid as the rights of person or
property. That is to say, they are integral conditions of a good
social order. A society in which a single honest man of normal
capacity is definitely unable to find the means of maintaining
himself by useful work is to that extent suffering from malorganization. There is somewhere a defect in the social system,
a hitch in the economic machine. Now, the individual workman cannot put the machine straight. He is the last person to
have any say in the control of the market. It is not his fault if
there is over-production in his industry, or if a new and
cheaper process has been introduced which makes his particular skill, perhaps the product of years of application, a drug
in the market. He does not direct or regulate industry. He is
not responsible for its ups and downs, but he has to pay for
them. That is why it is not charity but justice for which he is

asking. Now, it may be infinitely difficult to meet his demand. To do so may involve a far-reaching economic reconstruction. The industrial questions involved may be so little understood that we may easily make matters worse in the attempt to make them better. All this shows the difficulty in finding means of meeting this particular claim of justice, but it does not shake its position as a claim of justice. A right is a right none the less though the means of securing it be imperfectly known; and the workman who is unemployed or underpaid through economic malorganization will remain a reproach not to the charity but to the justice of society as long as he is to be seen in the land.

If this view of the duty of the State and the right of the workman is coming to prevail, it is owing partly to an enhanced sense of common responsibility, and partly to the teaching of experience. In the earlier days of the Free Trade era, it was permissible to hope that self-help would be an adequate solvent, and that with cheap food and expanding commerce the average workman would be able by the exercise of prudence and thrift not only to maintain himself in good times, but to lay by for sickness, unemployment, and old age. The actual course of events has in large measure disappointed these hopes. It is true that the standard of living in England has progressively advanced throughout the nineteenth century. It is true, in particular, that, since the disastrous period that preceded the Repeal of the Corn Laws and the passing of the Ten Hours' Act, social improvement has been real and marked. Trade Unionism and co-operation have grown, wages upon the whole have increased, the cost of living has diminished, housing and sanitation have improved, the death rate has fallen from about twenty-two to less than fifteen per thousand. But with all this improvement the prospect of a complete and lifelong economic independence for the average workman upon the lines of individual competition, even when supplemented and guarded by the collective bargaining of the Trade Union, appears exceedingly remote. The increase of wages does not appear to be by any means proportionate to the general growth of wealth. The whole standard of living has risen; the very provision of education has brought with it new needs and has almost compelled a higher standard of life in order to satisfy them. As a whole, the working classes of England, though less thrifty than those of some Continental countries, cannot be accused of undue negligence with regard to the future. The accumulation of savings in Friendly Societies, Trade Unions, Co-operative Societies, and Savings Banks shows an increase which has more than kept pace with the rise in the level of wages; yet there appears no likelihood that the average manual worker will attain the goal of that full independence, covering all the risks of life for self and family, which can alone render the competitive system really adequate to the demands of a civilized conscience.

71)   *The Times*, 21 October 1907.

ASQUITH SPEECH AT EAST FIFE, 1907

Anyone who looked around with unprejudiced eyes at the structure of society as it actually is and realized not only the enormous disparities in the distribution of material comfort and happiness, but the still more striking discrepancies between opportunity on the one side and talent and character on the other, would not only find it difficult to reconcile what he saw with even the rudest standard of ideal justice, but would be tempted to be amazed at the patience and inertness with which the mass of mankind acquiesced in what they deemed to be their lot. . . . Large areas of our social and industrial life had had to be set free from the misdirected and paralysing activity of the State, trade had had to be set free from throttling tariffs, the practice of religion had had to be set free from invidious and discriminating tests, both in national and municipal government, the barriers of caste had had to be broken down and a way opened to the democracy. That task of emancipation was still far from complete. But there was another side to the matter. The experience of our own and of every other progressive country had shown that there were wants, needs, services which could not be safely left to the unregulated operation of the forces of supply and demand, and for which only the community as a whole could make adequate and effective provision. Each case must be judged on its own merits by the balance of experience so long as we kept in mind that a large part of the evils and apparent injustices of society were due to causes beyond the reach of merely mechanical treatment. There was not a single stage in that process of emancipation and liberation which had not been denounced as a form of Socialism; but did any man now regret it? Did any one wish us as a nation to retrace our steps? Could anyone be blind enough to think the process was complete?

If they asked him at what point it was that Liberalism and what they called Socialism in the true and strict sense of the term parted company, he answered, When liberty in its positive, and not merely its negative, sense was threatened. Liberty meant more than the mere absence of coercion or restraint; it meant the power of initiative, the free play of intelligence and wills, the right, as long as a man did not become a danger or a nuisance to the community, to use as he thought best the faculties of his nature or his brain and the opportunities of his life. The great loss counterbalancing all apparent gains of a reconstruction of society upon what were called Socialistic lines would be that liberty would be slowly but surely starved to death, and that with the superficial equality of fortunes and conditions, even if that could be attained, we should have the most startling despotism the world had ever seen. To Socialism, so understood, Liberals were prepared to offer a convinced and uncompromising opposition. But he was not so much afraid of its advent in this country as many excellent people seemed to be.

72) 'Unionist Party' in *New Encyclopedia of Social Reform* (Funk & Wagnalls, 1908), 1248.

In opposition to socialism, the Unionist pamphlets say:

OPPOSITION TO SOCIALISM

Socialism means the end of liberty—the Socialists would make every man a puppet and a slave to the Socialist god— the State. All men would become machines for the use of the State, their work parceled out when, how, and where the State thought fit, and its results snatched from them for the purposes of the State.

Socialism would seize from every man his home and belongings. Under socialism no man must *own* anything; everything would belong to the State. All the savings of years of thrift would be taken and thrown into the common pool.

Socialism would destroy family life and take away those

sweet things that make the English idea of home the best thing in the world.

For 'home,' socialism would substitute gigantic barracks where you would be compelled to live and have your meals divided out to you, of such kind and quantity as the State decided, in such company as the State chose for you. If you wanted more tea, more beer, more tobacco, however honestly you had earned it, you could not have it. You must have no more than your neighbors. Socialism would kill all enterprise and stop progress, individual and national. Under socialism no man could rise. Can you conceive what life would be without ambition or hope? Without the possibility of reaching to better things? Without the chance of carving out for yourself a higher future? With the deadening knowledge that as you are so you shall remain, with your life State-planned, State-run, State-crushed? Is not this black despair? Under our present conditions, however low down a man may start, he has it in his power to make his future. Consider the thousands of men who have risen from nothing to eminence.

There is no need for socialism. Not because the present state of things is perfect. But every year sees the worker's lot improved. The aim of every piece of labor legislation is to bring into being benefits which could not be possible under socialism. And with it all the marked liberty is not lessened; it is increased. Why, then give up liberty for nothing?

73)   Lord Hugh Cecil, *Conservatism* (Williams & Norgate, 1912), 195–6.

A policy of State interference is not, as such, alien from Conservatism. The questions that arise as to the respective spheres of the State and the individual cannot, in short, be answered by Conservatives with any general answer. The only proposition of a general character that can be laid down is that the State must not treat individuals unjustly, that is, must not inflict upon them undeserved injury. This condition granted, any scheme for enlarging the function of the State must be judged by Conservatives merely on its merits without reference to any general formula, but from a standpoint prudently distrustful of the untried, and preferring to develop what exists rather than to demolish and reconstruct. Conservative social reform need not, therefore, proceed on purely individualist lines. There is no antithesis between Conservatism and Socialism, or even between Conservatism and Liberalism. Subject to the counsels of prudence and to a preference for what exists and has been tried over the unknown, Conservatives have no difficulty in welcoming the social activity of the State.

CHAPTER EIGHT

Tariff Reform

Some sectors of British industry were under increasing pressure from foreign competition. Too many industrialists lacked enterprise and some even lacked interest (74). Sharp criticism was voiced on this account from each side of the fiscal controversy, both by *The Times* (75), which supported tariff reform, and by free traders such as Alfred Marshall (1842–1924), the Cambridge economist, who opposed it. Marshall was asked by the Treasury in 1903 to advise how far free trade had ceased to be the best policy for Britain (76). He was also one of fourteen university economists who wrote a joint letter to *The Times* emphasizing how tariff reform might mean dearer bread (77). Free trade politicians made great play with this fear, arguing that the need was not for protection but for greater enterprise in British industry and for better technical education (78). Joseph Chamberlain agreed about this weakness, but insisted that even if industry became more enterprising it would still need the support of imperial preference. He was most interested in preferential tariffs, however, as a means of fostering Empire unity (79, 80, 81). Sharp debate raged round Chamberlain's proposals throughout the second half of 1903 (82, 83, 84). On grounds both of economic principle and political prudence Balfour, the Prime Minister, sought a middle position (85). But little of this controversy was understood by ordinary electors, despite the propaganda efforts of the Tariff Reform League, though ignorance did not prevent Edwardians taking sides, more against tariff reform than for it (86, 87).

74)   E. E. Williams, *Made in Germany* (Heinemann, 2nd ed., 1896), 172–5.

But let me again reiterate that help from the State is not enough. Fair Trade, Commercial Consuls, Technical Colleges —good and necessary as they are—will not avail to stem the inroad of the German, unless our manufacturers and merchants brace themselves for exertions more strenuous and better directed, and a more forward and spirited policy generally, than have been the rule with them for many years.

They must be more studious of the tastes and wishes of their customers. Evidence on this head is accumulating daily; scarce a British Consul's report but emphasises the paramount need of English manufacturers paying more regard to the desires of those with whom they do, or would do, business.

They must send out travellers who know the language of the country which they are to canvass.

They must cease to scorn the small order. Witnesses to the folly of contemning orders derisively described by English houses as 'mere retail business' are numerous. The manufacturers usually awake to the fatal results which follow this policy of pinchbeck magnificence when the trade has gone.

They must pay more heed to the merits of careful packing, and the like details of well-conducted commerce.

Yet more important: **They must have an up-to-date equipment in their workshops.** Much of the disaster which has overtaken our Iron and Steel Trades is attributed to the better machinery of the Continental ironmasters. Much of the havoc wrought in our Chemical trades is due to parsimony in equipment.

They must adopt the Metric System of Weights and Measures, for their Export Business at any rate. It is difficult to refer to this subject without exhibiting impatience. Statesmen approve the reform in their speeches; Chambers of Commerce resolve that it is a necessity; the Decimal System forms part of the Board School repertory: no one has a word to say against its adoption. Yet our traders persist—knowing it to be to their own hurt—in the antiquated and clumsy table of Weights and Measures used by our forefathers before international commerce was born. Also, **whatever the system of money and measures in vogue in a country in which Englishmen** purpose to trade, they must conform to that system, or be prepared to see the puzzled native transfer his orders to the accommodating German.

They must be more artistic. It is well enough—it is very well—to be thorough and substantial, but articles for sale must take the eye of the purchaser, and English goods are very often inferior to German in this respect. The defect must be remedied: it is hard to believe that elegance is beyond the reach of English designers and craftsmen. If our people will only recognise the importance of graceful form, pleasing design, and artistic finish, and cultivate the necessary skill, they can repair the deficiency, in a great measure. Any way, the experiment is worth trying. Arts and Crafts Exhibitions should not be regarded as the property of Mr. John Burns's 'aesthetic dawdlers.'

They must practise the Imitative Art. Englishmen have done this in the past—witness the foreign names of many English manufactures: 'holland', to take one example: which indicate an originally foreign industry captured by our own people. But the Germans have shown themselves even better and more thorough masters of the art, as Englishmen know to their cost. Englishmen must practise it more sedulously.

They must advertise more boldly. The fear of exhibitions is a craven fear, and must be overcome. Just now, particularly, when English goods are being supplanted by German our manufacturers, when their manufactures are worthy of praise, should take advantage of any chance that may offer of putting them before the public side by side with the German equivalent. Foreigners who want to imitate English wares can secure the necessary specimens; they are not confined to looking at them through a glass case.

Labour Troubles must be avoided. English manufacturers should recognise that it is necessary for their servants to enjoy decent conditions of life. Well paid workers—other things being equal—are the best workers, and a raising of wages or a shortening of hours is often a profitable investment. It is poor policy on the part of the masters to risk or throw away trade for the sake of a few pence. And the men on their part should be careful how they foster disputes; the rules of a trade-union should not be rigid in non-essentials, but should emulate the elasticity of the market and the changing conditions of industry. Trade-unionism is a beneficent power, when it is wielded with discretion. One often observes signs of a lack in this regard.

Lastly, **Englishmen must be more progressive.** They must not rest on their reputation; they must be ever alert and watchful, ready to take instant and full advantage of new discoveries, ready to accommodate themselves to the continual changes in the wants of the peoples of all nations. Let the fate of the Dyeing Trade serve for a common warning.

. . . .

Are these counsels of perfection? They are counsels, nevertheless, which are, every one of them, necessary to salvation. Every one of them is followed in Germany, and I decline to believe that England's industrial character has so deteriorated that she is unable, an she will, to pull herself up to the German standard of conduct. *Her unique position as unchallenged mistress of the Industrial World is gone, and is not likely to be regained.* But some of the departed glory may yet be restored to her. At least let us see to it that she fares no worse.

75) 'Obsolete Engineering Works', *The Times*, 17 April 1912.

The long experience of engineering enjoyed by some of the old-established concerns appears to have had the effect of making the owners very conservative, and they are rather too prone to think that what was good enough in their fathers' and grandfathers' days is good enough now. They grudge every penny spent in improvements, and will renew nothing until they are absolutely obliged, with the result that they find it continually more difficult to secure orders at profitable rates. Such people often complain about unfair competition, but if any suggestion is made to them about improvements they excuse themselves in busy times by saying that they cannot afford to stop any part of their works for alterations, and in slack times they say that they have no money to spend on new ideas and must wait until trade improves. . . .

If the proprietors of the out-of-date works of all kinds which are to be found in every old manufacturing centre of this country would only shake themselves free from their complacent or despondent frame of mind, as the case may be, pay more attention to what other people are doing in their line of business, and be content to take less money out of their works for their personal use and leave more in for improvements, they would find that there are still good profits to be made, and they would have the satisfaction not only of being able to leave a sound business to those who come after them, but also of feeling that they were doing what they could to maintain the reputation of their country. This trade and reputation will need to be worked for harder than ever in the future now that other countries can produce articles of as good a quality as we can ourselves in practically every branch of engineering, and produce them at equal or less cost; but we are as favourably situated on the whole as any other country for turning out engineering products, and if we let trade slip through our fingers it is because too many of our manufacturers persist in fighting with obsolete weapons.

76)   A. Marshall, *Official Papers* (Macmillan, for the Royal Economic Society, 1926), 405–6.

64.   The greatness and rapidity of her loss is partly due to that very prosperity which followed the adoption of Free Trade. She had the full benefit of railways, and no other country at that time had. Her coal and iron, better placed relatively to one another than elsewhere, had not begun to run short, and she could afford to use largely Bessemer's exacting but efficient process. Other Western nations partially followed her movements towards Free Trade, and in distant lands there was a rapidly increasing demand for manufactures, which she alone was able to supply in large quantities. This combination of advantages was sufficient to encourage the belief that an Englishman could expect to obtain a much larger real income and to live much more luxuriously than anybody else, at all events in an old country; and that if he chose to shorten his hours of work and take things easily, he could afford to do it.

65.   But two additional causes of self-complacency were added. The American Civil War and the successive wars in which Germany was engaged, partially diverted the attention of these countries from industry: it checked the growth of their productive resources; and it made them eager to buy material of war, including railway plant and the more serviceable textile materials, at almost any cost. And lastly, the influx of gold enriched every English manufacturer who could borrow

money with which to buy materials, could apply moderate intelligence in handling them, and could then sell them at a raised level of prices and discharge his debt with money of less purchasing power than that which he had borrowed.

66. This combination of causes made many of the sons of manufacturers content to follow mechanically the lead given by their fathers. They worked shorter hours, and they exerted themselves less to obtain new practical ideas than their fathers had done; and thus a part of England's leadership was destroyed rapidly. In the nineties it became clear that in the future Englishmen must take business as seriously as their grandfathers had done, and as their American and German rivals were doing: that their training for business must be methodical, like that of their new rivals; and not merely practical, on lines that had sufficed for the simpler world of two generations ago; and lastly that the time had passed at which they could afford merely to teach foreigners and not learn from them in return.

67. This estimate of leadership is different from, almost antagonistic to, measurement of a country's leadership by the *volume* of her foreign trade without reference to its *quality*. Measurement by mere quantity is misleading.

77) *The Times*, 15 August 1903.

Sir,

We, the undersigned, beg leave to express our opinions of a more or less technical character connected with the fiscal proposals which now occupy the attention of the country.

One of the main objects aimed at in these proposals—the cultivation of friendly feelings between the United Kingdom and other parts of the Empire—is ardently desired by us; and we should not regard it as a fatal objection to a fiscal scheme adapted to this purpose that it was attended with a considerable sacrifice of material wealth. But the suggested means for attaining this desirable end do not seem to us advisable, first, because there would probably be incurred an immense and permanent sacrifice, not only of material, but also of higher goods; and, secondly, because the means suggested would be likely, in our judgement, to defeat rather than attain the end in view.

First, having regard to the prevalence of certain erroneous

opinions, to which we advert below, we think that any system of preferential tariffs would most probably lead to the reintroduction of protection into the fiscal system of the United Kingdom. But a return to protection would, we hold, be detrimental to the material prosperity of this country, partly for reasons of the same kind as those which, as now universally admitted, justified the adoption of free trade—reasons which are now stronger than formerly, in consequence of the great proportion of food and raw materials imported from foreign countries, and the greater extent and complexity of our foreign trade. The evil would probably be a lasting one since experience shows that protection, when it has once taken root, is likely to extend beyond the limits at first assigned to it, and is very difficult to extirpate. There are also to be apprehended those evils other than material which protection brings in its train, the loss of purity in politics, the unfair advantage given to those who wield the powers of jobbery and corruption, unjust distribution of wealth, and the growth of 'sinister interests'.

Secondly, we apprehend that the suggested arrangements, far from promoting amity, may engender irritating controversies between the different members of the Empire. The growing sense of solidarity would be strained by an opposition of interests such as was experienced by our country under protection, and has been noticeable in the history of the United States and of other countries. Such an opposition of interests would be all the more disruptive in the case of the British Empire, as it is not held together by a central government.

Our convictions on this subject are opposed to certain popular opinions, with respect to which we offer the following observations.—

1.   It is not true that an increase of imports involved the diminished employment of workmen in the importing country. The statement is universally rejected by those who have thought about the subject, and is completely refuted by experience.

2.   It is very improbable that a tax on food imported into the United Kingdom would result in an equivalent—or more than equivalent—rise in wages. The result which may be anticipated as a direct consequence of the tax is a lowering of the real remuneration of labour.

3.   The injury which the British consumer would receive from an import tax on wheat might be slightly reduced in the

possible, but under existing circumstances very improbable, event of a small proportion of the burden being thrown permanently on the foreign producer.

4. To the statement that a tax on food will raise the price of food, it is not a valid reply that this result may possibly in fact not follow. When we say that an import duty raises price, we mean, of course, unless its effect is overborne by other causes operating at the same time in the other direction. Or, in other words, we mean that in consequence of the import duty the price is generally higher by the amount of the duty than it would have been if other things had remained the same.

5. It seems to us impossible to devise any tariff regulation which shall at once expand the wheat-growing areas in the Colonies, encourage agriculture in the United Kingdom, and at the same time not injure the British consumer.

6. The suggestion that the public, though clearly damnified by an impost, may yet obtain a full equivalent from its yield is incorrect, because it leaves out of account the interference with the free circulation of goods, the detriment incidental to diverting industry from the course which it would otherwise have taken, and the circumstance that, in the case of a tax on foreign wheat— English and Colonial wheat being free—while the consumer would have to pay the whole or nearly the whole tax on all the wheat, the Government would get the tax only on foreign wheat.

7. In general, those who lightly undertake to reorganise the supply of food and otherwise divert the course of industry do not adequately realise what a burden of proof rests on the politician who, leaving the plain rule of taxation for the sake of revenue only, seeks to attain ulterior objects by manipulating tariffs.

78) *Speeches by the Rt. Hon. H. H. Asquith* (*The Times*, 1908), 185–6.

ASQUITH SPEECH AT CINDERFORD, 1903

All roads converge to the same point. You cannot have retaliation effectively as against your principal foreign competitors without ultimately taxing raw materials and food. Preference admittedly you cannot have without ultimately taxing food, and as I have endeavoured to show, you cannot have that logically and consistently without ultimately taxing raw materials and also manufactures. The moment you try to put *ad valorem* duties on manufactures you lead to the same conclusion, Among the things imported into this country of those on which no further British capital or labour is to be expended the proportion is so insignificant that it would not yield you any substantial revenue at all. By whatever way you approach it you come to the same goal. This is a proposal to tax British industry, to tax the food of the people and thereby to diminish their wages, to tax the raw material out of which our wealth is made. It is a scheme which is based upon unfounded assumptions and unproved inferences. There is no ground whatever for saying either that British trade, as a whole, is stagnant or decaying, or that the Empire can only be maintained by reverting to fiscal devices which were tried and found wanting in the old days of Protection. Free influx of food and raw materials from every possible source of supply into this country is not only as essential, but is more essential to our national strength and prosperity than it was in the days of Cobden and Peel.

THE ALTERNATIVE POLICY

Do not, however—and this shall be my final word—do not let it be supposed that because we are driven to defend the citadel of Free Trade we, therefore, think that all is for the best and are content with a policy of folded hands. That there are disquieting features in our industrial as in our social conditions no honest observer, certainly no member of the party of progress, will be found to deny. We have seen industries in which we ought to have maintained our supremacy falling behind, and in some cases entirely taken away from us by our competitors. Defective knowledge, inferior processes, lack of flexibility or versatility, a stubborn industrial conservatism, these are the real enemies of British trade, and have done us infinitely more harm than all the tariffs and all the dumping syndicates that were ever created. Better education, better training, better methods, a larger outlook than for our primary needs—and it says little for our political sagacity that we should allow our minds to be diverted from them by quarrels as to the quantum of dogmatic theology that is to be administered to little children, or by demands to revive the fallacies of Protection.

No, that is not the way in which we should improve our condition. True it is also that in spite of the continuous growth of our national prosperity we still have with us the unemployed, the ill-fed, the aged poor; but here, again, let us look to natural and not to artificial remedies. Instead of raising the price of bread let us try to raise the standard of life. Temperance, better housing, the tenure and taxation of land, these are matters as to which we have allowed our legislation to fall deplorably into arrear. To take up the task in a spirit of faith and of resolute purpose is, I hope and believe, the mission of the Liberal party in a Liberal Parliament.

79) J. Amery, *Life of Joseph Chamberlain*, volume five (Macmillan, 1969), 177–8.

CHAMBERLAIN IN CONVERSATION WITH HIS ELECTION AGENT,
APRIL 1903

Now I want to look forward to the next General Election and consider what policy we should go to the country on. I said that I should not be sorry if we went out for a short time; but of course we must fight to win, if we can. I will tell you what I should be disposed to do, if I were Prime Minister, and had a free hand. I should like to know what you think of it and what view you think our friends here would take.

First, there is the licensing question . . .

The other thing that I have in mind is imperialism. I would say that we have done a great deal; but after all it is only a beginning, and, if we do not go forward, we cannot help going back. We expect the Colonies to do more for us; in fact we must get them to do more for us. But there is another side to the question: what can we do for them? They are protectionist; we cannot help that; and while we stick rigidly to Free Trade, we have nothing to give them. Now I believe in Free Trade,— just as I believe in peace. We believe in the blessings of peace just as much, and for the same reasons, as the Little-Englanders. The difference is that we say that sometimes we must go to war, or else our enemies would take away all we have. I should not pretend that a protective tariff would do us any good; only I do say that by Free Trade we are giving up a weapon that we want in order to hit back at our enemies. Take the case of Canada. They have given us a preference of 33 per cent. It has not done quite all that was expected, because the tariff is still protective, and in some cases prohibitive. Still it is a fact that our trade with Canada was falling away to nothing; and now it is increasing. Well, the Germans complained of the preference against them. The Canadians said that Germany had no right to complain; Canada was just as much a part of the British Empire as Yorkshire. Then the Germans reply that they do not recognise that; that they have put Canada in the worst position in their tariff. The Canadians find that they are hard hit in their trade with Germany, while we are giving them no advantage over Germany. Then it is proposed in South Africa to give us a 25 per cent advantage. It is not certain anyhow to go through the Cape Parliament, because of the Dutchmen who are not disposed to make sacrifices for the Empire. They have this argument, that, if they give this preference, Germany will hit back and injure the South African export trade in wool, while England has nothing to give them by way of compensation.

I think that if it were put in this way we might get some support from the present feeling of enmity to Germany. Only of course we might lose the support of those of our friends who are rigid Freetraders, just as on the other question we should lose our teetotal friends. What I want you to consider and find out is whether there are many of our friends here that would take offence at a Fair Trade policy. . . . For myself I have never been able to get over the difficulty that in fact the protectionist countries like America have prospered under protection. They ought not—but they do. There must be something wrong in the argument. Anyhow that is my idea of the future policy. I think I shall try to lead up to it on May 15th, without of course proposing any definite measure. I wish you would get some information as to the reception it is likely to get from our people, and let me know.'

80)   C. W. Boyd (ed.), *Mr. Chamberlain's Speeches* (Constable, 1914), II, 129–40.

CHAMBERLAIN SPEECH AT BIRMINGHAM, 15 MAY 1903

When, in the late war, this old country of ours showed that it was still possessed by the spirit of our ancestors, that it was still prepared to count no sacrifice that was necessary in order to maintain the honour and the interests of the Empire that was committed to its charge, then you found such a response from your brethren, your children, across the seas, as had never been known before, astonishing the world by an undeniable proof of affection and regard. I have said that that was a new chapter, the beginning of a new era. Is it to end there? Is it to end with the end of the war, with the termination of the crisis that brought it forth? Are we to sink back to the old policy of selfish isolation which went very far to try, and even to sap, the loyalty of our colonial brethren? I do not think so. I think these larger issues touch the people of this country. I think they have awakened to the enormous importance of a creative time like the present, and will take advantage of the opportunity that is offered to make permanent that which has begun so well. . . . The Empire is in its infancy. Now is the time when we can mould that Empire, and we and those who live with us can decide its future destinies. . . .

Here, in the United Kingdom, there are some forty millions of us. Outside, there are more than ten millions either directly descended from ancestors who left this country, or persons who, themselves in their youth, left this country in order to find their fortunes in our possessions abroad. Now how long do you suppose that this proportion of the population is going to endure? How long are we going to be four times as many as our kinsfolk abroad? The development of those colonies has been delayed by many reasons—partly, as I think, by our inaction, partly by the provincial spirit which we have not done enough to discourage, that spirit which attaches undue importance to the local incidents and legislation of each separate State, and gives insufficient regard to the interests of the whole, but mainly, probably, by a more material reason, by the fact that the United States of America have offered a greater attraction to British immigration. But that is changing. The United States of America, with all their vast territory, are filling up, and even now we hear of thousands and tens of thousands of emigrants leaving the United States of America in order to take up the fresh and rich lands of our Dominion of Canada. And it seems to me to be not at all an impossible assumption that, before the end of this half century, we may find that our fellow-subjects beyond the seas may be more numerous than we are at home.

I want you to look forward. I want you ·to consider the

infinite importance of this, not only to yourselves but to your descendants. Now is the time when you can exert influence. Do you wish that, if these ten millions become forty millions, they shall still be closely, intimately, affectionately united to you? Or do you contemplate the possibility of their being separated, going off each in his own direction under a separate flag? Think what it means to your power and influence as a country; think what it means to your position among the nations of the world; think what it means to your trade and commerce. I put that last. The influence of the Empire is the thing I think most about, and that influence, I believe, will always be used for the peace and civilisation of the world.

But the question of trade and commerce is one of the greatest importance. Unless that is satisfactorily settled, I, for one, do not believe in a continued union of the Empire. I am told—I hear it stated again and again by what I believe to be the representatives of a small minority of the people of this country, whom I describe, because I know no other words for them, as Little Englanders—I hear it stated by them, what is a fact, that our trade with our colonies is less than our trade with foreign countries, and therefore it appears to be their opinion that we should do everything in our power to cultivate that trade with foreigners, and that we can safely disregard the trade with our children. Now, sir, that is not my conclusion. My conclusion is exactly the opposite. I say it is the business of British statesmen to do everything they can, even at some present sacrifice, to keep the trade of the colonies with Great Britain; to increase that trade, to promote it, even if in doing so we lessen somewhat the trade with our foreign competitors. Are we doing everything at the present time to direct the patriotic movement not only here, but through all the colonies, in the right channel? Are we, in fact, by our legislation, by our action, making for union, or are we drifting to separation? That is a critical issue. In my opinion, the germs of a Federal Union that will make the British Empire powerful and influential for good beyond the dreams of any one now living are in the soil; but it is a tender and delicate plant, and requires careful handling. . . .

Sir, my idea of British policy—I mean the policy of the United Kingdom—is that here, at the beginning of things, at the beginning of this new chapter, we should show our cordial appreciation of the first step taken by our colonies to show their solidarity with us. Every advance which they make should be reciprocated. We should ourselves set a great example by acknowledging the community of interest, and, above all, that community of sacrifice on which alone the Empire can permanently rest. I have admitted that the colonies have hitherto been backward in their contributions towards Imperial defence. They are following their own lines. I hope they will do better in the future; but in the meantime they are doing a great deal, and they are trying to promote this union, which I regard as of so much importance, in their own way and by their own means.

And first among those means is the offer of preferential tariffs. Now that is a matter which, at the present moment, is of the greatest possible importance to every one of you. It depends upon how we treat this policy of the colonies—not a policy inaugurated by us, but a policy which comes to us from our children abroad—it depends upon how we treat it, whether it is developed in the future, or withdrawn as being unacceptable to those whom it is sought to benefit. . . . Canada is, of all our colonies, the most backward in contributing to common defence, but Canada has been the most forward in endeavouring to unite the Empire by other means—by strengthening our commercial relations, and by giving to us special favour and preference. And if we appreciate this action properly, it seems to me that not only is it certain that every other colony of the Empire will necessarily and in due time follow this example, but Canada herself and the other colonies, as the bonds are drawn closer, and as we become more and more one people, united by interest as well as by sentiment, will be more and more ready to take their fair share in these burdens of defence to which I have referred. The policy which I wish to make clear to you is not to force our colonies—that is hopeless, for they are as independent as we are—but to meet everything they do. If they see a way of drawing the Empire together, let us help them in that, even if they may not be prepared to join us in some other way from which we think the same result would be achieved. But let us be prepared to accept every indication on their part of this desire. Let us show we appreciate it; and, believe me, it will not be long before all will come into line, and the results which follow will be greater than, perhaps, it would be prudent now to anticipate. . . .

The ministers of Canada, when they were over here last

year, made me a further definite offer. They said: 'We have done for you as much as we can do voluntarily and freely and without return. If you are willing to reciprocate in any way, we are prepared to reconsider our tariff with a view of seeing whether we cannot give you further reductions, especially in regard to those goods in which you come into competition with foreigners; and we will do this if you will meet us by giving us a drawback on the small tax of 1s. per quarter which you have put upon corn.' That was a definite offer which we have had to refuse. I need not say that, if I could treat matters of this kind solely in regard to my position as Secretary of State for the Colonies, I should have said, 'That is a fair offer, that is a generous offer, from your point of view, and it is an offer which we might ask our people to accept.' But, speaking for the Government as a whole, and not solely in the interests of the colonies, I am obliged to say that it is contrary to the established fiscal policy of this country; that we hold ourselves bound to keep open market for all the world, even if they close their markets to us; and that, therefore, so long as that is the mandate of the British public, we are not in a position to offer any preference or favour whatever, even to our own children. We cannot make any difference between those who treat us well and those who treat us badly. Yes, but that is the doctrine which, I am told is the accepted doctrine of the Free Traders, and we are all Free Traders. I have considerable doubt whether the interpretation of Free Trade which is current amongst a certain limited section is the true interpretation. I am perfectly certain that I am not a Protectionist; but I want to point out that, if the interpretation is that our only duty is to buy in the cheapest market without regard to where we can sell—if that is the theory of Free Trade that finds acceptance, then, in pursuance of that policy, you will lose the advantage of the further reduction in duty which your great colony of Canada offers to you, the manufacturers of this country. And you may lose a great deal more; because in the speech which the Minister of Finance made to the Canadian Parliament the other day he says that if they are told definitely that Great Britain, the mother country, can do nothing for them in the way of reciprocity, they must reconsider their position and reconsider the preference that they have already given.

These are big questions, and this particular question is

complicated in a rather unexpected manner. The policy which prevents us from offering an advantage to our colonies prevents us from defending them if they are attacked. Now, I suppose, you and I are agreed that the British Empire is one and indivisible. You and I are agreed that we absolutely refuse to look upon any of the States that form the British Empire as in any way excluded from any advantage or privilege to which the British Empire is entitled. We may well, therefore, have supposed that an agreement of this kind by which Canada does a kindness to us, was a matter of family arrangement, concerning nobody else. But, unfortunately, Germany thinks otherwise. There is a German Empire. The German Empire is divided into States. Bavaria, and, let us say, Hanover, Saxony, and Würtemberg, may deal between themselves any way they please. As a matter of fact, they have entire Free Trade among themselves. We do not consider them separate entities; we treat the German Empire as a whole, and we do not complain because one State gives an advantage to another State within that Empire, and does not give it to all the rest of the world. But in this case of Canada, Germany insists upon treating Canada as though it were a separate country. It refuses to recognise it as a part of one Empire, entitled to claim the privileges of that Empire. It regards this agreement as being something more than a domestic agreement, and it has penalised Canada by placing upon Canadian goods an additional duty.

Now the reason for this is clear. The German newspapers very frankly explain that this is a policy of reprisal, and that it is intended to deter other colonies from giving to us the same advantage. Therefore, it is not merely punishment inflicted by Germany upon Canada, but it is a threat to South Africa, to Australia, and to New Zealand. This policy, a policy of dictation and interference, is justified by the belief that we are so wedded to our fiscal system that we cannot interfere, and that we cannot defend our colonies, and that, in fact, any one of them that attempts to establish any kind of special relations with us does so at its own risk, and must be left to bear the brunt of foreign hostility. To my mind, that is putting us in a rather humiliating position. I do not like it at all. I know what will follow if we allow it to prevail; it is easy to predict the consequences. How do you think that, under such circumstances, we can approach our colonies with appeals to aid us in promoting the union of the Empire, or ask them to bear a share of the common burdens? Are we to say to them, 'This is your Empire, take pride in it, share its privileges?' They will say, 'What are its privileges? The privileges appear to be that if we treat you as relations and friends, if we show you kindness, if we give you preference, you who benefit by our action, can only leave us alone to fight our own battles against those who are offended by our action.' Now, is that Free Trade? I am not going further to-night. My object is to put the position before you, and, above all, as I have just come home from great colonies, I want you to see these matters as they appear to our colonial fellow-subjects. There is no doubt what they think, and there is no doubt what great issues hang upon their decision. I asked just now, 'Is this Free Trade?' No; it is absolutely a new situation; there has been nothing like it in our history. It is a situation that was never contemplated by any of those whom we regard as the authors of Free Trade. . . .

I leave the matter in your hands. I desire that a discussion on this subject should be opened. The time has not yet come to settle it; but it seems to me that, for good or for evil, it is an issue much greater in its consequences than any of our local disputes. Make a mistake in legislation—it can be corrected. Make a mistake in your Imperial policy—it is irretrievable. You have an opportunity; you will never have it again. And, for my own part, I believe in a British Empire, in an Empire which, although it should be one of its first duties to cultivate friendship with all the nations of the world, should yet, even if alone, be self-sustaining and self-sufficient, able to maintain itself against the competition of all its rivals. And I do not believe in a Little England which shall be separated from all those to whom it should in the natural course look for support and affection—a Little England which shall thus be dependent absolutely on the mercy of those who envy its present prosperity; and who have shown they are ready to do all in their power to prevent the future union of the British race throughout the world.

81) C. W. Boyd (ed.), *Mr. Chamberlain's Speeches* (Constable, 1914), II, 141–8, 156–9.

CHAMBERLAIN SPEECH AT GLASGOW, 6 OCTOBER 1903

I do not regard this as a party meeting. I am no longer a party leader. I am an outsider, and it is not my intention—I do not think it would be right—to raise any exclusively party issues. . . .

What are our objects? They are two. In the first place, we all desire the maintenance and increase of the national strength and the prosperity of the United Kingdom. That may be a selfish desire; but in my mind it carries with it something more than mere selfishness. You cannot expect foreigners to take the same views as we of our position and duty. To my mind Britain has played a great part in the past history of the world, and for that reason I wish Britain to continue. Then, in the second place, our object is, or should be, the realisation of the greatest ideal which has ever inspired statesmen in any country or in any age—the creation of an Empire such as the world has never seen. We have to cement the union of the states beyond the seas; we have to consolidate the British race; we have to meet the clash of competition, commercial now— sometimes in the past it has been otherwise—it may be again in the future. Whatever it be, whatever danger threatens, we have to meet it no longer as an isolated country; we have to meet it fortified and strengthened, and buttressed by all those of our kinsmen, all those powerful and continually rising states which speak our common tongue and glory in our common flag. . . .

I tell you that it is not well to-day with British industry. We have been going through a period of great expansion. The whole world has been prosperous. I see signs of a change, but let that pass. When the change comes, I think even the Free Fooders will be converted. But meanwhile, what are the facts? The year 1900 was the record year of British trade. The exports were the largest we had ever known. The year 1902— last year—was nearly as good, and yet, if you will compare your trade in 1872, thirty years ago, with the trade of 1902— the export trade—you will find that there has been a moderate increase of £22,000,000. That, I think, is something like 7½ per cent. Meanwhile, the population has increased 30 per cent.

Can you go on supporting your population at that rate of increase, when even in the best of years you can only show so much smaller an increase in your foreign trade? The actual increase was £22,000,000 under our Free Trade. In the same time the increase in the United States of America was £110,000,000, and the increase in Germany was £56,000,000. In the United Kingdom our export trade has been practically stagnant for thirty years. It went down in the interval. It has now gone up in the most prosperous times. In the most prosperous times it is hardly better than it was thirty years ago.

Meanwhile the protected countries which you have been told, and which I myself at one time believed, were going rapidly to wreck and ruin, have progressed in a much greater proportion than ours. That is not all; not merely the amount of your trade remained stagnant, but the character of your trade has changed. When Mr. Cobden preached his doctrine, he believed, as he had at that time considerable reason to suppose, that while foreign countries would supply us with our food-stuffs and raw materials, we should remain the mart of the world, and should send them in exchange our manufactures. But that is exactly what we have not done. On the contrary, in the period to which I have referred, we are sending less and less of our manufactures to them, and they are sending more and more of their manufactures to us. . . .

How is it that that has not impressed the people before now? Because the change has been concealed by our statistics. I do not say they have not shown it, because you could have picked it out, but they are not put in a form which is understanded of the people. You have failed to observe that the maintenance of your trade is dependent entirely on British possessions. While to these foreign countries your export of manufactures has declined by £46,000,000, to your British possessions it has increased £40,000,000, and at the present time your trade with the colonies and British possessions is larger in amount, very much larger in amount, and very much more valuable in the categories I have named, than our trade with the whole of Europe and the United States of America. It is much larger than our trade to those neutral countries of which I have spoken, and it remains at the present day the most rapidly increasing, the most important, the most valuable of the whole of our trade. One more comparison. During this period of thirty years in which our exports of manufactures have fallen £46,000,000 to foreign countries, what has happened as regards their exports of manufactures to us? They have risen from £63,000,000 in 1872 to £149,000,000 in 1902. They have increased £86,000,000. That may be all right. I am not for the moment saying whether that is right or wrong, but when people say that we ought to hold exactly the same opinion about things that our ancestors did, my reply is that I dare say we should do so if circumstances had remained the same.

But now, if I have been able to make these figures clear, there is one thing which follows—that is, that our Imperial trade is absolutely essential to our prosperity at the present time. If that trade declines, or if it does not increase in proportion to our population and to the loss of trade with foreign countries, then we sink at once into a fifth-rate nation. Our fate will be the fate of the empires and kingdoms of the past. We shall have reached our highest point, and indeed I am not certain that there are not some of my opponents who regard that with absolute complacency. I do not. As I have said, I have the misfortune to be an optimist. I do not believe in the setting of the British star, but then, I do not believe in the folly of the British people. I trust them. I trust the working classes of this country, and I have confidence that they who are our masters, electorally speaking, will have the intelligence to see that they must wake up. They must modify their policy to suit new conditions. They must meet those conditions with altogether a new policy.

I have said that if our Imperial trade declines we decline. My second point is this. It will decline inevitably unless while there is still time we take the necessary steps to preserve it. . . . Can we invent a tie which must be a practical one, which will prevent separation, and I make the same answer as Mr. Rhodes, who suggested reciprocal preference, and I say that it is only by commercial union, reciprocal preference, that you can lay the foundations of the confederation of the Empire to which we all look forward as a brilliant possibility. Now I have told you what you are to gain by preference. You will gain the retention and the increase of your customers. You will gain work for the enormous number of those who are now unemployed; you will pave the way for a firmer and more enduring union of the Empire. What will it cost you? What do the colonies ask? They ask a preference on their particular products. You cannot give them, at least it would be futile to offer them, a preference on manufactured goods, because at the present time the exported manufacture of the colonies is entirely insignificant. You cannot, in my opinion, give them a preference on raw material. It has been said that I should propose such a tax; but I repeat now, in the most explicit terms, that I do not propose a tax on raw materials, which are a necessity of our manufacturing trade. What remains? Food.

Therefore, if you wish to have preference, if you desire to gain this increase, if you wish to prevent separation, you must put a tax on food. The murder is out. I said that in the House of Commons, but I said a good deal more, but that is the only thing of all that I said that my opponents have thought it particularly interesting to quote, and you see that on every wall, in the headlines of the leaflets of the Cobden Club, in the speeches of the devotees of free imports, in the arguments of those who dread the responsibilities of Empire, but do not seem to care much about the possibility of its dissolution—all these, then, put in the forefront that Mr. Chamberlain says, 'You must tax food.' I was going to say that this statement which they quote is true. But it is only half the truth, and they never give you the other half. You never see attached to this statement that you must tax food the other words that I have used in reference to this subject, that nothing that I propose would add one farthing to the cost of living to the working man, or to any family in this country. How is that to be achieved? I have been asked for a plan. I have hesitated, because, as you will readily see, no final plan can be proposed until a Government is authorised by the people to enter into negotiations upon these principles. Until that Government has had the opportunity of negotiating with the colonies, with foreign countries, and with the heads and experts in all our great industries, any plan must be at the present time more or less of a sketch plan.

But at the same time I recognise that you have a right to call upon me for the broad outlines of my plan, and those I will give you if you will bear with me. You have heard it said that I propose to put a duty of 5s. or 10s. a quarter on wheat. That is untrue. I propose to put a low duty on foreign corn, no duty at all on the corn coming from our British possessions. But I propose to put a low duty on foreign corn not exceeding 2s. a quarter. I propose to put no tax whatever on maize, partly because maize is a food of some of the very poorest of the population, and partly also because it is a raw material for the farmers, who feed their stock with it. I propose that the corresponding tax which will have to be put on flour should give a substantial preference to the miller, and I do that in order to re-establish one of our most ancient industries in this country, believing that if that is done not only will more work be found in agricultural districts, with some tendency, perhaps, operating against the constant migration from the country into the towns, but also because by re-establishing the milling industry in this country, the offals, as they are called—the refuse of the wheat—will remain in the country and will give to the farmers or the agricultural population a food for their stock and their pigs at very much lower rates. That will benefit not merely the great farmer, but it will benefit the little man, the small owner of a plot or even the allotment owner who keeps a single pig. I am told by a high agricultural authority that if this were done so great an effect would be produced upon the price of the food of the animal that where an agricultural labourer keeps one pig now he might keep two in the future. I propose to put a small tax of about 5 per cent. on foreign meat and dairy produce. I propose to exclude bacon, because once more bacon is a popular food with some of the poorest of the population. And, lastly, I propose to give a substantial preference to our colonies upon colonial wines and perhaps upon colonial fruits. Well, those are the taxes, new taxes, or alterations of taxation which I propose as additions to your present burden.

But I propose also some great remissions. I propose to take off three-fourths of the duty on tea and half of the whole duty on sugar, with a corresponding reduction on cocoa and coffee. Now, what will be the result of these changes: in the first place upon the cost of living; in the second place upon the Treasury? As regards the cost of living, I have accepted, for the purpose of argument, the figures of the Board of Trade as to the consumption of an ordinary workman's family, both in the country districts and in the towns, and I find that if he pays the whole of the new duties that I propose to impose it would cost an agricultural labourer $16\frac{1}{2}$ farthings per week more than at present, and the artisan in the town $19\frac{1}{2}$ farthings per week. In other words, it would add about 4d. per week to the expenditure of the agricultural labourer and 5d. per week on the expenditure of the artisan. But, then, the reduction which

I propose, again taking the consumption as it is declared by the Board of Trade, the reduction would be—in the case of the agricultural labourer 17 farthings a week; in the case of the artisan 19½ farthings a week.

Now, gentlemen, you will see, if you have followed me, that upon the assumption that you pay the whole of the new taxes yourselves, the agricultural labourer would be half a farthing per week to the better, and the artisan would be exactly in the same position as at present. I have made this assumption, but I do not believe in it. I do not believe that these small taxes upon food would be paid to any large extent by the consumers in this country. I believe, on the contrary, they would be paid by the foreigner.

82)   W. J. Ashley, *The Tariff Problem* (King, 3rd ed., 1911), 111–13, 262–3.

We are now in a position to complete our forecast of the probable industrial future of Great Britain, so long as the present forces at work continue to operate unchecked. The great countries of the world will each seek to manufacture for themselves the chief staples of which they have need, and they will do this with increasing success even if they have to resort to high protection to effect their purpose. They will more and more advance from the preliminary to the later stages, from the rougher to the finer processes of the several industries—*e.g.*, in the case of cotton goods, from low numbers of yarn to high, and from yarn to piece goods. In the markets which remain 'neutral' the British manufacturer will probably be more and more distanced by the greater economy of production possible to America by its larger scale of operations, this larger scale being itself due to the larger secure home market. At home certain of our primary industries, especially those of iron and steel, will be battered with crushing blows by the American manufacturer in every recurring period of depression. The cheap material thus provided may give a temporary fillip to some other industries—thus cheap steel will for the time assist our shipbuilders. But while the gain will be of doubtful duration, the loss by the destruction of the material-supplying industry will be profound, and will be widely demoralising. Fortunately the growth of our population is somewhat slackening. But it will still increase, and we shall be more and more dependent on imported food. For this food we shall manage to pay, for a very considerable time, by turning more and more to those branches of production in which we shall continue to have an 'advantage.' We shall more and more rapidly exhaust our resources of coal, and we shall devote ourselves more and more to those industries which flourish on cheap labour. The habits of our population will also probably continue to give us advantages in the production of spirits on a large scale, and their sale to the rest of the world. More and more of our capital will probably be invested in the establishment of manufactures abroad. And while London and a few other great towns will become even larger agglomerations of labouring population, the rest of England will remain an agreeable place of residence for *rentiers*, big and little, and will flourish on the 'tourist industry'. And—though with some new features—the history of Holland will have been repeated. . . .

The struggle to create an effective British Empire is, at bottom, an attempt to counteract, by human foresight, the working of forces, which, left to themselves, involve the decadence of this country. Even if the industrial life of the country is bound to undergo profound changes in the future as in the past, that is no reason why we should be in a hurry to bring on the exhaustion of our present resources by an increasing dependence on the export of coal. Even if, for some unavoidable reasons, the United States can manufacture certain commodities more cheaply than we can, that is no reason why we should allow our own cost of production to further increase by the narrowing of our market with its inevitable effect on the economies of manufacture. Even if Great Britain is to lose some of its trades, it will be better to lose them to other parts of our Empire between whose several members there shall be a vitalising movement of thought and activity, than to become a stagnant backwater left on one side by the main currents of human endeavour. No man can be absolutely sure that a preferential system will secure the unity of the Empire; but to me, at any rate, it presents itself as the only direction in which there is a fighting chance. It may be that the decline of this people and the loss of its colonies are inevitable. But until we have tried soberly to build up a preferential system we cannot know this; and meanwhile the preferential movement is surely —as one of my friends among American economists has characterised it—'good Economics and good Politics.'

83)   J. A. Hobson, 'Protection as a Working-Class Policy' in
H. W. Massingham (ed.), *Labour and Protection* (Fisher
Unwin, 1903), 33–5.

That Britain is no longer the workshop of the world is true,
and it would be folly to expect it so to be. It is physically impossible for that position to be maintained. It is as undesirable as it
is inexpedient. The people who urge this as an ideal fail to realise
that the world exists for some other purpose than the exploitation
of foreign nations by British factory-owners and landlords employing armies of people in monotonous occupations. Work is
an important, but not the only, phase of individual and national
life. England has more than its equitable share of the world's
work, and the pity of it is that so much of the product of its energies should be wasted in war, where it is not misspent upon
drink or gambling, betting and luxury. A nation that spends
£180,000,000 a year on drink, £70,000,000 on war and
£50,000,000 on horse-racing and betting need not tax the
food of its poor or exclude the cheap sugar of foreign countries
because it wishes to raise a few millions of revenue or to help
its Colonies. Here, in three branches of its wasteful expenditure—drink, war, gambling—lies the total amount of its export trade with the Colonies and the world. Here is a true
margin for economy. Within these bloated figures are the
means for Old Age Pensions, extended trade, diminished
burdens, increased health, vigour, and capacity for all classes
of the community. Certain it is that we must view with alarm
the statement made by that competent publicist, Mr Arthur
Sherwell, that in June 1903, at Edinburgh, out of 405,000
working hours which 4250 workmen should have worked in a
fortnight in a typical Scotch industry, 100,650 hours, or 25 per
cent., were lost by avoidable causes, *the overwhelming proportion
of that lost time being due to intemperance*. Thus it is not in our
Fiscal stars but in ourselves that we are underlings.

No; the country has wealth enough and to spare. Let her
use it for the elevation of her people, for the growth of gentler
manners, simpler ways, soberer habits, more refined pleasures,
and the upbuilding of Commonwealths beyond the seas, free
from the curse of militarism, of which Protection is the product
in Europe, and of which Preferential Tariffs will be the pre-
cursor in the Colonies. As for the Colonies, let them remain
supreme in their separate and autonomous development, freely

attached to the Mother Country by the strongest of ties—those of sentiment begotten of kinship and respect created by independence. How much better such a relation than the restrictions and bargains that a system of mutual Protection demands!

84) H. Cox (ed.), *British Industries under Free Trade* (Fisher Unwin, 1903), vii–ix.

THE COBDEN CLUB CASE BY ITS SECRETARY, COX

What then are the principles which Adam Smith taught, and which England some fifty years later began cautiously to practice, and then after a fierce political struggle finally adopted? The main principle, so far as the present controversy is concerned, is this: *That it is impossible to add to the wealth of a nation by preventing the free importation of foreign goods.* This proposition would be self-evident but for the fact that the use of money blinds the average man to the realities of trade. If trade were in appearance, what it is in reality, an exchange of goods for goods, nobody would be so insane as to question the advantage to a nation of freely receiving all the good things that other nations can be induced to send it. But trade has for many centuries in all civilised countries presented the appearance of an exchange of goods against money, and the average man forgets that money is merely a go-between; nor does he perceive that the exchange of goods for money is only half of a transaction which must subsequently be completed by the exchange of money for goods. To realise this essential characteristic of money it is only necessary to try and imagine what would happen if the persons who sold goods were content to keep the money they receive. It is clear that as soon as they had sold all their existing stock they would get no more money, and meanwhile they would be naked and starving amid a pile of useless pieces of metal.

It seems almost infantile to have to remind the reader of these obvious considerations, but such a reminder is not altogether unnecessary when even Cabinet ministers show their ignorance of the real nature of trade. Whatever be the mechanism of trade, whether it be the simple barter of the primitive savage, or whether it be conducted with coins of copper or of silver or of gold, or with banknotes, or with cheques, or with bills of exchange, under all these conditions trade in its essence always has been, and always must be, an exchange of goods for goods, of one good thing for another good thing. Furthermore, trade is always conducted between individuals.[1] Strictly speaking, there is no such thing as trade between nations. The individual Englishman trades with the individual Frenchman, the Frenchman with a Chinaman, the Chinaman with a Yankee, the Yankee with a Canadian, the Canadian with a Scot, the Scotchman with an Englishman. All these men are each seeking their own profit in the exchanges they make. They will find that profit better if left to themselves than if their operations are subject to the control of politicians and bureaucrats, who may be corrupt, and who certainly will be ignorant. But the national wealth is the sum total of the wealth of the individuals composing the nation. It can therefore only be diminished by any system of trade regulation which deprives individuals of the liberty to obtain profit where they can find it best.

85)   Blanche E. C. Dugdale, *Arthur James Balfour* (Hutchinson, 1939), I, 266–7.

BALFOUR TO THE KING, 15 SEPTEMBER 1903

The root principle for which Mr. Balfour pleads is liberty of fiscal negotiation. Hitherto it has been impossible for us to negotiate effectively with other Governments in respect of commercial treaties because we have neither anything to give which they wish to receive nor anything to take away which they are afraid to lose. Our negotiations are therefore barren; and we have been obliged to look on helplessly while in all the most advanced countries a tariff barrier is being built up against our manufactures which is an ever-growing obstacle to our legitimate trade development. Mr. Balfour does not contemplate that at this stage the evil can be removed; but if there are means of mitigating it, those means should be tried; and they cannot be tried if the canons of taxation at present in force are not respected. In Mr. Balfour's opinion the change he contemplates would promote, not hinder, 'free trade'.

There are, however, two quite different shapes in which this 'freedom to negotiate' may be employed—one against foreign Governments, the other in favour of our own Colonies. In

[1] In the comparatively rare cases where governments engage in trade they act on the same principles as individual trading firms.

dealing with foreign Governments we may threaten—and if
need be employ—'retaliation.' In dealing with our own
Colonies we can only offer 'preference.' The second is perhaps
the most important; if, that is, a really good bargain could be
struck between the Mother Country and her children. But it is
also far the most difficult. It is difficult because a bargain is
always difficult; it is especially difficult because it is hard to
see how any bargain could be contrived which the Colonies
would accept, and which would not involve some taxation of
food in this country.

In Mr. Balfour's opinion there are ways in which such
taxation might be imposed, which would in no degree add to
the cost of living of the working classes. But he is also of
opinion that in the present state of public feeling, no such plan
could get a fair hearing; to make it part of the Government
programme would be to break up the Party, and to endanger
the other half of the policy—that which authorises retaliation
—for which the country is beter prepared. Mr. Balfour therefore, as at present advised, intends to say that, though Colonial
Preference is eminently desirable in the interests both of British
commerce and Imperial unity, it has not yet come within the
sphere of practical politics.

86)   R. Tressell, *The Ragged Trousered Philanthropists* (Lawrence
      & Wishart, complete edition, 1965), 21–2.

None of them really understood the subject: not one of them
had ever devoted fifteen consecutive minutes to the earnest
investigation of it. The papers they read were filled with vague
and alarming accounts of the quantities of foreign merchandise
imported into this country, the enormous number of aliens
constantly arriving, and their destitute conditions, how they
lived, the crimes they committed, and the injury they did to
British trade. These were the seeds which, cunningly sown in
their minds, caused to grow up within them a bitter undis-
criminating hatred of foreigners. To them the mysterious thing
they variously called the 'Friscal Policy', the 'Fistical Policy',
or the 'Fissical Question' was a great Anti-Foreign Crusade.
The country was in a hell of a state, poverty, hunger and
misery in a hundred forms had already invaded thousands of
homes and stood upon the thresholds of thousands more. How
came these things to be? It was the bloody foreigner! There-

fore, down with the foreigners and all their works. Out with them. Drive them b——s into the bloody sea! The country would be ruined if not protected in some way. This Friscal, Fistical, Fissical or whatever the hell policy it was called, *was* Protection, therefore no one but a bloody fool could hesitate to support it. It was all quite plain—quite simple. One did not need to think twice about it. It was scarcely necessary to think about it at all.

This was the conclusion reached by Crass and such of his mates who thought they were Conservatives—the majority of them could not have read a dozen sentences aloud without stumbling—it was not necessary to think or study or investigate anything. It was all as clear as daylight. The foreigner was the enemy, and the cause of poverty and bad trade.

87)   Tariff Reform League leaflet.   No. 104.

What is Tariff Reform?

WHY SHOULD I VOTE FOR IT?

These are questions everyone wants to be able to answer; and everyone **ought** to be able to answer them, for the answer is easy.

First: What is a 'Tariff'?

A 'Tariff' is a list of duties or tolls paid to Government, at seaport or frontier towns, on foreign goods brought into a country.

Every civilised country has a Tariff, because every civilised country puts duties on **some** of the goods it buys from other countries.

We have always had a Tariff.

WE HAVE A TARIFF NOW.

Last year we raised nearly

13 MILLION POUNDS

from heavy duties on **tea, sugar, coffee, cocoa and dried fruits.**

In addition we raised

ANOTHER 13 MILLION POUNDS

from heavy duties on **tobacco,** which nine men out of ten think as necessary as food.

Who pays these duties? We do!

Why? Because we do not grow any tea, or sugar, or coffee, or cocoa, or tobacco, in this country. Consequently those who send us these things have no British competition to meet which would force them to pay the duties themselves by lowering the price they charge us.

Therefore these duties are paid out of our pockets.

Every man and woman who drinks tea or coffee, or smokes tobacco, pays a tax on every cup and every pipeful.

Secondly: What is Tariff Reform?

Tariff Reform simply means **reforming** or **re-arranging** this existing Tariff of ours, so as to **increase employment and wages,** and at the same time to **lighten the burden of taxation we now have to bear.**

CAN WE DO THIS?

Yes! If we put duties on foreign goods that **do** compete with things we grow ourselves, the **foreigner** would have to pay these duties if he wanted to get into our market.

Instead of putting the duties on tea and coffee and sugar and tobacco, we could put them on foreign corn, foreign meat, foreign butter, and other things that **compete** with British produce injuring British agriculture and **throwing British Agricultural Labourers out of work and wages.**

We could **also** put duties on a number of the **Foreign Manufactures** which come into our market to compete with British manufactures, and either **throw British Workmen out of employment or lower their wages.**

Duties on things like motor-cars, silks, satins, velvets, or bows could not possibly hurt poor people, who do not buy such things and these duties also would be **largely paid by the foreigner** who wanted to do business in our market on fair terms.

REMEMBER that our present tariff taxes **you.**

REMEMBER that **Tariff Reform** proposes to tax the **foreigner.**

REMEMBER that our present tariff allows the foreigner to **throw British workpeople out of employment and wages.**

REMEMBER that **Tariff Reform** will prevent his doing so and will thus **increase employment and wages in this country.**

Printed and published by Jas. Truscott & Son, Ltd., London.
For further Copies apply LEAFLET, 7, VICTORIA STREET, S.W.
Price 4d. per 100, *or* 2s. *per* 1,000.

CHAPTER NINE

The Empire

On the eve of the Boer War (1899–1902) confidence remained high in the strength and self-sufficiency of the British Empire (88). But foreign hostility and British difficulties in overcoming the Boer farmers confirmed Joseph Chamberlain in his belief that the Empire needed to secure greater strength through greater unity (89). Boer War jingoism was sharply criticized by radicals such as J. A. Hobson (90). Hobson sought to prove how high finance was manipulating 'imperialism' for profit, though he did accept the need for colonization in the name of 'civilization' (91). This was Kipling's 'white man's burden' (92). Ramsay MacDonald was refreshingly unpatronizing and perceptive (93), in contrast to Sir Francis Younghusband (1863–1942), explorer and colonial administrator who was totally unperceptive (94). On the brink of war in 1914 H. N. Brailsford was re-stating the Hobson thesis (95). The hopes voiced by Chamberlain and Milner for a tighter system of Imperial government met with little response from the self-governing colonies (96, 97). But by the later Edwardian period politicians were beginning to feel their way towards what was to become, after the First World War, the undemanding 'Commonwealth' partnership (98, 99, 100). This partnership was not envisaged by Balfour as likely to embrace the coloured peoples of the Empire (101). Radicals pointed out the hypocrisy and danger of such an attitude, especially in relation to South Africa (102). The Liberal Government hoped for the best there under the 1910 union (103), though reports sent back were not encouraging (104). India too was uncertain and unsettled (105), but the Morley-Minto reforms produced some temporary easement (106). Though the British Empire had progressed markedly between 1901 and 1914, in the latter year the question still being asked was: 'Will the Empire Live?' (107).

88)   E. Sanderson, *The British Empire in the Nineteenth Century*
       (Blackie, 1899), VI, 352–4.

The Colonial and Indian Exhibition held in London in 1886
was a display full of interest, beauty, and instruction, and one
which was very successful in awaking the British people at
home to a sense of the reality and greatness of the empire of
which, in territorial area, the islands that they inhabit form
only an eightieth part. That grand show of the resources which
have been described in our pages gave us visible proof that,
with advantage to themselves, our fellow-subjects abroad can
furnish us with endless supplies of beef and mutton, alive and
dead, fresh and frozen; of bacon and hams, of cheese and
butter; with a boundless store of grain and flour, including
maize; with unlimited quantities of pine-apples and bananas,
mangoes and limes, apples, lime-juice, and many preserved
fruits of temperate, sub-tropical, and tropical climes. It was
there seen that, if China utterly failed us in her staple product,
the British housewife could, at the same or at a lower cost,
make any amount of excellent tea with leaves from India and
Ceylon; that the best cocoa, coffee, and sugar in the world are
abundantly produced within the British dominions; that good
wine and the finest rum could never fail; and that the smoker,
if all foreign sources were closed, could still have excellent
tobacco and cigars. If all the rest of the world refused to
furnish medicinal relief for our sick, the British Empire would
supply a profusion of drugs; of perfumes for the sick-room and
the boudoir, of spices for the confectioner and the cook; of
dye-woods for the manufacturer of silks and woollens. From
our own colonies we could obtain immense supplies of animal
and vegetable fats and oils for illuminating, lubricating, and
other purposes, with some gums and resins of great value,
including gutta percha. The mills of Lancashire, if they were
dependent on our colonies alone, would not be destitute of the
finest cotton, or of good silk; and if all the sheep in the British
Isles were to perish, there would be no lack—nay, a boundless
import—of the best wool from our own possessions. We can
obtain at will, from the same countries, an enormous quantity
of valuable fibres for cordage, for textile fabrics, and for paper-
making, in flax and hemp, jute, and the *Phormium tenax* of New
Zealand. As long as our colonial empire exists and thrives,
hides and leather and tanning materials and furs, with many

kinds of serviceable skins, cannot cease to be ready for the home-market. Nor need the user of timber for all kinds of purposes fear the failure of colonial supplies in many species of the most durable and ornamental woods that the world can show.

As we look round this vast and prosperous realm, which can be paralleled by nothing in the history of any other State, we see an empire that is, in its various parts, washed by all oceans; an empire in which the sovereign rules over Mohammedans, Buddhists, Brahmans, pagans, and Parsees; over Roman Catholics, as over Protestants of all shades of belief; over men of many races, of all colours, of hundreds of varieties of language and ways of life. In saying that the sun never sets upon the dominions of Great Britain we really assert that, in some part or other of the world, British subjects are ever awake and alert. At the midnight hour for the British Isles, the early risers among 220 millions of people under our sway in India have begun or are beginning the labours of the day which, for us, has yet some hours before dawn. At the same midnight hour for dwellers in the home-country, the Canadian Dominion, at its farthest point on the Pacific shore, sees British subjects in mid-afternoon of the day whose sun has, in the British Isles, long sunk beneath Atlantic waves. Take flight in thought across the great Pacific, in south-westerly course from the Dominion to New Zealand, and you find the people about to have a mid-day meal. Sail or steam where you will over distant seas, you can scarcely avoid the sight of the flag waving over fortress or signal-post or Government-house or man-of-war or stately steamer of some merchant-line. Looking round again over this earth-encircling series of states under one monarch, from London, the mighty heart where the empire's life pulsates in its utmost force; writing at a time when we hear foreign vapouring and babble concerning the 'isolation of Great Britain', accompanied by scarcely veiled threats of blocking our commercial routes to India and Australasia, and of reducing us to the rank of a third-class nation, we pronounce that there is one moral to the story which it has been our privilege to tell. If we are 'narrow and selfish, factious and self-indulgent, impatient of necessary burdens; if we see in public affairs not our Empire but our country, not our country but our parish, and in our parish our house, the Empire is doomed'. We cordially echo Lord Rosebery's words. Let Britons keep with undaunted resolution what has been gained

through the possession and the exercise of all the great qualities and faculties that make men and nations conquerors and
colonizers of the earth which man was bidden to replenish and
subdue. Let the 'citizens of no mean city', dwellers in the land
that has produced Cromwell and Chatham; Marlborough and
Wellington; Clive and Wolfe; Blake, Rodney, Duncan, Nelson
and many other sea-captains of immortal renown, decide
whether, by neglecting to prepare for the day of conflict, they
shall see the heritage bequeathed by their sires destroyed or
maimed, or whether they will successfully defend it, as they
may if they are wise in time, even against a world in arms.

89)   C. W. Boyd (ed.), *Mr. Chamberlain's Speeches* (Constable,
      1914), II, 367–72.

JOSEPH CHAMBERLAIN'S LAST SPEECH, 1906

The character of the individual depends upon the greatness
of the ideals upon which he rests, and the character of a nation
is the same. The moral grandeur of a nation depends upon its
being sometimes able to forget itself, sometimes able to think
of the future of the race for which it stands. England without
an empire! Can you conceive it? England in that case would
not be the England we love. If the ties of sympathy which have
gradually been woven between ourselves and our children
who are soon to become great nations, across the seas, if these
ties were weakened or destroyed, if we suffered their affection
to die for want of food for it, if we allowed them to drift apart,
then this England of ours would sink from the comparative
position which it has enjoyed throughout the centuries. It
would no longer be a power, if not supreme, at all events of
the greatest influence, generally well exercised on the civilization and the peace of the world. It would be a fifth-rate nation,
existing on the sufferance of its more powerful neighbours. We
will not have it. . . .
    The remedy is at hand, and if we are not too careless, too
apathetic as to the future, if we are not too timid to act, I say
there is even now time to hold for ourselves and our people our
own trade. And we can hold it against all fair competition.
And we can do more. We can extend our trade in the best
markets, with our best friends. We can benefit them in trading
with them, while they give us reciprocal advantage in the

preference which they give for our manufactures. We can do this. We can strengthen the union. We can draw closer the growing nations, the sister states, and by a commercial union we can pave the way for that federation which I see constantly before me as a practical object of aspiration—that federation of free nations which will enable us to prolong in ages yet to come all the glorious traditions of the British race.

Ladies and gentlemen, if we are to fulfil these aspirations, believe me, we must cultivate the affection and the sympathy of these children of ours in the colonies. We must learn to understand them better, to appreciate more highly their mission and their work. They are our pioneers sent out from here, fighting against nature, fighting against dangers and difficulties of every kind. They have worthily maintained the honour of the flag and the interests of the Empire, and they deserve the sympathy which I claim you should give them. But are we going the right way to produce this kindly feeling? You may be, who agree with the words I say, but what about those who profess to represent you? What are they doing at this time to draw closer together the British Empire? . . .

The union of the Empire must be preceded and accompanied, as I have said, by a better understanding, by a closer sympathy. To secure that is the highest object of statesmanship now at the beginning of the twentieth century, and, if these were the last words that I were permitted to utter to you I would rejoice to utter them in your presence and with your approval. I know that the fruition of our hopes is certain. I hope I may be able to live to congratulate you upon our common triumph, but in any case I have faith in the people. I trust in the good sense, the intelligence, and the patriotism of the majority, the vast majority, of my countrymen. I look forward to the future with hope and confidence, and

> *'Others I doubt not, if not we,*
> *The issue of our toil shall see.'*

90)   J. A. Hobson, *The Psychology of Jingoism* (Grant Richards, 1901), 3–4.

Among large sections of the middle and the labouring classes, the music-hall, and the recreative public-house into which it shades off by imperceptible degrees, are a more potent educator than the church, the school, the political meeting, or even than the press. Into this 'lighter self' of the city populace the artiste conveys by song or recitation crude notions upon morals and politics, appealing by coarse humour or exaggerated pathos to the animal lusts of an audience stimulated by alcohol into appreciative hilarity.

In ordinary times politics plays no important part in these feasts of sensationalism, but the glorification of brute force and an ignorant contempt for foreigners are ever-present factors which at great political crises make the music-hall a very serviceable engine for generating military passion. The art of the music-hall is the only 'popular' art of the present day: its words and melodies pass by quick magic from the Empire or the Alhambra over the length and breadth of the land, re-echoed in a thousand provincial halls, clubs, and drinking saloons, until the remotest village is familiar with air and sentiment. By such process of artistic suggestion the fervour of Jingoism has been widely fed, and it is worthy of note that the present meaning of the word was fastened upon it by the popularity of a single verse.

Nicer critics may even be disposed to dilate upon the context of this early use of the new political term—the affected modesty of the opening disclaimer, the rapid transition to a tone of bullying braggadocio, with its culminating stress upon the money-bags, and the unconscious humour of an assumption that it is our national duty to defend the Turk.

Indeed, without descending to minute analysis, we may find something instructive in the crude jumble of sentiment and the artistic setting which it finds—

> 'We don't want to fight,
>   But, by Jingo, if we do,
> We've got the men,
>   We've got the ships,
> We've got the money too'—

crowned by the domineering passion blurted out in the concluding line—

> 'The Russians shall not have Constantinople.'

91) J. A. Hobson, *Imperialism* (Fisher Unwin, 1902), part I, chs, IV, VI; part II, ch. IV.

What is the direct economic outcome of Imperialism? A great expenditure of public money upon ships, guns, military and naval equipment and stores, growing and productive of enormous profits when a war, or an alarm of war, occurs; new public loans and important fluctuations in the home and foreign Bourses; more posts for soldiers and sailors and in the diplomatic and consular services; improvement of foreign investments by the substitution of the British flag for a foreign flag; acquisition of markets for certain classes of exports, and some protection and assistance for trades representing British houses in these manufactures; employment for engineers, missionaries, speculative miners, ranchers and other emigrants.

Certain definite business and professional interests feeding upon imperialistic expenditure, or upon the results of that expenditure, are thus set up in opposition to the common good, and, instinctively feeling their way to one another, are found united in strong sympathy to support every new imperialistic exploit. . . .

If, contemplating the enormous expenditure on armaments, the ruinous wars, the diplomatic audacity of knavery by which modern Governments seek to extend their territorial power, we put the plain, practical question, *Cui bono?* the first and most obvious answer is, The investor. . . .

Investors who have put their money in foreign lands, upon terms which take full account of risks connected with the political conditions of the country, desire to use the resources of their Government to minimise these risks, and so to enhance the capital value and the interest of their private investments. The investing and speculative classes in general also desire that Great Britain should take other foreign areas under her flag in order to secure new areas for profitable investment and speculation. . . .

It is true that the motor-power of Imperialism is not chiefly financial: finance is rather the governor of the imperial engine, directing the energy and determining its work: it does not constitute the fuel of the engine, nor does it directly generate the power. Finance manipulates the patriotic forces which politicians, soldiers, philanthropists, and traders generate; the enthusiasm for expansion which issues from these sources, though strong and genuine, is irregular and blind; the financial interest has those qualities of concentration and clear-sighted calculation which are needed to set Imperialism to work. An ambitious statesman, a frontier soldier, an over-zealous missionary, a pushing trader, may suggest or even initiate a step of imperial expansion, may assist in educating patriotic public opinion to the urgent need of some fresh advance, but the final determination rests with the financial power. The direct influence exercised by great financial houses in 'high politics' is supported by the control which they exercise over the body of public opinion through the Press, which, in every 'civilised' country, is becoming more and more their obedient instrument. While the specifically financial newspaper imposes 'facts' and 'opinions' on the business classes, the general body of the Press comes more and more under the conscious or unconscious domination of financiers. The case of the South African Press, whose agents and correspondents fanned the martial flames in this country, was one of open ownership on the part of South African financiers, and this policy of owning newspapers for the sake of manufacturing public opinion is common in the great European cities. . . . Apart from the financial Press, and financial ownership of the general Press, the City notoriously exercises a subtle and abiding influence upon leading London newspapers, and through them upon the body of the Provincial Press, while the entire dependence of the Press for its business profits upon its advertising columns involves a peculiar reluctance to oppose the organised financial classes with whom rests the control of so much advertising business. Add to this the natural sympathy with a sensational policy which a cheap Press always manifests, and it becomes evident that the Press is strongly biassed towards Imperialism, and lends itself with great facility to the suggestion of financial or political Imperialists who desire to work up patriotism for some new piece of expansion. . . .

The play of these forces does not openly appear. They are essentially parasites upon patriotism, and they adapt themselves to its protecting colours. In the mouths of their representatives are noble phrases, expressive of their desire to extend the area of civilisation, to establish good government, promote Christianity, extirpate slavery, and elevate the lower races. Some of the business men who hold such language may entertain a genuine, though usually a vague, desire to accomplish these ends, but they are primarily engaged in business, and they are not unaware of the utility of the more unselfish forces in furthering their ends. Their true attitude of mind is expressed by Mr. Rhodes in his famous description of 'Her Majesty's Flag' as 'the greatest commercial asset in the world'. . . .

If the consuming public in this country raised its standard of consumption to keep pace with every rise of productive powers, there would be no excess of goods or capital clamorous to use Imperialism in order to find markets: foreign trade would indeed exist, but there would be no difficulty in exchanging a small surplus of our manufactures for the food and raw material we annually absorbed, and all the savings that we made could find employment, if we chose, in home industries. . . .

An economy that assigns to the 'possessing' classes an excess of consuming power which they cannot use, and cannot convert into really serviceable capital, is a dog-in-the-manger policy. The social reforms which deprive the possessing classes of their surplus will not, therefore, inflict upon them the real injury they dread; they can only use this surplus by forcing on their country a wrecking policy of Imperialism. The only safety of nations lies in removing the unearned increments of income from the possessing classes, and adding them to the wage-income of the working classes or to the public income, in order that they may be spent in raising the standard of consumption. . . .

Trade Unionism and Socialism are thus the natural enemies of Imperialism, for they take away from the 'imperialist' classes the surplus incomes which form the economic stimulus of Imperialism. . . .

It is the great practical business of the century to explore and develop, by every method which science can devise, the hidden natural and human resources of the globe.

That the white Western nations will abandon a quest on which they have already gone so far is a view which does not deserve consideration. That this process of development may be so conducted as to yield a gain to world-civilisation, instead of some terrible *débâcle* in which revolted slave races may trample down their parasitic and degenerate white masters, should be the supreme aim of far-sighted scientific statecraft.

To those who utter the single cry of warning, '*laissez faire*, hands off, let these people develop their resources themselves with such assistance as they ask or hire, undisturbed by the importunate and arrogant control of foreign nations,' it is a sufficient answer to point out the impossibility of maintaining such an attitude.

If organised Governments of civilised Powers refused the

task, they would let loose a horde of private adventurers, slavers, piratical traders, treasure hunters, concession mongers, who, animated by mere greed of gold or power, would set about the work of exploitation under no public control and with no regard to the future; playing havoc with the political, economic, and moral institutions of the peoples, instilling civilised vices and civilised diseases, importing spirits and firearms as the trade of readiest acceptance, fostering inter-necine strife for their own political and industrial purposes, and even setting up private despotisms sustained by organised armed forces. . . . The contact with white races cannot be avoided, and it is more perilous and more injurious in pro-portion as it lacks governmental sanction and control. The most gigantic modern experiment in private adventure is slowly yielding its full tale of horrors in the Congo Free State, while the handing over of large regions in Africa to the virtually unchecked government of Chartered Companies exposes every-where the dangers of a contact based on private commercialism.

To abandon the backward races to these perils of private exploitation, it is argued forcibly, is a barbarous dereliction of a public duty on behalf of humanity and the civilization of the world. Not merely does it leave the tropics to be the helpless prey of the offscourings of civilised nations; it opens grave dangers in the future, from the political or military ambitions of native or imported rulers, who, playing upon the religious fanaticism or the combative instincts of great hordes of semi-savages, may impose upon them so effective a military disci-pline as to give terrible significance to some black or yellow 'peril'. Complete isolation is no longer possible even for the remotest island; absolute self-sufficiency is no more possible for a nation than for an individual: in each case society has the right and the need to safeguard its interests against an injurious assertion of individuality.

Again, though there is some force in the contention that the backward natives could and would protect themselves against the encroachments of private adventurers, if they had the assurance that the latter could not call upon their Government for assistance or for vengeance, history does not lead us to believe that these powers of self-protection, however adequate against forcible invasions, would suffice to meet the more insidious wiles by which traders, prospectors, and political adventurers insinuate their poisons into primitive societies like that of Samoa or Ashanti.

So far, we have established two tentative principles. First, that all interference on the part of civilised white races with 'lower races' is not *prima facie* illegitimate. Second, that such interference cannot safely be left to private enterprise of individual whites. If these principles be admitted, it follows that civilised Governments *may* undertake the political and economic control of lower races—in a word, that the characteristic form of modern Imperialism is not under all conditions illegitimate.

What, then, are the conditions which render it legitimate? They may be provisionally stated thus: Such interference with the government of a lower race must be directed primarily to secure the safety and progress of the civilisation of the world, and not the special interest of the interfering nation. Such interference must be attended by an improvement and elevation of the character of the people who are brought under this control. Lastly, the determination of the two preceding conditions must not be left to the arbitrary will or judgment of the interfering nation, but must proceed from some organised representation of civilized humanity.

92)   THE WHITE MAN'S BURDEN
                        1899
           (*The United States and the Philippine Islands*)
               Take up the White Man's burden—
                   Send forth the best ye breed—
               Go bind your sons to exile
                   To serve your captives' need;
               To wait in heavy harness
                   On fluttered folk and wild—
               Your new-caught, sullen peoples,
                   Half devil and half child.

               Take up the White Man's burden—
                   In patience to abide,
               To veil the threat of terror
                   And check the show of pride;
               By open speech and simple,
                   An hundred times made plain,
               To seek another's profit,
                   And work another's gain.

Take up the White Man's burden—
   The savage wars of peace—
Fill full the mouth of Famine
   And bid the sickness cease;
And when your goal is nearest
   The end for others sought,
Watch Sloth and heathen Folly
   Bring all your hope to nought.

Take up the White Man's burden—
   No tawdry rule of kings,
But toil of serf and sweeper—
   The tale of common things.
The ports ye shall not enter,
   The roads ye shall not tread,
Go make them with your living,
   And mark them with your dead!

Take up the White Man's burden—
   And reap his old reward:
The blame of those ye better,
   The hate of those ye guard—
The cry of hosts ye humour
   (Ah, slowly!) toward the light:—
'Why brought ye us from bondage,
   'Our loved Egyptian night?'

Take up the White Man's burden—
   Ye dare not stoop to less—
Nor call too loud on Freedom
   To cloak your weariness;
By all ye cry or whisper,
   By all ye leave or do,
The silent, sullen peoples
   Shall weigh your Gods and you.

Take up the White Man's burden—
   Have done with childish days—
The lightly proffered laurel,
   The easy, ungrudged praise.
Comes now, to search your manhood
   Through all the thankless years,
Cold-edged with dear-bought wisdom.
   The judgment of your peers!

93) J. Ramsay MacDonald, *Socialism and Government* (ILP, 1909). II, 80–91.

I do not mean that the aim of the native policy of white races must necessarily be the establishment of democratic government, as we understand it, amongst natives. The democracy of these northern lands is probably native to the soil and to the race. To go with it north and south, east and west, as though it were the inevitable end of all government is to make a fetish of it. Democracy is only one of the forms— the only possible form for us, perhaps—by which government by public opinion shows itself. We cannot treat the native past as though it had given him no inheritance of habit and mind. He, like ourselves, is nothing apart from his inheritance. We cannot get him to begin again. We have, therefore, to judge him from his own standpoint and not from ours. The institutions which are to give him freedom are most likely altogether different from those which are to give us freedom. The success of native policy, therefore, depends on whether the white races can put themselves in the position of native guides along roads which it is natural for the natives themselves to travel, and not merely on ways which suit the convenience and views of the whites themselves. They can, however, recognise the power of his chiefs and his headmen, his tribal laws and customs, his tribal economics; they can assist him to throw off excrescences of degeneracy. The spirit which demands individual freedom and democratic control here, is satisfied by the self-development of different communities, provided always that that entails no breach of fundamental moral order—such, for instance, as wanton destruction of human life.

Native education and the goal of native policy cannot be separated. If we are not to establish democratic control in native States, we should not educate them in democratic ways. Our education is part of the preparation for our civic life. How deep is our folly, for instance, in educating Indians in the principles of civil liberty at our English schools and Universities and then sending them home to obey a government which we maintain on principles of such absolute authority that a Charles the First would hardly claim its powers even as a corollary to his divine right. If India is not to receive self-government, sanity demands that Indians should not be instructed in Western political philosophy. For the effect of superimposing an education based upon principles of Western civil liberty upon minds which are expected to accept conditions of Eastern subjection, is introducing into the subject dominions, and into the Empire as a whole, a divergence between mind and experience which is bound ultimately to end in civil disaster.

It follows, if what I have argued be true, that it is a profound mistake to regard the native as a child, or as a potential white man who ought to be educated in school and State as though he were a white man. It is an unscientific view. The democrat may recognise that his Democracy depends on circumstances and still remain a democrat. From the point of view of scientific politics and organic social relationships the recognition of historical and racial differences, of varied evolutions, of diverse forms of tribal and national organisation is as natural as observation amongst the peoples of the world makes it necessary. It is one of the fundamental differences between the new Socialism and the old Radicalism that the former is endowed with the historical spirit whilst the latter was moved only by political legalism. The equality of Socialism is not uniformity. It recognises differences. It has no cast iron system which is to be applied to all races and all conditions —no panacea, no universal mode of thought. It therefore does not consider the native race as a white one at an early stage of evolution. It cannot, consistently with its spirit, make the mistake of regarding the East as the West in the making. It has a spirit, a sentiment, a moral outlook. This spirit it regards as universal but not the forms which embody it.

The natural and inevitable difficulties which beset attempts to govern natives are greatly augmented by the breaking up of tribal organisation by whites, and the scattering of natives throughout white settlements. Invariably, the result of this is to rouse racial antipathy, which is sometimes attributed to economic antagonism. But it is in the blood. There is a repulsion between the white and the coloured races which becomes active when they live together and the conditions of social equality begin to arise. The repulsion is more or less quiescent when the native is docile in his servitude; it awakes when he acquires the civil and economic advantages which, were there no bar, would entitle him to social recognition, or when he makes political demands. To some extent the irritant which rouses the antipathy may be economic, but the feeling itself is much more deeply seated than that, and its explanation is probably hidden away with the meaning of heredity in the hitherto unexplored caverns of the human mind. Mainly by reason of this antipathy it is futile to hope that the governing majority should be composed of natives where the natives are in a majority, but where the white men have established their own government and are no longer guests of the native race. Nature does not work that way. To mourn over this is to mourn over creation—an utterly useless pastime.

Whether the white man should have been in such a hurry to establish his own government in such lands is open to question. He might have done far better if he had remained a guest, if he had accepted native sovereignty, if he had taught the native to accommodate himself to the new conditions—giving the native rulers the necessary moral and political protection. But he chose the easier and the more brutal part. He exerted his power; he killed the native or brushed him aside; he destroyed and did not help to fulfil; he established his own government. That is the accomplished fact which makes the problem. I regret it. It is an unseemly blot on the white man's escutcheon. And, what has been done cannot be undone—as regards the Congo native, as regards the United States negro. The question therefore is: What ought to be the position of the native under such a government? Much will depend on the native's own plane of evolution. The Burmese may justify one answer, the Masai another. But the following rules may be assumed: The government must have some respect for native public opinion; where self-government is possible, it should be established. The type of government included within the extreme realisation of these principles may vary from undisturbed kraal government in special reserves, to self-government of practically a Western kind, such as is possible in parts of India.

Two great States have enfranchised the native and coloured citizen—Cape Colony and the United States. The experience of each has differed because the circumstances of each were different. In the latter the experience has not been altogether happy because the methods of enfranchisement were most unhappy; in the former the experience has been most fortunate. Some friends of the native races demand as an immediate concession a full franchise to natives. They believe that equality between whites and natives is the only guarantee of security which the latter can have. At present such demands will not be granted, and by being pressed only raise racial prejudices. Equality may be the goal, but the white race must undergo much spiritual change before that goal can be reached. Meanwhile, in the interests of the natives themselves, let us try to devise some practical settlement. For the time being a majority of native votes in mixed communities is not conducive to good government. The native, except in special cases, is not a citizen developed up to bearing democratic responsibilities. . . .

The Cape Colony method is the best. Even when it is accompanied by some special native qualification, it fulfils its purpose, because whilst a property or educational standard would be a test of class in a community of uniform race, it is not so in a mixed community. It secures the representation of the native race and makes its public opinion part of the public opinion which the legislature has to take into account, and it prevents that race from acquiring a preponderating electoral interest.

But behind our failures and our mistakes is the fact that the races rarely understand each other. They look at and hold communion with each other over a gulf. They are like people meeting in the night. Neither race discovers the password to the soul of the other. Amongst the vast crowds of men whom we send abroad to govern for us a handful are so spiritually endowed that they penetrate to the hearts of the people under them.

94) Sir F. Younghusband, 'Inter Racial Relations', *Sociological Review*, III (Sherratt & Hughes, 1910), 151–3.

The time when men were most nearly equal was when they were all primitive barbarians a quarter of a million years ago. Ever since then they have been becoming more and more unequal, and the evidence is not only that there are grades but that those grades are increasing and steepening. Not only is the Hottentot not equal to the Frenchman but the distance between them is likely to increase: it was less great a thousand years ago than it is now and it seems a fair inference that it is less now than it will be a thousand years hence.

We may fairly assume that nations will always remain on different grades. This being so, and the earth's area being limited, it is obvious that certain border races must inevitably come under the control, the protection, the administrative tutelage of certain higher races. The less-gifted Mongolians, Turkis and Tibetans are under the protection and tutelage of the more highly-civilised Chinese. The aboriginal tribes of India come under the tutelage of Hindu Chiefs and these again under British protection. We still retain an uncomfortable feeling that there is something wrong in exercising such tutelage—something unjust, high-handed and oppressive. We still retain the false idea of the equality of all men and feel half guilty in assuming a position of superiority. But it seems to me far more reasonable for the higher nations to regard themselves as possessing a high and important trust for common humanity to protect and guide and inspire the lower races. For let us look facts in the face. Even in the present generation Siberia and Manchuria have been threaded by a railway. Peking has been brought within seventeen days of Paris and London. Central Asia has been pacified. Order has been brought into the midst of Africa, and its deepest depths have been made accessible. Egypt, Tunis and Algiers have been restored to prosperity. And in many other directions the control and guidance by one or other of the powerful higher nations has worked not only for the good of that nation, and not only for the benefit of the less-developed race which has been brought under its administrative tutelage, but also—and this is the point—to the advantage of *all* nations, for the good of mankind as a *whole*. Common humanity benefits where the administrative tutelage has been judiciously and humanely exercised. Every nation benefits by the presence of the Russians in Siberia and Central Asia, of the Chinese in Mongolia and Turkestan, of the British in India, Egypt and Central and Southern Africa, and of the French in Tunis and Algeria. Neither the Asiatics, Africans nor Europeans would benefit by Russia, England and France declaring that all men were equal and retiring from their task of administrative tutelage. Protection, guidance, and tutelage of the weak by the strong, of the lower by the higher are, to my mind, an essential part of human development.

Yet, while I see the necessity for this tutelage, I also recognise that the proper way of exercising it has not yet been worked out by a single one of the higher nations. All of them are either too indifferent, or too clumsy, or too fitful and undecided. And the practical point to which energy will have in future to be directed is how to effect that tutelage without emasculating the protected people. The aim will be to develop individuality. And how to preserve order without crushing individuality is the great administrative problem of to-day. The French and the Italians with their refined taste and delicacy of touch possess advantages in which the harder and in some respect clumsier nations of the North are lacking. But they are often wanting in persistency and purposefulness, and do not get that support from the mother-country which the Englishman, in spite of his diatribes against interference from Downing Street, does receive in a far greater degree than any one else except, perhaps, the Russian.

If I might be permitted to offer a hint as to the solution of this most delicate and intricate problem I should say that it lay along the lines which Professor Caldecott has indicated—that is to say, not along the lines of fusion and inter-marriage but along the lines of organised co-operation, or in English, of working together. Let us imagine the higher nations freed of the last shred of doubt as to the necessity and more than necessity, the duty and obligation of guiding and controlling lower and less fortunate races. Let us imagine them throwing their whole heart into the work, not jealously distrustful of one another's intentions, but whole-heartedly co-operating with one another in the conviction that each is the gainer by the good work of the other, and that the work done is for the good of all humanity. And let us imagine further that to carry out their intentions they have evolved agents with all the warm sympathy of the Irishman, the delicacy, the method and the imagination of the Frenchman, and the self-reliance and long-persistency of the Englishman. Then we may catch a glimpse of the ideal method by which administrative tutelage may bring forth, foster and develop all the individuality in the lower race, and raise the higher races still higher by exercising them in sympathy and by convincing them that they are daily contributing to that drawing together and uplifting of common humanity which must be the highest aim of every individual and of every nation.

It is naturally easier for a nation to ignore this obligation. The tutelage of less-favoured people is a difficult and often thankless task. It is a drain on the manhood of the controlling nation. Many of her ablest sons are drained away from the

mother-country and are not available for her own development. Often the work has to be carried on in an uncongenial
climate where the physique suffers. Often again home ties are
strained and domestic happiness is sacrificed. And at all times
it is difficult to adjust the political ideals of the mother-country
to the administrative needs of the protected people. It is for
this reason that so many Americans shrink from protectorates
in Cuba, the Phillipines or elsewhere. They want to concern
themselves only with their own purely domestic democratic
ideals and wish to be perfectly free from any of the obligations
which the administrative tutelage of other peoples implies.
And such reluctance to be concerned with any one else's affairs
than their own, and such repugnance to anything which
savours of domination and suppression is easily intelligible.
Nevertheless there is a point of view, the one which I have
indicated above, from which such abnegation may appear
more like refined and fastidious selfishness than like high-
souled generosity, and may be less really humane than the
action of another who believes that for the good of humanity
as a whole it is essential that the more advanced nations should
take the more backward in hand in much the same way as the
higher classes in a nation do not shut themselves off from and
ignore the lower classes, but deliberately and in the interests of
the whole nation take them in hand and fit them more and
more for the exercise of responsibility.

Moreover those who have doubts as to the rights or advantages of one race controlling another may take this further
point into consideration, that there are peoples who flourish
best and who can most effectively develop their especial
individuality when they are under the protection of a
stronger, more practical race, who will do the, as it were,
'dirty' work of governing for them. There are peoples whose
minds are more particularly directed to spiritual matters,
who develop better when relieved of the necessity of governing and protecting themselves. The Tibetans *prefer* being
under some strong temporal power, whom they think they
will influence spiritually while they themselves receive adequate protection. And the Jews, though they did not come
under Roman protection as a matter of choice, nevertheless,
did, when under that protection, make their greatest contribution to the welfare of mankind, for it was then that
Christianity arose.

95)   H. N. Brailsford, *The War of Steel and Gold, a Study of the Armed Peace* (Bell, 4th ed., 1915), 79–82.

Why, then, is it that capital seeks to export itself? There are many cogent reasons abroad. At home the fundamental fact is the rapid accumulation of surplus capital. It grows in the hands of trust magnates, bankers, and ground landlords more rapidly than the demand for it at home. It tries continually to get itself employed at home, and the result is that periodic over-production, which shows itself in a 'slump' of trade and a crisis of unemployment. Capital, like labour, has its periods of unemployment, and its favourite method of meeting them is emigration. When rates of interest fall at home, it begins to look abroad for something at once remunerative, and not too risky, and it is to diplomacy that it turns to protect it from risks. If, further, we go on to ask why capital cannot get itself profitably employed at home as fast as it is accumulated, the answer is briefly that its too rapid accumulation has stood in the way of a simultaneous development of the consumers who might have given it employment. Had a little more of the profits of a trade 'boom' gone to labour, and a little less to capital, it is manifest that labour would have had more money to spend, and the new surplus capital—less considerable in amount—might have been employed in meeting this new demand. The shareholders of a Lancashire mill make their 35 per cent. in a good year—such cases occur. Had they and their fellows been content with something less than 35 per cent., and added to wages what they subtracted from dividends, the workers all over the country would have been spending more than before on the necessaries and the luxuries which these mills provide. There need then have been no slump, and the new capital might even have been used to make more cotton goods for the home market. But the shareholders insist on their 35 per cent., and the workers are foolish enough, or weak enough, to let them take it. What, then, is the too fortunate shareholder to do with his money? He spends as much as he can on motor-cars and grouse-moors, town-houses and domestic display. But even to this, unless he is a mere spendthrift, there is a limit. He, therefore, invests what he is pleased to call his 'savings'—meaning by that term the money which he has saved from other people's wages, and failed to expend on his own pleasures. The home market is 'glutted'—

which means that the masses have nothing more to spend. He therefore, looks abroad. An Egyptian Khedive wants money to squander on ballet-girls and palaces and operas. Japan wants money to build ironclads. Russia wants money to pay for the repression of her subjects. Or perhaps gold has been discovered in Ashanti, or the niggers of West Africa have developed a taste for gin. Into such enterprises goes the capital that cannot find employment at home. The reason for the too rapid export of capital abroad is, in short, the bad division of wealth at home. For there is 'work' enough in these islands to 'employ' more than all their surplus capital, if only the consuming power of the masses could be increased. Raise wages, raise with them the standard of comfort, and this restless capital need no longer wander abroad. There ought to be enough for it to do at home. It might build working-class dwellings in reclaimed slums instead of palaces for an Egyptian Khedive. It might 'colonise England' instead of speculating in tropical land. It might exert itself in providing the English labourer with a more frequent change of clean shirts for his back and clean sheets for his bed, instead of enabling the Russian Government to build in Russian dockyards at an extravagant cost warships which it does not need, to be navigated by sailors whose only hope is mutiny and revolt. Capital conducts itself to-day much as the primitive agriculturist behaves. It must be for ever conquering fresh territory and bringing new fields under culture, simply because it does not know how to make a good use of the fields it already possesses. The primitive farmer —in Russia, for example—must become a conqueror, because he has never learned to apply manure. The capitalist must rush abroad, because he will not fertilise the demand for more commodities at home by the simple expedient of raising wages.

The other reason which is most potent in inducing capital to flow abroad is the elementary fact that coloured labour can be more ruthlessly exploited than white. The supposed risks of a foreign investment, moreover, enable the capitalist to charge usurious interest. It follows that on both grounds the profits to be made abroad are greater than the profits to be made at home.

In one of the classics of the Imperialist muse, Mr. Rudyard Kipling remarks that there are no ten commandments east of Suez. That may be an attraction to Tommy Atkins. The capitalist hears the East 'a calling mainly because there are no Factory Acts east of Suez.

96)   M. Ollivier (ed.), *The Colonial and Imperial Conferences from 1887 to 1937* (HMSO, Ottawa, 1954), I, 153–5.

JOSEPH CHAMBERLAIN SPEECH AT 1902 COLONIAL CONFERENCE

We do require your assistance in the administration of the vast Empire which is yours as well as ours. The weary Titan staggers under the too vast orb of its fate. We have borne the burden for many years. We think it is time that our children should assist us to support it, and whenever you make the request to us, be sure that we shall hasten gladly to call you to our Councils. If you are prepared at any time to take any share, any proportionate share, in the burdens of the Empire, we are prepared to meet you with any proposal for giving to you a corresponding voice in the policy of the Empire. And the object, if I may point out to you, may be achieved in various ways. Suggestions have been made that representation should be given to the Colonies in either, or in both, Houses of Parliament. There is no objection in principle to any such proposal. If it comes to us, it is a proposal which His Majesty's Government would certainly feel justified in favourably considering, but I have always felt that the most practical form in which we could achieve our object, would be the establishment or the creation of a real Council of the Empire to which all questions of Imperial interest might be referred, and if it were desired to proceed gradually, as probably would be our course—we are all accustomed to the slow ways in which our Constitutions have been worked out—if it be desired to proceed gradually, the Council might in the first instance be merely an advisory council. It would resemble in some respects, the advisory council which was established in Australia, and which, although it was not wholly successful, did nevertheless pave the way for the complete federation upon which we now congratulate them. But although that would be a preliminary step, it is clear that the object would not be completely secured until there had been conferred upon such a Council executive functions, and perhaps also legislative powers, and it is for you to say, gentlemen, whether you think the time has come when any progress whatever can be made in this direction.

In the absence of any formal constitution of the Empire, the nearest approach to such a Council is to be found in the Conference which we open today—a conference, a meeting, of the principal representatives of the motherland and also of the nations which, together with the United Kingdom, constitute the Empire. And I observe upon the paper of subjects which will be distributed to you, and of which notice has been given for consideration at further meetings of the Conference, that the Premier of New Zealand, on behalf of that Colony, has made a proposal for transforming these Conferences—which have been held hitherto rather casually, and only in connection with special occasions,—into a periodical meeting. If this were done, or if an Imperial Council were established, it is clear that the two subjects which would immediately call for its attention are those which I have already mentioned—of Imperial defence and commercial relations. And we invite your special attention to these two objects on the present occasion.

As regards Imperial defence, I propose to lay before you, for your information, a paper which will show the comparative amount of the ordinary naval and military expenditure of the United Kingdom and of the different self-governing Colonies. You will find that in the case of the United Kingdom the cost of our armaments has enormously increased since 1897. That increase is not entirely due to our initiative, but it is forced upon us by the action of other Powers who have made great advances, especially in connection with the Navy, which we have found it to be our duty and necessity to equal. But the net result is extraordinary. At the present moment the Estimates for the present year for naval and military expenditure in the United Kingdom—not including the extraordinary war expenses, but the normal estimates—involve an expenditure per head of the population of the United Kingdom of 29s. 3d. —29s. 3d. per head per annum.

Sir WILFRID LAURIER: Is the military and naval together?

The SECRETARY OF STATE: Military and Naval together. In Canada the same items involve an expenditure of only 2s. per head of the population, about one fifteenth of that incurred by the United Kingdom. In New South Wales—I have not the figures for the Commonwealth as a whole, but I am giving those as illustrations—and I find that in New South Wales the expenditure is 3s. 5d.; in Victoria 3s. 3d.; in New

Zealand 3s. 4d.; and in the Cape and Natal, I think it is between 2s. and 3s. Now, no one, I think, will pretend that that is a fair distribution of the burdens of Empire. No one will believe that the United Kingdom can, for all time, make this inordinate sacrifice. While the Colonies were young and poor, in the first place they did not offer anything like the same temptation to the ambitions of others, and, in the second place, they were clearly incapable of providing large sums for their defence, and therefore it was perfectly right and natural that the mother country should undertake the protection of her children. But now that the Colonies are rich and powerful, that every day they are growing by leaps and bounds, their material prosperity promises to rival that of the United Kingdom itself, and I think it is inconsistent with their position —inconsistent with their dignity as nations—that they should leave the mother country to bear the whole, or almost the whole, of the expense. Justification of union is that a bundle is stronger than the sticks which compose it, but if the whole strain is to be thrown on one stick, there is very little advantage in any attempt to put them into a bundle. And I would beg of you in this relation to bear in mind that you are not asked— your people are not asked—to put upon their own shoulders any burden for the exclusive advantage of the mother country. On the contrary, if the United Kingdom stood alone, as a mere speck in the Northern Sea, it is certain that its expenditure for these purposes of defence might be immensely curtailed. It is owing to its duties and obligations to its colonies throughout the Empire; it is owing to its trade with those Colonies, a trade in which of course they are equally interested with ourselves, that the necessity has been cast upon us to make these enormous preparations. And I think, therefore, you will agree with me that it is not unreasonable for us to call your serious attention to a state of things which cannot be permanent.

97) Lord Milner, *The Nation and the Empire* (Constable, 1913), 90–1.

MILNER'S SOUTH AFRICAN FAREWELL SPEECH, 1905

This question, as I see it—the future of the British Empire— is a race, a close race, between the numerous influences so manifestly making for disruption, and the growth of a great, but still very imperfectly realised, political conception. Shall we ever get ourselves understood in time? The word Empire, the word Imperial, are, in some respects, unfortunate. They suggest domination, ascendancy, the rule of a superior state over vassal states. But as they are the only words available, all we can do is to make the best of them, and to raise them in the scale of language by a new significance. When we, who call ourselves Imperialists, talk of the British Empire, we think of a group of states, independent of one another in their local affairs, but bound together for the defence of their common interests, and the development of a common civilisation, and so bound, not in an alliance—for alliances can be made and unmade, and are never more than nominally lasting,—but in a permanent organic union. Of such a union, we fully admit, the dominions of our sovereign, as they exist to-day, are only the raw material. Our ideal is still distant, but we are firmly convinced that it is not visionary nor unattainable.

98)   A. B. Keith (ed.), *Selected Speeches and Documents on British Colonial Policy, 1763–1917* (Oxford University Press, 1918), II, 302–3.

ASQUITH SPEECH AT 1911 IMPERIAL CONFERENCE— THE CASE AGAINST IMPERIAL FEDERATION

It would impair if not altogether destroy the authority of the Government of the United Kingdom in such grave matters as the conduct of foreign policy, the conclusion of treaties, the declaration and maintenance of peace, or the declaration of war and, indeed, all those relations with Foreign Powers, necessarily of the most delicate character, which are now in the hands of the Imperial Government, subject to its responsibility to the Imperial Parliament. That authority cannot be shared, and the co-existence side by side with the Cabinet of the United Kingdom of this proposed body—it does not matter by what name you call it for the moment—clothed with the functions and the jurisdiction which Sir Joseph Ward proposed to invest it with, would, in our judgement, be absolutely fatal to our present system of responsible government.

That is from the Imperial point of view. Now from the point of view of the Dominions I cannot do better than repeat in my own words what was said by Sir Wilfrid Laurier. So far as the Dominions are concerned, this new machine could impose upon the Dominions by the voice of a body in which they would be in a standing minority (that is part of the case), in a small minority indeed, a policy of which they might all disapprove, of which some of them at any rate possibly and probably would disapprove, a policy which would in most cases involve expenditure and an expenditure which would have to be met by the imposition on a dissentient community of taxation by its own government.

We cannot, with the traditions and the history of the British Empire behind us, either from the point of view of the United Kingdom, or from the point of view of our self-governing Dominions, assent for a moment to proposals which are so fatal to the very fundamental conditions on which our Empire has been built up and carried on. Therefore, with the highest possible respect, as we all have, for the skill and ability with which Sir Joseph Ward has presented his case, and a great deal of sympathy with many of the objects he has in view, I think we must agree that on its merits this proposal is not a practical one, and that, even if it were so, even if it could be shown to be so, the fact that it not only does not receive the unanimous consent of all the representatives of the Dominions, but is repudiated by them all except Sir Joseph Ward himself, is for the purposes of this Conference a fatal and, indeed, an insuperable objection to its adoption.

99)   Lord Hugh Cecil, *Conservatism* (Williams & Norgate, 1912), 214–17.

Within the Empire a certain incoherence seems to become manifest in the presence of the conception of national vocation. Vocation implies a person called. It suggests a being, organic and homogeneous, setting about his proper function with entire mastery of all his powers. The British Empire at present is not like such a being. Part of it is indeed active, but part of it is rather a sphere of operation than itself operative. And, what is strangest, part of it can be called neither active nor passive; it neither does nor is done to; is neither a force nor a burden but lies betwixt the two, neither helping nor being helped. That the Empire should contain both what is active and what is passive is characteristic of it. Our vocation in the world has been to undertake the government of vast un-civilised populations and to raise them gradually to a higher level of life. Those populations form part of the Empire, but naturally can scarcely be reckoned as adding to its strength, at any rate in the earlier stages of development under our rule. After a time, as in India, they pass from being a sphere of national work to being part of the national strength; and if there are deductions to be made, those may fairly be reckoned as signs of the imperfection that attaches to all human effort. In what we call the Dependencies of the Crown, therefore, there is nothing abnormal, nothing inconsistent with the obvious characteristics of our vocation. But the great self-governing Dominions play at present a strangely ambiguous part, for they are, like the United Kingdom, inhabited by a population of our race, who are governed according to our standards of civilisation and live essentially lives like ours; but yet the Dominions are not so organised as to be a regular part of our national force. They do indeed come to our help, as in South Africa, but such action is avowedly the action of independent allies rather than the co-operation of different parts of a single body. They lie outside the idea of a person called to a high function. Though reckoned, and proud to be reckoned, as of the same people as ourselves, they are too detached to be thought of, even in a metaphor, as part of the same organism. And if we personify the Empire, our imaginations recoil like Frankenstein from the monster that we have made, the monster of a heterogeneous personality.

This brings us to the greatest problem of imperial affairs, the problem of how to make the Empire a single organism without destroying or imperilling the full liberty which each part of it rightly and uncompromisingly claims. We want the people of the Dominions to be in the fullest sense part of the national power. We want them to hearken with a single ear to the dictates of the national vocation. We want the whole body to go forth on its appointed task with a single mind and will. But we want also that all citizens of our race, in whatever part of the King's Dominions they may live, shall be equally sharers in the great inheritance of free self-government. To the solution of this problem Conservatism is already addressing itself. Nor is there any partisan dispute about the ultimate purpose in view. The policy of preferential trade has been propounded as a step in the desired direction; and if this policy has been resisted by Liberals and a few Conservatives, it is not because its unifying object is not desired, but because there are doubts as to the reality of its unifying effect. It is disputed whether giving British subjects in different parts of the Empire trade advantages at the cost of other British subjects in the imperial markets, will really make for unifying and organising the whole body. But the policy of drawing the Empire together is and will remain a chief object of Conservatism to-day; and if it should turn out that preference is an impossible or ineffi-cacious method of achieving the object, it will only serve to turn the minds of Conservatives to new expedients for attain-ing what they desire.

It is important to remember that a main purpose of uniting the Empire is to organise it for war and what belongs to war, for the foreign policy that leads up to war and for the arma-ments and other means of defence that are necessary for carrying war on. It is in respect to our relations to foreign countries and to our dependencies that we feel principally the lack of imperial union and the consequent difficulty of fulfilling our national vocation as a single people. Organised unitedly for war, we should have the machinery which would be also available for carrying out any imperial policy within the de-pendencies of the Empire. We should, in short, act as a unit in so far as our vocation required. But that further and closer union for all purposes which we enjoy in the United Kingdom and which depends not a little on geographical propinquity is, however theoretically desirable, probably unattainable for the whole of an Empire so scattered as ours. We do not desire to press the cause of union in a way inconsistent with the facts of distance, and consequently with well-informed and skilful government. We do not, in short, wish to interfere with any powers the colonial Dominions now possess. But we wish to bring them into activity as part of the operative power of the Empire as a whole, in order that a single national unit may fulfil to the world its appointed vocation.

100)   *The Times,* 24 May 1911.

BALFOUR SPEECH AT THE ALBERT HALL, LONDON, 1911

There never has been a departure—a new departure—in the Imperial aggregation of great masses of population at all comparable with ours, and we have no lessons to learn from the great historic Empires of the past. We are the beginners, the founders, of a new world-wide Constitution. We are architects in a new style. We neither can nor if we can could we imitate our great predecessors. The British Empire has grown to its present condition . . . by steps at the same time so insensible and so unique that I do not believe that the great mass of foreign observers, or domestic observers, really see how novel is the departure which we are making, and how great are the humanitarian interests which depend upon the success of the great experience of Empire. For, ladies and gentlemen, the difficulty did not emerge when these communities which now are the great self-governing Dominions were in their infantile state. Then there was no real question of equality as between what we then called Colonies and the Mother Country. They depended upon us for their capital, for their population, for their defence, for their laws. They bore, indeed, the same relation to us that a child in its first infancy bears to its parents. They owed us everything, and from us they got everything. In that condition of things there was no difficulty, and there had not emerged the new conditions which have made this one of the most critical moments in the history, not, believe me, of this country alone, but in the history of the development of political institutions.

Now what has happened? What has happened is this; that we, and in the history of the world we alone, have known how to produce great communities springing from us, originally dependent upon us, but who are gradually growing to self-conscious maturity, and who, while growing to self-conscious maturity, are anxious to remain elements in one great constituent whole. That is new. . . . Hitherto what has happened is one of two things—either the parent country has endeavoured to retain control and domination over its children, usually with disastrous results, usually with a violent severance when those children reached maturity; or else, as in the old Greek times, the colony that went out, whatever sentiment it may have maintained for the Mother Country, for the parent State, was from the beginning independent, self-sufficient and self-contained.

Our experiment is new. We know, we feel, we rejoice to see that these Dominions—our children—are going to have the same self-conscious and independent life that we in these islands have enjoyed and mean to go one enjoying. The last thing that any responsible politician in this country has ever either said or thought is to suppose that we mean to continue those trammels—if trammels they were—that may be useful in the first months of childhood, but which become not merely superfluous but absolutely harmful when the offspring reaches that stage which our great Dominions have long reached— that in which they are capable of managing their own affairs, and have as great a right to manage their own affairs, as you who are assembled in this hall or as we who live in these islands.

The problem therefore is—How are you going to carry out what is the ideal and the ambition of all the great self-governing millions in the Empire, which is a new ideal and a new ambition, that of at once combining the self-conscious national life with the consciousness of belonging to a yet larger whole, belonging to an Empire as well as belonging to a Dominion or to a territory? That is the difficulty, the problem we have to face; and, believe me, it cannot be faced, at all events it cannot be solved, unless both here and overseas we approach it, not in a spirit of pettifogging calculation, but with that far-seeing imagination which, believe me, is the true wisdom of statesmanship . . . if the future of the British Empire be what I hope it will be, if the ideal I have ventured to sketch be really carried out for the first time in the world's history in practice, the relations between the constituent autonomous elements of one great Empire must be like those which bind together the independent members of a single family— members of a family all of whom have reached years of discretion, but yet feel how much they gain by the mutual interchange of services, by mutual affection, by regarding each other as in some respects nearer than the outside world; and that is not founded in family life, and it cannot be founded in the Empire of the future merely by conventions, treaties, and formal arrangements between the constituent parties. . . .

I cannot help feeling when I argue either in the House of Commons or on the platform, with those who do not take our view about Colonial Preference—I cannot help feeling that our difference is not merely one of hard reasoning; I feel that they do not understand or appreciate the true sentiments which ought to animate every citizen of each of those separate

Dominions towards the communities as a whole with whom they share the responsibilities of Empire. . . .

I see in this policy of Preference a great and integral element in the general policy of Tariff Reform. I see in that not merely a method by which British capital at home and British labour at home may be placed in a better position than they are now —I see in it something far greater and not less intimately connected, believe me, with the real material well-being of this country and the Empire—I see sentiments of common interest growing up between us and our Colonies, and I see a solution of the problem which I ventured to put before you at the beginning of my speech, that new and that unique problem which we who are here and in the Dominions are now setting ourselves by Providence to solve.

101) *Parliamentary Debates*, fourth series, CXXXII (1904), 304.

BALFOUR SPEECH IN 'CHINESE LABOUR' DEBATE, 1904

More than one speaker on the other side has hinted that the statements made by us to show that you cannot get the white man and the black man to work together on equal terms are statements made in the interests of that mysterious locality, Park Lane, and have no relation to the facts of African life. Unfortunately the theories of the eighteenth and early nineteenth centuries, that all men were born equal, have been refuted in this, as in many other instances, by the advance of science. Men are not born equal. They cannot be made equal by education extending over generation after generation within the ordinary historical limit. The differences between one family and another of mankind lie deep in the remote and unfathomable past, and it is folly to suppose that your petty educational regulations, be they what they may, can obliterate distinctions deep-seated under the laws of nature. And that being so, you will not get the white man and the black man to work together as equals; and if you could effect the impossible you would injure not only the white man but the black man, and not only the black man but the white man . . . this unbridgable abyss separates the two races. Do not let us aim at an impossible ideal.

102)   J. A. Hobson, *The Crisis of Liberalism: New Issues of Democracy* (King, 1909), 244–5.

So it has come about that a Government has been established in South Africa, in form resembling that of Canada, Australia, and New Zealand, in substance very different. To describe as a self-governing nation the white oligarchy that has, with our connivance, fenced itself against admission of the ablest and most progressive members of races living in their midst and by general admission capable of a civilisation at least as high as that of the ordinary white wage-earner, is an outrage to political terminology. Deliberately to set out upon a new career as a civilised nation with a definition of civilisation which takes as the criterion race and colour, not individual character and attainments, is nothing else than to sow a crop of dark and dangerous problems for the future. Such a government, such a civilisation, must fall between two stools. There is, indeed, no parallel without or within the Empire for a self-government in which five-sixths of the governed are excluded from all rights of citizenship. In other colonies where the population is mainly composed of 'lower races' bureaucracy is never more than tempered by representation, and that representation is mostly free from colour-lines: such government can at least secure order, if at the cost of progress. It is conceivable (though our Empire affords no present instance) that sound order and political security might be obtained by a white oligarchy which kept in economic servitude the lower ₋aces of inhabitants, barred them from skilled industries, from any large participation in modern city life, and from religious and intellectual instruction of any kind. This was virtually the old Boer policy, though adopted as readily by British settlers on the land; it was absolutely successful. But it is not conformable to-day either to the conditions or the sentiments of the more progressive white citizens of South Africa, even in Natal. There is no intention to refuse all technical and intellectual education to Zulus, Fingos, and other natives capable of profiting by it: much of the hard work which Europeans will continue to require and will refuse to do themselves involves and evokes knowledge, intelligence, and a sense of personal responsibility. Not even the most carefully sophisticated Christianity furnished by 'kept' white missionaries, can prevent the democratic doctrines of the New Testament from doing this revolutionary work.

To take away the political liberties enjoyed for a third of a century in Cape Colony would prove too dangerous: to leave them will be to set a continuously growing ferment at work throughout the length and breadth of the Union. For there are very deep and very real native grievances. In the Transvaal and Orange River Colony the elementary freedom of movement from one place to another is denied, the right of buying and holding land is denied: whenever in South Africa a dispute arises between a white and a coloured man it is tried in a white man's court, by white man's justice. Indeed it is needless to labour such an issue: political rights are everywhere the indispensable condition of civil rights, and without them can be no security of life, liberty and property for an 'inferior' race or class.

I am well aware that public opinion is very unenlightened among the bulk of the white population of South Africa. Many of the political leaders confess themselves favourable to a carefully restricted native franchise, but insist that 'the people will not have it.' But I cannot help feeling that if these statesmen had taken a little more time to forecast the troubles which are certain to arise from an essentially inconsistent native policy, such as I have here described, they would have thrown the full weight of their personal authority, never likely to be greater than now, against the popular prejudice, and have welcomed the aid of our Liberal Government to support a Constitution free from this stain of colour.

103) *Parliamentary Debates, House of Commons*, fifth series, IX
      (1909), 1656–8.

ASQUITH SPEECH ON THE SOUTH AFRICA BILL, 1909

In submitting this Motion to the House, I wish to take the opportunity of putting on record the fact that this Bill, consisting of over 150 clauses and a very complicated Schedule, after very careful consideration by this House, has been passed without Amendment. It is not to be understood—it would be a totally false impression if it were suggested—that as regards all the provisions of the Bill there is unanimity of opinion in the House. In particular, as regards some of the clauses which deal with the treatment of natives and the access of native Members to the Legislature, there is, as everybody who has followed these Debates will have seen, not only no difference of opinion in this House, but absolute unanimity of opinion in the way of regret that particular provisions of the Bill have been inserted. I wish, before this Bill leaves the Imperial Parliament, to make it perfectly clear that we here have exercised, and I think wisely and legitimately exercised, not only restraint of expression, but reserve of judgment in regard to matters of this kind, simply because we desire this great experiment of the establishment of complete self-government in South Africa to start on the lines and in accordance with the ideas which our fellow citizens there have deliberately and after long deliberation come to. It is perfectly true, the Imperial Parliament cannot divest itself of responsibility in this matter. We do not do so, and if we yielded as we have yielded in points of detail, on some points on which many hon. Members feel very strongly, if we yielded to the deliberate judgment of South Africa, it has been because we have thought it undesirable at this stage, the last stage in the completion of an almost unprecedentedly difficult task, to put forward anything that would be an obstacle to the successful working in the future.

Speaking for myself and for the Government, I venture to express not only the hope but the expectation in some of these matters which have been the subject of discussion here in the House, both on the Second Reading and the Committee Stage, that the views which have been so strongly and practically, without any discordant expression of opinion, given utterance to here, will be sympathetically considered by our fellow citizens there. For my part I think, as I have said throughout, that it would be far better that any relaxation of what many of us, almost all of us, regard as unnecessary restrictions from the electoral rights or rights of eligibility of our fellow subjects should be carried out spontaneously, and on the initiative of the South African Parliament, rather than they should appear to be forced upon them by the Imperial Parliament here. While we part from this measure without any substantial, or any Amendment of any sort or kind, I am sure our fellow subjects will not take it in bad part if we respectfully and very earnestly beg them at the same time that they, in the exercise of their undoubted and unfettered freedom, should find it possible sooner or later, and sooner rather than later, to modify the provisions.

But, Sir, having said that, may I add that whatever particular criticisms may be made of special provisions of the Bill,
this Imperial Parliament, without distinction of party, regards
it as one of the greatest steps that has ever been taken in our
legislative history. By free concerted action of the communities
which only a few years ago seemed to be fatally and irremedi-
ably divided by history, by sentiment, and even by interest, all
worked together to make this not only a component part of the
British Empire, but a community which, forgetting all the bad
traditions of the past, will undertake new duties in a spirit of
loyalty and patriotism and concord. We here, if I may venture
to voice the opinion of the House, wish this great and magnificent experiment all possible success. It starts on its voyage with
every good wish that we can give it; we trust and believe that
in South Africa, as throughout the other parts of the British
Empire, the fullest concession of local autonomy and free and
unfettered powers of self-government may be found to be the
best safeguard for Imperial unity.

104)   H. Hamilton Fyfe, *South Africa To-Day* (Bell, 1911),
        43–6.

'What are we to do?' From end to end of Africa goes up this
despairing cry. It rings through the world. It arouses uneasy
echoes wherever it is realised that the pressure of events is
before long going to bring all the white races up against
Asiatics and Africans in a struggle for mastery. At present
there is no 'native policy.' The whites are simply training the
blacks to supplant them. From time to time attempts are made
to 'do something.' Lately, for instance, it was proposed to
make marriages between white persons and persons with any
degree of colour illegal. This roused the Archbishop of Cape
Town to declare that such unions 'could not be illegal in the
sight of God,' and therefore the Church would, in any case,
continue to celebrate them. . . .
    That there is any immediate 'danger' no one believes, so far
as a concerted movement is concerned. The Basutos might
give trouble, would give trouble, if their land were interfered
with. But that is not seriously feared. There are, nevertheless,
various currents of disturbance flowing beneath the surface.
The Ethiopian Church, founded in 1892 by a native Wesleyan,

is actively hammering 'Africa for the Africans' into woolly heads. Windy, rhetorical notions of nationality and 'freedom' are even in the wilderness upsetting untrained minds. From the United States come negro preachers to urge the union of the black races in all parts of the world. Newspapers in native languages are widely circulated, stirring up strife between black and white people, urging that it is time to drive the British into the sea (an echo of Boer threats), and angrily asking why mixed marriages should be condemned. . . .

The one advantage of this still very limited but increasing unsettlement is that, as I have said in an earlier chapter, it makes any further war between the white races in South Africa an impossibility. They must keep a united front. In time the same cause will stop wars between white peoples everywhere. There will probably be one other European war. But that will be the last, and even that may possibly be staved off until we are awake to the unwisdom of fighting among ourselves in the presence of dangers threatening us all.

105) V. Chirol, *Indian Unrest* (Macmillan, 1910), xv–xvi [introduction by Sir Alfred Lyall (1835–1911), Indian civil servant and writer].

The truth is that in India the English have been throughout obliged to lay out their own roads, and to feel their way, without any precedents to guide them. No other Government, European or Asiatic, has yet essayed to administer a great Oriental population, alien in race and religion, by institutions of a representative type, reckoning upon free discussion and an unrestricted Press for reasonable consideration of its measures and fair play, relying upon secular education and absolute religious neutrality to control the unruly affections of sinful men. It is now seen that our Western ideas and inventions, moral and material, are being turned against us by some of those to whom we have imparted an elementary aptitude for using them. And thus we have the strange spectacle, in certain parts of India, of a party capable of resorting to methods that are both reactionary and revolutionary, of men who offer prayers and sacrifices to ferocious divinities and denounce the Government by seditious journalism, preaching primitive superstition in the very modern form of leading articles. The mixture of religion with politics has always produced a highly explosive compound, especially in Asia.

These agitations are in fact the symptoms of what are said by Shakespeare to be the 'cankers of a calm world'; they are the natural outcome of artificial culture in an educational hothouse, among classes who have had for generations no real training in rough or hazardous politics. The outline of the present situation in India is that we have been disseminating ideas of abstract political right, and the germs of representative institutions, among a people that had for centuries been governed autocratically, and in a country where local liberties and habits of self-government had been long obliterated or had never existed. At the same time we have been spreading modern education broadcast throughout the land, where, before English rule, learning had not advanced beyond the stage of Europe in the middle ages. These may be taken to be the primary causes of the existing Unrest; and meanwhile the administrative machine has been so efficiently organized, it has run, hitherto, so easily and quietly, as to disguise from inexperienced bystanders the long discipline and training in affairs of State that are required for its management. Nor is it clearly perceived that the real driving power lies in the forces held in reserve by the British nation and in the respect which British guardianship everywhere commands. That Indians should be liberally invited to share the responsibilities of high office is now a recognized principle of public policy. But the process of initiation must be gradual and tentative; and vague notions of dissolving the British connexion only prove incompetence to realize the whole situation, external and internal, of the country. Across the frontiers of India are warlike nations, who are intent upon arming themselves after the latest modern pattern, though for the other benefits of Western science and learning they show, as yet, very little taste or inclination. They would certainly be a serious menace to a weak Government in the Indian plains, while their sympathy with a literary class would be uncommonly slight. Against intruders of this sort the British hold securely the gates of India; and it must be clear that the civilization and future prosperity of the whole country depend entirely upon their determination to maintain public tranquility by strict enforcement of the laws; combined with their policy of admitting the highest intellects and capacities to the Councils of the State, and of

assigning reasonable administrative and legislative independence to the great provinces in accord with the unity of a
powerful Empire.

106)   Lord Morley, *Indian Speeches 1907–1909* (Macmillan,
       1909), 91–2, 96–7.

We are not prepared to divest the Governor-General in his
Council of an official majority. In the Provincial Councils we
propose to dispense with it, but in the Viceroy's Legislative
Council we propose to adhere to it. Only let me say that here
we may seem to lag a stage behind the Government of India
themselves—so little violent are we—because that Government
say, in their despatch—'On all ordinary occasions we are
ready to dispense with an official majority in the Imperial
Legislative Council, and to rely on the public spirit of non-
official members to enable us to carry on the ordinary work of
legislation.' My Lords, that is what we propose to do in the
Provincial Councils. But in the Imperial Council we consider
an official majority essential. It may be said that this is a most
flagrant logical inconsistency. So it would be, on one condition. If I were attempting to set up a Parliamentary system in
India, or if it could be said that this chapter of reforms led
directly or necessarily up to the establishment of a Parliamentary system in India, I, for one, would have nothing at all
to do with it. I do not believe—it is not of very great consequence what I believe, because the fulfilment of my vaticina-
tions could not come off very soon—in spite of the attempts in
Oriental countries at this moment, interesting attempts to
which we all wish well, to set up some sort of Parliamentary
system—it is no ambition of mine, at all events, to have any
share in beginning that operation in India. If my existence,
either officially or corporeally, were prolonged twenty times
longer than either of them is likely to be, a Parliamentary
system in India is not at all the goal to which I would for one
moment aspire. . . .

As an illustrious Member of this House wrote—'We found a
society in a state of decomposition, and we have undertaken
the serious and stupendous process of reconstructing it.'

Macaulay, for it was he, said—'India now is like Europe in
the fifth century.'

Yes, a stupendous process indeed. The process has gone on with marvellous success, and if we all, according to our various lights, are true to our colours, that process will go on. Whatever is said, I for one—though I am not what is commonly called an Imperialist—so far from denying, I most emphatically affirm, that for us to preside over this transition from the fifth European century in some parts, in slow, uneven stages, up to the twentieth—so that you have before you all the centuries at once as it were—for us to preside over that, and to be the guide of peoples in that condition, is, if conducted with humanity and sympathy, with wisdom, with political courage, not only a human duty, but what has been often and most truly called one of the most glorious tasks ever confided to any powerful State in the history of civilised mankind.

107)   H. G. Wells, 'Will the Empire Live?' in *An Englishman Looks at the World* (Cassell, 1914), 33–4, 37–41.

What will hold such an Empire as the British together, this great, laxly scattered, sea-linked association of ancient states and new-formed countries, Oriental nations, and continental colonies? What will enable it to resist the endless internal strains, the inevitable external pressures and attacks to which it must be subjected? This is the primary question for British Imperialism; everything else is secondary or subordinated to that.

There is a multitude of answers. But I suppose most of them will prove under examination either to be, or to lead to, or to imply very distinctly this generalisation, that if most of the intelligent and active people in the Empire want it to continue it will, and that if a large proportion of such active and intelligent people are discontented and estranged, nothing can save it from disintegration. I do not suppose that a navy ten times larger than ours, or conscription of the most irksome thoroughness, could oblige Canada to remain in the Empire if the general will and feeling of Canada were against it, or coerce India into a sustained submission if India presented a united and resistant front. Our Empire, for all its roll of battles, was not created by force; colonisation and diplomacy have played a far larger share in its growth than conquest; and there is no such strength in its sovereignty as the rule of pride and pressure demand. It is to the free consent and participation of its constituent peoples that we must look for its continuance. . . .

Physically, our Empire is incurably scattered, various, and divided, and it is to quite other links and forces, it seems to me, than fiscal or military unification that we who desire its continuance must look to hold it together. There never was anything like it before. Essentially it is an adventure of the British spirit, sanguine, discursive, and beyond comparison insubordinate, adaptable, and originating. . . . Beneath the thin legal and administrative ties that hold it together lies the far more vital bond of a traditional free spontaneous activity. It has a common medium of expression in the English tongue, a unity of liberal and tolerant purpose amidst its enormous variety of localised life and colour. And it is in the development and strengthening, the enrichment, the rendering more conscious and more purposeful, of that broad creative spirit of the British that the true cement and continuance of our Empire is to be found.

The Empire must live by the forces that begot it. It cannot hope to give any such exclusive prosperity as a Zollverein might afford; it can hold out no hopes of collective conquests and triumphs—its utmost military rôle must be the guaranteeing of a common inaggressive security; but it can, and, if it is to survive, it must, give all its constituent parts such a civilisation as none of them could achieve alone, a civilisation, a wealth and fullness of life increasing and developing with the years. Through that, and that alone, can it be made worth having and worth serving.

And in the first place the whole Empire must use the English language. I do not mean that any language must be stamped out, that a thousand languages may not flourish by board and cradle and in folk-songs and village gossip—Erse, the Taal, a hundred Indian and other Eastern tongues, Canadian French —but I mean that also English must be available, that everywhere there must be English teaching. And everyone who wants to read science or history or philosophy, to come out of the village life into wider thoughts and broader horizons, to gain appreciation in art, must find ready to hand, easily attainable in English, all there is to know and all that has been said thereon. It is worth a hundred Dreadnoughts and a million soldiers to the Empire, that wherever the imperial posts reach, wherever there is a curious or receptive mind, there in English and by the imperial connection the full thought of the race should come. To the lonely youth upon the New Zealand sheep farm, to the young Hindu, to the trapper under a Labrador tilt, to the half-breed assistant at a Burmese oil-well, to the self-educating Scottish miner or the Egyptian clerk, the Empire and the English language should exist, visibly and certainly, as the media by which his spirit escapes from his immediate surroundings and all the urgencies of every day, into a limitless fellowship of thought and beauty.

Now I am not writing this in any vague rhetorical way; I mean specifically that our Empire has to become the medium of knowledge and thought to every intelligent person in it, or that it is bound to go to pieces. It has no economic, no military, no racial, no religious unity. Its only conceivable unity is a unity of language and purpose and outlook. If it is not held together by thought and spirit, it cannot be held together. No other cement exists that can hold it together indefinitely.

Not only English literature, but all other literatures well translated into English, and all science and all philosophy, have to be brought within the reach of everyone capable of availing himself of such reading. And this must be done, not by private enterprise or for gain, but as an Imperial function. Wherever the Empire extends there its presence must signify all that breadth of thought and outlook no localised life can supply.

Only so is it possible to establish and maintain the wide understandings, the common sympathy necessary to our continued association. The Empire, mediately or immediately, must become the universal educator, news-agent, book-distributor, civiliser-general, and vehicle of imaginative inspiration for its peoples, or else it must submit to the gravitation of its various parts to new and more invigorating associations.

No empire, it may be urged, has ever attempted anything of this sort, but no empire like the British has ever yet existed. Its conditions and needs are unprecedented, its consolidation is a new problem, to be solved, if it is solved at all, by untried means. And in the English language as a vehicle of thought and civilisation alone is that means to be found.

Now it is idle to pretend that at the present time the British Empire is giving its constituent peoples any such high and rewarding civilisation as I am here suggesting. It gives them a certain immunity from warfare, a penny post, an occasional spectacular coronation, a few knighthoods and peerages, and the services of an honest, unsympathetic, narrow-minded, and unattractive officialism. No adequate effort is being made to render the English language universal throughout its limits, none at all to use it as a medium of thought and enlightenment.

CHAPTER TEN

The Problem of Poverty

Under the influence of stark facts revealed by Booth, Rowntree and others the Edwardians began to abandon Victorian attitudes towards the treatment of poverty (108), and to accept the need for greater official intervention (109). Rowntree, in particular, described and defined poverty with a degree of sophistication previously unattained (110), providing a model for subsequent investigations (111). The provision of school meals for underfed children, as recommended by the Inter-Departmental Committee on Physical Deterioration (112), marked a significant movement away from old ideas about exclusive parental responsibility (113, 114). The 1902 Education Act recast the national system of English school education along lines of 'equality of opportunity' which remained substantially unchanged until 1944 (115). The Act passed and was applied despite Nonconformist resistance encouraged by the Liberals (116, 117). Such resistance was coming to seem outdated, nineteenth-century in spirit. Decidedly of the new century was the work of Margaret McMillan, who combined high educational aspirations for adults with influential pioneering work for the medical inspection and treatment of elementary schoolchildren and for the provision of nursery schools (118). Charles Booth was an early campaigner for old-age pensions (119), finally enacted by the Liberals in 1908. Thereafter the tide of the 'new Liberalism' ran in swiftly (120), though little influenced by either the Majority or Minority Reports of the Poor Law Commission (121, 122). The introduction of Labour Exchanges owed much to William Beveridge (123), but more to Churchill (124). The 1909 budget brought a new approach to taxation in the name of social reform (124), a novelty attractive to Lloyd George (125), repugnant to Balfour (126). Reduction of the powers of the Lords (127), and social insurance (128), both promised in 1909 were finally enacted in 1911, even though the insurance scheme was opposed as unjust not only by the privileged (129), but also (for contrasting reasons) by socialists such as Snowden (130). Undeterred Lloyd George intended to follow National Insurance with land reform (131, 132).

108)　Helen Bosanquet, *The Strength of the People* (Macmillan, 1902), 331–2, 339–40.

To have classified a man as belonging to the poor, or the residuum, or the submerged, means that we no longer expect from him the qualities of independence and responsibility which we assume as a matter of course in all others; and by this view of him, combined with our careless policy of relief and charity, we go far to annihilate in reality the qualities which we have already denied him in imagination. A man is one of the poor, then we must feed his children and provide for his old age, and leave him with nothing but his own immediate wants to think of; he belongs to the residuum, then we cannot expect him to be a good workman even in his own degree; he is one of the submerged, then we deny him all manliness, and expect no effort on his part to raise himself above the waves; he lives in a slum or a ghetto or a mean street, it is impossible, then, for him to have any intelligent interests or amusements, or be anything but a drinking brute. So we say and think, and our mode of treating him is naturally based upon our sayings and thoughts about him. Moreover, the knowledge of such language is not confined to those who initiate it—it is only too well appreciated by those to whom it is applied; and how can it fail to have a bad effect upon them? Bitter resentment or degrading acquiescence—we may well wonder which state of mind is likely to be most harmful; but one or the other must inevitably result under the continued and repeated insult. . . .

But when all is said and done which well-wishers can say or do, it still remains true that the strength of the people lies in its own conscious efforts to face difficulties and overcome them. 'Difficulties to overcome, and freedom to overcome them,' is an essential condition of progress for human beings of whatever position in life. Any class or any individual which is either unconscious of difficulties, or unable to make the effort to master them, must stagnate and ultimately deteriorate. Every generation, almost every year, brings its own problems to be solved; and we cannot foretell what they will be, still less foretell their solution. But one thing we can say—that the real solution will rest in the hands, or rather the minds, of the people most nearly affected. If they cannot be made to care for it and seek for it, it can never be given to them from outside.

But though we cannot give to each other, either as individuals or classes or legislators, we can do much on the one hand to provide opportunities, on the other to set free the energies which are essential to the appropriation of those opportunities. Freedom from self-indulgence and from tyrannous appetites and blind vacancy can only be attained by the interests which draw a man out of himself; and these he will find largely in the difficulties which he has to overcome in life, and in the education which we put within his reach. Freedom from excessive toil can come only from economic improvement; and that, we have seen reason to think, can be best attained by raising a larger number to the ranks of skilled workers. But the one thing to avoid in all our work, whether legislative, social, or personal, is the risk of diminishing the saving interests in the life of an individual or a class by doing for them what they could do for themselves.

109)   C. Booth, *Life and Labour of the People in London*, volume I (Macmillan, 1902 ed.), 166–7.

To bring class B under State regulation would be to control the springs of pauperism; hence what I have to propose may be considered as an extension of the Poor Law. What is the Poor Law system? It is a limited form of Socialism—a Socialistic community (aided from outside) living in the midst of an Individualist nation. Socialistic also to a great extent are our Board schools, hospitals, and charitable institutions, where the conditions of relief are not the services which the applicant can render in return, but the services of which he stands in need. My idea is to make the dual system, Socialism in the arms of Individualism, under which we already live, more efficient by extending somewhat the sphere of the former and making the division of function more distinct. Our Individualism fails because our Socialism is incomplete. In taking charge of the lives of the incapable, State Socialism finds its proper work, and by doing it completely, would relieve us of a serious danger. The Individualist system breaks down as things are, and is invaded on every side by Socialistic innovations, but its hardy doctrines would have a far better chance in a society purged of those who cannot stand alone. Thorough interference on the part of the State with the lives of a small fraction of the population would tend to make it possible, ultimately, to dispense with any Socialistic interference in the lives of all the rest.

This, in rough outline and divested of all detail, is my theory.

110) B. S. Rowntree, *Poverty, a Study of Town Life* (Nelson, 1914 ed.), 167–72, 350–6.

And let us clearly understand what 'merely physical efficiency' means. A family living upon the scale allowed for in this estimate must never spend a penny on railway fare or omnibus. They must never go into the country unless they walk. They must never purchase a halfpenny newspaper or spend a penny to buy a ticket for a popular concert. They must write no letters to absent children, for they cannot afford to pay the postage. They must never contribute anything to their church or chapel, or give any help to a neighbour which costs them money. They cannot save, nor can they join sick club or Trade Union, because they cannot pay the necessary subscriptions. The children must have no pocket money for dolls, marbles, or sweets. The father must smoke no tobacco, and must drink no beer. The mother must never buy any pretty clothes for herself or for her children, the character of the family wardrobe as for the family diet being governed by the regulation, 'Nothing must be bought but that which is absolutely necessary for the maintenance of physical health, and what is bought must be of the plainest and most economical description.' Should a child fall ill, it must be attended by the parish doctor; should it die, it must be buried by the parish. Finally, the wage-earner must never be absent from his work for a single day.

If any of these conditions are broken, the extra expenditure involved is met, *and can only be met*, by limiting the diet; or, in other words, by sacrificing physical efficiency.

That few York labourers receiving 20s. or 21s. per week submit to these iron conditions in order to maintain physical efficiency is obvious. And even were they to submit, physical efficiency would be unattainable for those who had three or more children dependent upon them. It cannot therefore be too clearly understood, nor too emphatically repeated, *that whenever a worker having three children dependent on him, and receiving not more than 21s. 8d. per week, indulges in any expenditure beyond that required for the barest physical needs, he can do so only at the cost of his own physical efficiency, or of that of some members of his family. . . .*

The life of a labourer is marked by five alternating periods of want and comparative plenty. During early childhood, unless his father is a skilled worker, he probably will be in poverty; this will last until he, or some of his brothers or sisters, begin to earn money and thus augment their father's wage sufficiently to raise the family above the poverty line. Then follows the period during which he is earning money and living under his parents' roof; for some portion of this period he will be earning more money than is required for lodging, food, and clothes. This is his chance to save money. If he has saved enough to pay for furnishing a cottage, this period of comparative prosperity may continue after marriage until he has two or three children, when poverty will again overtake him. This period of poverty will last perhaps for ten years, *i.e.* until the first child is fourteen years old and begins to earn wages; but if there are more than three children it may last longer.[1] While the children are earning, and before they leave the home to marry, the man enjoys another period of prosperity—possibly, however, only to sink back again into poverty when his children have married and left him, and he himself is too old to work, for his income has never permitted his saving enough for him and his wife to live upon for more than a very short time.

A labourer is thus in poverty, and therefore underfed—

(a) In childhood—when his constitution is being built up.

(b) In early middle life—when he should be in his prime.

(c) In old age.

---

[1] It is to be noted that the family are in poverty, and consequently are underfed, during the first ten or more years of the children's lives.

The accompanying diagram may serve to illustrate this:—

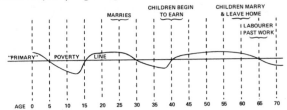

It should be noted that the women are in poverty during the greater part of the period that they are bearing children.

We thus see that the 7230 persons shown by this inquiry to be in a state of 'primary' poverty, *represent merely that section who happened to be in one of these poverty periods at the time the inquiry was made.* Many of these will, in course of time, pass on into a period of comparative prosperity; this will take place as soon as the children, now dependent, begin to earn. But their places below the poverty line will be taken by others who are at present living in that prosperous period previous to, or shortly after, marriage. Again, many now classed as above the poverty line were below it until the children began to earn. The proportion of the community who at one period or other of their lives suffer from poverty to the point of physical privation is therefore much greater, and the injurious effects of such a condition are much more widespread than would appear from a consideration of the number who can be shown to be below the poverty line at any given moment. . . .

Families regarded as living in poverty were grouped under two heads:—

(*a*) Families whose total earnings were insufficient to obtain the minimum necessaries for the maintenance of merely physical efficiency. Poverty falling under this head was described as 'primary' poverty.

(*b*) Families whose total earnings would have been sufficient for the maintenance of merely physical efficiency were it not that some portion of it was absorbed by other expenditure, either useful or wasteful. Poverty falling under this head was described as 'secondary' poverty.

To ascertain the total number living in 'primary' poverty it was necessary to ascertain the minimum cost upon which families of various sizes could be maintained in a state of physical efficiency. This question was discussed under three heads, viz. the necessary expenditure for (1) food; (2) rent;

and (3) all else.

In Chapter IV it was shown that for a family of father, mother, and three children, the minimum weekly expenditure upon which physical efficiency can be maintained in York is 21s. 8d., made up as follows:—

						s.	d.
Food	.	.	.	.	.	12	9
Rent (say)	.	.	.	.	.	4	0
Clothing, light, fuel, etc.	.	.	.	.	.	4	11
						21	8

The necessary expenditure for families larger or smaller than the above will be correspondingly greater or less. This estimate was based upon the assumptions that the diet is selected with a careful regard to the nutritive values of various food stuffs, and that these are all purchased at the lowest current prices. It only allows for a diet less generous as regards variety than that supplied to able-bodied paupers in work-houses. It further assumes that no clothing is purchased which is not absolutely necessary for health, and assumes too that it is of the plainest and most economical description.

No expenditure of any kind is allowed for beyond that which is absolutely necessary for the maintenance of *merely physical efficiency*.

The number of persons whose earnings are so low that they cannot meet the expenditure necessary for the above standard of living, stringent to severity though it is, and bare of all creature comforts, was shown to be no less than 7230, or almost exactly 10 per cent of the total population of the city. These persons, then, represent those who are in 'primary' poverty.

The number of those in 'secondary' poverty was arrived at by ascertaining the *total* number living in poverty, and subtracting those living in 'primary' poverty. The investigators, in the course of their house-to-house visitation, noted those families who were obviously living in a state of poverty, *i.e.* in obvious want and squalor. Sometimes they obtained definite information that the bulk of the earnings was spent in drink or otherwise squandered; sometimes the external evidence of poverty in the home was so clear as to make verbal evidence superfluous.

In this way 20,302 persons, or 27.84 per cent of the total population, were returned as living in poverty. Subtracting

those whose poverty is 'primary', we arrive at the number
living in 'secondary' poverty—viz. 13,072, or 17.93 per cent
of the total population. The figures will be clearer if shown in
tabular form:—

		Proportion of total Population of York.
Persons in 'primary' poverty . . .	7,230	9.91 per cent
Persons in 'secondary' poverty. . .	13,072	17.93 ,,
Total number of persons living in poverty	20,302	27.84 ,,

One naturally asks, on reading these figures, how far they
represent the proportion of poverty in other towns. The only
statistics which enable us to form an opinion upon this point
are those collected in London by Mr. Charles Booth, and set
forth in his *Life and Labour of the People in London.* The objects of
Mr. Booth's inquiry, as explained by himself, were 'to show
the numerical relation which poverty, misery, and depravity
bear to regular earnings, and to describe the general conditions under which each class lives.'[1]

In East London Mr. Booth obtained information from the
School Board visitors regarding every family scheduled by the
Board in which there were children of school age. These
families represented about one-half of the working-class population, and Mr. Booth assumed that the condition of the whole
population was similar to that of the part tested.

In the other districts of London Mr. Booth, in order to
complete his inquiry in a reasonable time was obliged to adopt
a rougher classification.

From the information thus obtained, which he checked and
supplemented in various ways, Mr. Booth estimated that 30.7
per cent of the total population of London were living in
poverty.[2] *Supposing, then, that the same standard of poverty had been
adopted in the two inquiries,* a comparison between the poverty
in York and that of London would be possible. From the
commencement of my inquiry I have had opportunities of
consulting with Mr. Booth, and comparing the methods of
investigation and the standards of poverty adopted. As a result
I feel no hesitation in regarding my estimate of the total
poverty in York as comparable with Mr. Booth's estimate of

[1] *Life and Labour of the People in London,* by Charles Booth, vol. i. p. 6.
[2] In estimating the poverty in London Mr. Booth made no attempt to
differentiate between 'primary' and 'secondary' poverty.

the total poverty in London, and in this Mr. Booth agrees.

The proportions arrived at for the total population living in poverty in London and York respectively were as under:—

| London | . | . | . | 30.7 | per cent |
| York | . | . | . | 27.84 | ,, |

The proportion of the population living in poverty in York may be regarded as practically the same as in London, especially when we remember that Mr. Booth's information was gathered in 1887–1892, a period of only *average* trade prosperity, whilst the York figures were collected in 1899, when trade was unusually prosperous.

This agreement in result is so striking that it is perhaps best to say that I did not set out upon my inquiry with the object of proving any pre-conceived theory, but to ascertain actual facts, and that I was myself much surprised to obtain the above result.

We have been accustomed to look upon the poverty in London as exceptional, but when the result of careful investigation shows that the proportion of poverty in London is practically equalled in what may be regarded as a typical provincial town, we are faced by the startling probability that from 25 to 30 per cent of the town populations of the United Kingdom are living in poverty. If this be the fact, its grave significance may be realized when it is remembered that, in 1901, 77 per cent of the population of the United Kingdom is returned as 'urban' and only 23 per cent as 'rural'.

111)   A. Ponsonby, *The Camel and the Needle's Eye* (Fifield, 1910) 144–61.

The following authentic information, based on actual facts and not hearsay, will give some small idea of what this suggested investigation might produce. Extracts are also given from reports on the state of the poor for the sake of completeness rather than contrast.

For instance, we read a brief description of the household of a man of 'no occupation':

'Married. Two rooms; two children; parish relief; ill, incapable. Two little girls, one consumptive. The rooms are miserable, badly ventilated and damp. This house shares one closet with six other houses, and one water tap with three others.'

Or of a 'regular loafer':

'Married. Two rooms; one child. Wife sews. House very dark on account of high buildings opposite. Kept tidy and clean. This house shares one closet with two other houses, and one water tap with six others.'[1]

Surely we ought to know the description. though it cannot be so brief, of the household of another man of 'no occupation':

'Married. Two children. Four houses. London house, ——— Street, W. Sixty-two rooms; one of the country houses considerably larger. Thirty-six indoor servants:

    1 house steward.
    2 grooms of the chamber.
    1 valet.
    2 under butlers.
    3 footmen.
    2 steward's room footmen.
    1 gate porter.
    1 hall porter.
    1 usher of the servants' hall.
    2 odd men.
    1 house carpenter.
    1 chef.
    1 kitchen porter.
    4 kitchen and scullery maids.
    2 still-room maids.
    6 housemaids.
    1 linen maid.
    1 lady's maid.
    1 housekeeper.
    2 nurses.

Owns about 20,000 acres of land. (A larger staff of servants than this could be quoted. In one country house as many as ten housemaids are kept.)' . . .

---

[1] Rowntree's *Poverty*.

Man, wife, and child for five weeks:[1]

	s.	d.
Meat and liver	8	5
Potatoes and vegetables	2	$3\frac{1}{2}$
Fish	0	9
Bacon, eggs, and cheese	3	$6\frac{1}{4}$
Suet	1	0
Butter and dripping	2	9
Bread	8	$9\frac{1}{4}$
Flour	4	$1\frac{1}{2}$
Rice	0	6
Fruit, jam, and sugar	8	$4\frac{1}{4}$
Milk	3	2
Tea and coffee	3	6
Pepper and salt...................	0	$2\frac{1}{2}$
£2	7	$4\frac{1}{4}$
Average for one week	9	$5\frac{1}{2}$

Or man, wife, two boys, and a girl:

	£	s.	d.
Food and drink for three weeks	2	0	$7\frac{1}{4}$
Average for one week	0	13	$6\frac{1}{2}$

The study of the diet of this family reveals a deficiency of 25% in the protein and 7% in fuel value.[2]

Household books for one week—seven in family, nineteen servants:

	£
Butcher	16[3]
Baker	5
Poulterer................................	12
Dairy	9
Fruit, flowers, vegetables	16
Fishmonger	9
Grocer................................	5
£72

(Two dinner parties were given during the week.)

[1] Booth, Vol. I.
[2] Rowntree's *Poverty*.
[3] Odd shillings omitted.

The household of an 'unemployed man,' living in ———
Square, S.W., four in family and fourteen servants:

	£	s.	d.
Butcher	15	2	7
Greengrocer	10	10	0
Ice merchant	1	18	0
Fishmonger	7	10	0
Grocer	5	5	0
Milkman	4	10	0
Poulterer	12	0	0
Baker	3	17	0
	£60	12	7

In addition, three hundred eggs were sent up from the
country, as well as fruit, vegetables, and a little poultry. One
or two guests were entertained at luncheon, but the family
dined out one night of the week. ...

If the suggested volume, *The Life and Leisure of some People,* or
Riches: a Study of Town Life is ever written, any comment on
the carefully tabulated investigations would be quite unnecessary. As in the case of the books on Poverty, the bare
statement of facts is eloquent enough by itself.

Mr. Rowntree concludes his book with this pregnant
phrase:

'That in this land of abounding wealth, during a time of,
perhaps, unexampled prosperity, probably more than a quarter
of the population are living in poverty is a fact that may well
cause great searchings of heart.'

This might be paraphrased:

'That in this land, where more than a quarter of the
population are living in poverty, the abounding wealth of the
country should be retained by a comparatively small number
of people, who squander their riches in a way that brings no
happiness to themselves and inflicts misery and hardships on
others, is a fact that may well cause great searchings of heart.'

112) *Report of the Inter-Departmental Committee on Physical
      Deterioration* (HMSO, 1904), Cd. 2175, I, 84–93.

423.   The following is a summary of the principal recommendations which the Committee desire to make:—

(1) *Anthropometric Survey.*

With a view to the collection of definite data bearing upon the physical condition of the population, the Committee think that a permanent Anthropometric Survey should be organised as speedily as possible upon the lines indicated in Part I of the Report. In the first instance, this Survey should have for its object the periodic taking of measurements of children and young persons in schools and factories, enlisting for this purpose the assistance, among others, of School Teachers and Factory Surgeons, supplemented by a small staff of professional Surveyors. Besides this, a more comprehensive and specialist survey, spread over a longer period, of the population of the country at large, might be undertaken.

(2) *Register of Sickness.*

It appears to the Committee in the highest degree desirable that a Register of Sickness, not confined to infectious diseases, should be established and maintained. For this purpose the official returns of Poor Law Medical Officers could, with very little trouble and expense, be modified so as to secure a record of all diseases treated by them. And, further, it ought not to be difficult to procure the co-operation of hospitals and other charitable institutions throughout the country, so as to utilise for the same purpose the records of sickness kept by such institutions.

(3) *Advisory Council.*

The Committee are emphatic in recommending the creation of an Advisory Council, representing the Departments of State, within whose province questions touching the physical well-being of the people fall, with the addition of members nominated by the medical corporations and others, whose duty it should be, not only to receive and apply the information derived from the Anthropometric Survey and the Register of Sickness, but also to advise the Government on all legislative and administrative points concerning public health in respect of which State interference might be expedient; and to them might be remitted for consideration and report all the problems affecting public health which the requirements of a complex social organisation are constantly bringing to the front. Such a Council, the composition of which might be modelled to some extent on *Le Comité Consultatif d'hygiène publique de France*, would be, the Committee believe, of great assistance, especially to the Local Government Board, and would be calculated to supply the knowledge and stimulus which are necessary in order to give to the Public Health side of the Board's administration a prominence which the multiplicity of its other functions may have tended to obscure, and to attract to its work that measure of public interest and support which has perhaps been lacking hitherto.

(4) *Overcrowding.*

The Committee believe that the time has come for dealing drastically with this problem. They advocate an experimental effort by the Local Authority in certain of the worst districts, in the direction of fixing a standard and notifying that after a given date no crowding in excess of such standard would be permitted. It is believed that, if the thing were carried through without hesitation or sentimentality, means would be found, through the ordinary channels of supply and demand, or within the sphere of municipal activity, for housing all but the irreclaimably bad.

(5) *Labour Colonies and Public Nurseries.*

It may be necessary, in order to complete the work of clearing overcrowded slums, for the State, acting in conjunction with the Local Authority, to take charge of the lives of those who, from whatever cause, are incapable of independent existence up to the standard of decency which it imposes. In the last resort, this might take the form of labour colonies on the lines of the Salvation Army Colony at Hadleigh, with powers, however, of compulsory detention. The children of persons so treated might be lodged temporarily in public nurseries or boarded out. With a view to the enforcement of parental responsibility, the object would be to make the parent a debtor to society on account of the child, with the liability, in default of his providing the cost of a suitable maintenance, of being placed in a labour establishment under State supervision until the debt is worked off.

(6) *Building and Open Spaces.*

Local Authorities in contiguous areas which are in process of urbanisation should co-operate with a view to securing proper building regulations, in furtherance of which end the making of Building Bye-laws to be approved by the Local Government Board should be made compulsory on both urban and rural authorities; attention should also be given to the preservation of open spaces with abundance of light and air. By the use of judicious foresight and prudence the growth of squalid slums may be arrested, and districts which hereafter become urbanised may have at least some of the attributes of an ideal garden city.

(7) *Smoke Pollution.*

The Committee strongly advocate that cases of pollution of the air by smoke and noxious vapours in manufacturing districts should be heard by a stipendiary magistrate. A stricter enforcement of the law, and a change in legislation, giving higher penalties, would produce a great improvement without imposing any serious burden on manufacturers. It should also be considered whether the responsibilities of the ordinary householder in regard to domestic smoke pollution might not be brought home to him.

(8) *Register of owners of houses.*

It should be the duty of the Local Authority in all towns above a certain size to establish and maintain an accurate register of owners; this is one of the first *desiderata* towards dealing with slum property.

(9) *Medical Officers of Health.*

A Medical Officer of Health in all areas above a certain population should be required to give his whole time to the work, and in no case, unless convicted of misconduct, should a Medical Officer of Health so engaged be removed without the consent of the Local Government Board.

(10) *County and District Councils.*

With a view to strengthening the chain of responsibility in matters of local administration, County Councils should be empowered when necessary, after a reference to the Local Government Board, to act in default of urban (other than municipal boroughs) and rural sanitary authorities within the area of their administration, for all purposes of the Public Health and Housing Acts, to which end the appointment of Medical Officers of Health who would give their whole time should be made obligatory on County Councils.

(11) *Reports from Local Authorities.*

The Local Sanitary Authority in each district should be required to furnish to the Local Government Board, through the County Authority, reports according to certain specified requirements, which would show accurately what was being done, or left undone, in matters of sanitation and administration generally, and would thus form a basis of comparison between different districts. Armed with this information it should be the duty of the Central Authority to watch closely local administration, and to endeavour constantly to level up backward districts to the standard attained in the best administered areas.

(12) *Law as to Insanitary and Overcrowded House Property.*

Nothing has been brought more prominently to the notice of the Committee than the ignorance that prevails, even in quarters which ought to be well informed, as to what the law and the powers it confers are. A statement on this subject was prepared for the Committee, with the assistance of the Local Government Board; and it appears to them that the Board could not do better than issue it, with such additions as they think proper, to all Local Authorities.

(13) *Medical Inspection of Factories.*

The existing powers of Certifying Factory Surgeons should be extended, (1) so as to enable them to examine employees for purposes of qualification at a later age than sixteen, (2) so as to enable them to re-examine, when necessary, at definite intervals. Further, even if it be necessary that Inspectors of Factories and Medical Officers of Health should have, to some extent, co-ordinate powers with regard to insanitary conditions in factories, an arrangement should be made whereby each authority should notify to the other any defects that may be apparent, although coming within the other's province. Similarly it should be the Certifying Surgeon's duty to notify to the Factory Inspector or the Medical Officer of Health, as the case may be, such defects as may come under his notice.

(14) *Over-fatigue.*

As a preliminary to any further legislation on the subject of hours of employment, particularly employment of women and children, it is, in the view of the Committee, highly desirable that there should be a strictly scientific enquiry into the physiological causation and effects of over-fatigue, as recommended by the Brussels Congress.

(15) *Coal Mines.*

The medical examination of young persons should be extended so as to cover those employed in coal mines.

(16) *Workshops.*

The inspection and supervision of these, as distinguished from factories, should be strengthened. On the question whether this work should be undertaken by the Local Authority or the Home Office, the Committee are not in a position to make a definite recommendation. But one point in particular that calls for consideration is the propriety of making employment of children and young persons in workshops, dependent, as it is in factories, on a medical certificate.

(17) *Alcoholism.*

The Committee believe that more may be done to check the degeneration resulting from 'drink' by bringing home to men and women the fatal effects of alcohol on physical efficiency than by expatiating on the moral wickedness of drinking. To this end they advocate the systematic, practical training of teachers to enable them to give rational instruction in schools on the laws of health, including the demonstration of the physical evils caused by drinking. At the same time, the Committee cannot lose sight of the enormous improvement which has been effected in some countries, and might be effected in this country, by wise legislation.

(18) *Education in Rural Schools.*

With a view to combating the evils resulting from the constant influx from country to town, the Committee recommend that every effort should be made by those charged with the conduct and control of rural schools to open the minds of the children to the resources and opportunities of rural existence.

(19) *Rural Housing and Allotments.*

Local Authorities in Rural Districts should apply themselves to remedying the dearth of cottages which exist in many parts of the country, by the exercise of their powers under Part III of the Housing Act, 1890, as amended by the Act of 1900. If necessary, these powers might be supplemented by the introduction of some such machinery for putting them in motion as is contained in the Labourers' (Ireland) Acts, 1883–1903. It should also be seriously considered whether the experiment, for which there are legislative facilities, of dividing land into small holdings, might not be tried more frequently.

(20) *Food and Cookery.*

For the purpose of bringing home to the people the importance of properly selected and carefully prepared food, there is much room for training of a socially educative character among girls and young women. To this end the teaching of cookery in schools should be guided by the principles laid down in Paragraph 232 of the Report. Even more may be done by mothers' meetings and lectures, and the distribution of leaflets on the subject. Continuation classes for girls beyond school age should be organized, attendance at which should be compulsory, subject to the exercise of a judicious discretion on the part of the School Authority.

(21) *Cooking Grates.*

It should be provided by law that every dwelling let for the occupation of a family, should include a grate suitable for cooking.

(22) *Adulteration.*

It would be highly expedient that the Local Government Board should be authorised to fix a standard of purity for all foods and drinks, in the same manner as standards for milk and butter have been fixed by the Board of Agriculture.

(23) *Infant Mortality and Employment of Women.*

In order to arrive at some conclusion as to the connection between these two, (1) the infant mortality rates should be localised for particular areas in industrial towns, (2) general infant mortality rates for selected industries throughout the country should be taken, (3) the occupations (if any) of all mothers (married or unmarried) should be shown in the Registrar-General's records.

(24) *Still-births.*

Still-births should be registered.

(25) *Medical Certificates as to Cause of Death.*

A medical certificate as to the cause of death should invariably be required before the death of any child, or indeed of any other person, is registered. Moreover, the medical certificate should be regarded as confidential, and its contents should never be divulged by the Registrar, as is permissible at present, to the friends of the deceased. It should be sent by the local Registrar direct to the Registrar-General.

(26) *Employment of Women in Factories.*

The Committee do not think that the period during which employment after confinement is prohibited could be extended without counterbalancing disadvantages. But the law should certainly be strengthened, so as to place upon the employer the burden of obtaining proof that the required period has elapsed since the confinement of the women he employs, or, in the alternative, so as to prohibit future employment in the absence of (1) a medical certificate that it will not be prejudicial to their physical well-being, and (2) proof that reasonable provision is made for the care of their infants. This might take the form of a crêche, or be secured by the recognition for the purpose of a duly licensed body of women.

(27) *Provident Societies and Maternity Funds.*

Charitable efforts in manufacturing towns might well be directed towards endowing and maintaining insurance organisations to which employees, assisted by voluntary subscriptions, could contribute while in work, and from which they might receive assistance during the period of confinement and afterwards.

(28) *Milk Supply.*

With a view to ensuring the purity of the supply of milk to the community, the Committee think that the measures indicated in Paragraph 273 of the Report should be taken; in default of the Local Sanitary Authority taking proper precautions, the County Council should in all cases be authorised to act, and it should be the duty of the Local Government Board to intervene in the ultimate resort.

(29) *Feeding of Infants.*

The Committee are impressed with the enormous sacrifice of infant life due to insufficient or improper feeding. The ultimate remedy lies in that social education already described, and the Committee advocate the systematic instruction in continuation classes of girls in the processes of infant feeding and management. They also recommend the issue to mothers in every district of leaflets on the rearing of babies similar to those used in Sheffield and Wakefield; this could be done by the municipality, by voluntary associations, or by the Registrar on the registration of every infant.

(30) *Milk Depôts.*

It is of great importance that the milk supply should pass through as few hands as possible, and that milk vendors should not be general dealers whose sale of milk is confined to a few quarts. In order to effect these objects, milk depôts should be formed in every town, obtaining their supply direct from the farms. The Committee believe this could be done without recourse to direct municipal action, but they think that in all improvement Bills promoted by Local Authorities, the insertion of provisions dealing with the milk supply within their area should be insisted on.

(31) *Sterilisation and Refrigeration.*

Having regard to the acute difference of medical opinion as to the effects of sterilisation, the Committee recommend an investigation into the whole subject by a small body of experts. Milk, when drawn from the cow, should at once be refrigerated to a temperature of 40 degrees Fahrenheit.

(32) *Midwives.*

The Committee desire to call the attention of Local Authorities to the provisions of the Midwives Act, 1902, which may be made an instrument of the greatest utility for the dissemination among mothers of proper knowledge and practical advice.

(33) *Training of Mothers—Health Associations.*

While laying special stress on the need for education of the young in matters of hygiene and domestic economy, the Committee believe even more may be done in the direction of training the mothers of the present generation in these matters. To this end, Health Societies on the lines of the Manchester and Salford Ladies' Health Society should be formed all over the country. Enough has been said of the value of the system by competent judges to justify the Committee in urging upon every locality the adoption of similar methods. They would further suggest to the Local Government Board the expediency of issuing to Local Authorities a circular explaining the objects to be sought and the means by which they can best be attained.

(34) *Elementary Schools in Ireland.*

It appears that the elementary school system prevailing in Ireland urgently requires amendment in regard to warming of schools and hygiene conditions generally.

(35) *School attendance in rural districts.*

The Committee think that school attendance in rural districts should not be compulsory till the age of six or possibly seven, and should be discouraged, if not absolutely prohibited, under five.

(36) *Games and exercises for school children.*

It is desirable that more attention should be given, with the assistance, where possible, of voluntary agencies, to organizing games for school children, and for that purpose much greater use should be made both of school and public playgrounds than at present. But the Committee are of opinion that no scheme of games alone can ever be made general enough to supply the place of methodical physical training, and they hope that the course of physical exercises referred to in Paragraph 308 will find general acceptance with Local Authorities. While they consider that such exercises should, when possible, be taken in the open air, they would urge upon Local Authorities the expediency of providing play-sheds or rooms other than the ordinary class-rooms in which the exercises may be conducted regularly without interruption from the weather.

(37) *Cookery, hygiene, and domestic economy.*

Instruction in these matters should, as far as possible, be made compulsory on the elder girls at school, and care should be taken that it is placed in the hands of properly qualified teachers, to which end it is expedient that some State aid should be given under proper conditions to schools of cookery at which teachers are trained, and that hygiene in its various branches should be made an essential element in the course of training for all teachers.

(38) *Partial exemption from school.*

It should be considered whether the present law might not be modified so as to make it possible for a child under fourteen years of age to obtain partial exemption from the obligation to attend school, on no other condition than that of continuing to attend school up to a later age for certain specified periods and for special subjects of instruction.

(39) *Special schools for 'retarded' children.*

The Committee think that special schools of the Day Industrial School type might with advantage be established for the temporary treatment of children who are not up to normal school standard and are yet not so defective as to warrant treatment as 'mentally deficient.'

(40) *Special magistrate for juvenile cases.*

In all cases touching the young where the assistance of a magistrate is invoked, he should, where possible, be a specially selected person sitting for the purpose.

(41) *Medical inspection of school children.*

The Committee are emphatic in recommending that a systematised medical inspection of children at school should be imposed as a public duty on every school authority, and they agree with the Royal Commission on Physical Training (Scotland) that a contribution towards the cost should be made out of the Parliamentary Vote. With the assistance of teachers properly trained in the various branches of hygiene, the system could be so far based on their observations and records that no large and expensive medical staff would be necessary. The lines on which the inspection should be conducted are laid down in paragraphs 323–326 of the Report.

(42) *Feeding of elementary school children.*

The Committee recommend that definite provision should be made by the various Local Authorities for dealing with the question of underfed children in accordance with the methods indicated in paragraphs 358–365 of the Report. The Committee, it will be seen, do not contemplate any one uniform method of procedure, but think that regard should be had to the varying circumstances of different localities. They also suggest safeguards against economic abuse.

(43) *Physical exercise for growing girls.*

If physical exercise of a recreative character were included in the curriculum in the obligatory evening continuation classes for girls, the establishment of which has already been recommended, it would be likely to add greatly to the value and ultimately, it may be, to the popularity of such classes.

(44) *Crêches.*

Wherever it was thought desirable, owing to the employment of married women in factories, or for other reasons, to establish municipal crêches, girls over fourteen might be made to attend occasionally, and the teaching of infant management to such girls should be eligible for aid from the grant for public education.

(45) *Open spaces and gymnastic apparatus.*

It should be the duty of Local Authorities to provide and maintain open spaces in some proportion to the density of the population, and such spaces, or some of them, should include shelters fitted with gymnastic apparatus. Every effort should also be made to put such apparatus to the best possible use by placing it in charge of a competent instructor.

(46) *Clubs and cadet corps.*

Having regard to the enormous value to the physique of growing lads of these institutions, and to the possible saving of expenditure in other directions resulting therefrom, the Committee are of opinion that some grant should be made from the National Exchequer in aid of all clubs and cadet corps in which physical or quasi-military training, on an approved scheme, is conducted, subject to public inspection.

(47) *Physical exercise for growing boys.*

Lads should be made to attend evening continuation classes, in which drill and physical exercises should take a prominent place; and, with a view to the encouragement of clubs and cadet corps, exemption from the obligation might be granted to all enrolled and efficient members of such organizations as submitted to inspection and conformed to the regulations qualifying them for public aid.

(48) *Organization of existing institutions for the welfare of lads and girls.*

In order to organize existing efforts on a comprehensive and effective basis, the Committee would like to see a central body, in touch with municipal activity, established in every large town, and charged with the duty of supervising and directing voluntary agencies with a view to bringing them up to a minimum standard of efficiency.

(49) *Juvenile Smoking.*

The Committee recommend that a Bill should be brought before Parliament at an early date, having for its object, (1) to prohibit the sale of tobacco and cigarettes to children below a certain age, (2) to prohibit the sale of tobacco and cigarettes in sweet shops and other shops frequented by children.

(50) *Syphilis.*

The Committee recommend the appointment of a Commission of Inquiry into the prevalence and effects of syphilis, having special regard to the possibility of making the disease notifiable and to the adequacy of hospital accommodation for its treatment.

(51) *Insanity in Ireland.*

The Committee recommend that investigation should be undertaken at an early date into the extent and character of the increase of lunacy in Ireland.

(52) *Teeth, Eyes, and Ears.*

The Committee are of opinion that the care of the teeth should receive special attention in the teaching of the elements of hygiene in schools, that daily cleansing of the teeth should be enforced by both parents and teachers, and that systematic inspection of the teeth, eyes, and ears of school children should be undertaken as part of that general medical inspection which has already been recommended.

(53) *Vagrancy; Defective Children.*

The Committee wish to record their belief that the proposed inquiries into these subjects will be of great value.

CONCLUSION

424. The Committee hope that the facts and opinions they have collected will have some effect in allaying the apprehensions of those who, as it appears on insufficient grounds, have made up their minds that progressive deterioration is to be found among the people generally. At any rate the Committee believe that their labours will result in giving matter for reflection to those who realize the importance of evidence towards the determination of issues of such uncertainty and complexity, and that these persons, who they would fain hope are the larger portion of the thinking community, will await the necessary steps being taken to secure that body of well-sifted and accurate information, without which it is impossible to arrive at any conclusion of value as to the general problem.

425. It may be argued that there is here no immediate remedy, and that years must elapse before the lack of knowledge is supplied; but in regard to those evils, the existence of which is admitted, the Committee have recognised what can be done in the interval, and are confident that if their recommendations are adopted a considerable distance will have been traversed towards an amendment of the conditions they have described.

426. In the carrying out of their recommendations for the rectification of acknowledged evils, the Committee do not rely upon any large measure of legislative assistance; the law may

with advantage be altered and elaborated in certain respects, but the pathway to improvement lies in another direction. Complacent optimism and administrative indifference must be attacked and overcome, and a large-hearted sentiment of public interest take the place of timorous counsels and sectional prejudice.

113)   *The Times,* 2 January 1905, leading article.

We have already made a serious inroad upon personal responsibility and personal independence by relieving parents of the duty of educating their children. That is now used as an argument for relieving them of the duty of feeding their children. When we have done that, the argument will be stronger than ever for relieving them of the duty of clothing their children. It will be said that we pay vast sums for teaching and feeding, but that the money is wasted if the children are not properly clad. *L'appêtit vient en mangeant.* From that it is an easy step to paying for their proper housing; for what, it will be asked, is the use of feeding, clothing, and teaching children, if they come to school from close and insanitary bed-rooms? . . . The proposed measure would go far to sap the remaining independence of the existing parents; but what are we to expect from the present children when they in turn become parents? The habit of looking to the State for their maintenance would be ingrained in them; everything we now give would be to them a matter of course; and they would infallibly make new demands of their own, which in turn would be to their children an irreducible minimum.

114)   *Parliamentary Debates,* fourth series, CLII (1906), 1397–8.

ARTHUR HENDERSON SPEECH IN EDUCATION
(PROVISION OF MEALS) BILL DEBATE, 1906

He knew that they would be told, as they had been told in previous discussions, that to adopt the course suggested would be interfering with parental responsibility, and that they would also be placing a premium on thriftlessness. He did not believe in either of those objections. He would be the last to suggest that they should in any way interfere, in the sense that had been suggested, with parental responsibility. What he was anxious to do was to bring home, as it had never been brought home before, that this object could not be attained by charitable means. Experience had proved that charity instead of bringing home parental responsibility was one of the most serious and insidious influences in sapping and destroying parental responsibility. Therefore, they were anxious, as his hon. friend in moving the Second Reading of the Bill had pointed out, to go the length of suggesting that if parents were in a position to provide for their children and they failed to do so, the law should step in and deal with the parents, even to the extent of recovering the cost, and in bad cases they would go so far as not only to scarify them, but further punish the parent for neglecting his obligations to his child. The class that they were asking the House to provide for might very naturally be divided into three sections. In the first place there were the destitute children, whose parents were in extreme poverty for reasons that were preventable. Secondly, there were those whose parents were in temporary poverty because of enforced idleness. And thirdly, and he thought they were the most important of all, there were those whose fathers' economic condition when they were in work was of such a nature as almost to exclude any possibility of making that provision for their children which they might so much desire. He would urge upon the House that whatever was the condition of the parent in this matter, their immediate and foremost concern, as the guardians of this great nation, ought to be not with the father, but with the child.

115)   *The Times*, 15 October 1902.

BALFOUR SPEECH AT MANCHESTER, 1902

The existing educational system of this country is chaotic, is ineffectual, is utterly behind the age, makes us the laughing-stock of every advanced nation in Europe and America, puts us not only behind our American cousins but the German and the Frenchman and the Italian . . . from a local government point of view, we have the absurdity of two rating authorities dealing with education, both with power to draw upon the local resources . . . you have the great county councils and borough councils of this country, corporations like the Corporation of Manchester, building technical schools . . . but without the smallest power to arrange the education in their district that those who are expected to profit by these great technical schools shall come to them with adequate preparation. . . .

To go a step lower, there is at this moment in England no public authority which is capable of supplying secondary education in its true sense, and when you come to that higher primary education which has been illegally carried on by the Board Schools, though I heartily sympathise with the objects they had in view, when you come to deal with them you inevitably have under the existing system, between the corporation on the one side and the Board Schools on the other, you have inevitable overlapping. . . . And when, leaving higher secondary education, I come to that primary education which is the necessity of every class in the community, and to which we justly desire every man in the land from the highest to the lowest to subject his children, what do we find? Under the existing system we find Board Schools which are in no relation either to the voluntary schools on the one side or to the secondary schools and higher technical schools on the other, and we find the voluntary schools, educating, remember, more than half the children of this country, we find them in many cases starved for want of funds and incapable of carrying out to perfection, at all events, the greatest duties entrusted to them by the community. . . .

And what is our solution? I am not going into it in detail, but in substance it is this—that we should put all the branches of education of which I have spoken under the control and supervision of those great public assemblies, the borough councils and county councils of this country. That is the central principle of the Bill. On that everything else hangs. . . . We want those great municipal and county authorities to co-ordinate the higher with the lower education, to provide secondary education and higher elementary education without overlapping. We want it—and this is almost the most important thing that requires to be done, one of the most important things that requires to be done—we require it to train teachers. . . . We want this municipal and county authority to provide the machinery for training teachers, and we want it to control all the schools so far as secular education is concerned. . . . Remember, then, that the Bill is an organic whole, which deals with a great and admitted evil. It deals with it on a fixed and intelligible plan, and no amendment ought to be admitted into the Bill which destroys it as an organic whole. . . .

The divisions of religious opinion among us are unhappily so great and are unhappily of such a character that it is quite impossible that if you are to have compulsory education in the public schools of the country you can so arrange it that every parent should always find at his doors a school in which religious education is taken according to his own particular beliefs . . . the only possible alternative in which there is even a semblance of justice is one which, while it permits so-called undenominational teaching in schools entirely supported out of the public funds, permits denominational teaching in schools which are not so wholly supported out of public funds. . . . You will observe, then, that I am brought as regards secular education to the single authority, that authority being the county council or the borough council, and that as regards religious education in this country I believe that we must as part of our system, so long as we maintain the Cowper-Temple Clause, maintain the right to have the children of that party which desires it taught in voluntary schools. . . .

We have reached a point in the educational history of this country which is of capital and paramount importance . . . if we hesitate to do our duty and carry through this great reform, then I say we shall receive the contempt of the parents of the children living and to be born, for the next generation, and that contempt which we shall receive we shall justly and richly earn.

116) C. T. Bateman, *John Clifford* (National Council of the Evangelical Free Churches, 1904), 283–5.

CLIFFORD ON PASSIVE RESISTANCE

I am resolutely opposed to any man, a Mahometan or Methodist, a Ritualist or a Romanist, a Quaker or a Baptist, being made to suffer in the slightest degree for his religious opinions. In my fixed conviction those opinions are entirely outside the functions of the State. Parliament has nothing whatever to do with them. I am as strongly opposed to the establishment by Parliament of what is called 'undenominational teaching,' as I am to Romanism; *i.e.,* I protest with all my might against teaching at the expense of the ratepayers a set of dogmatic theological opinions on which Christians generally are supposed to be agreed, as I protest against the teaching of any distinctively Roman or Anglican doctrine. I wish theological dogma to be taught, but taught by the Churches, and entirely at the expense of the Churches; and not by the officers of Parliament, and at the expense of the ratepayers. I have fought for Roman Catholics in municipal and Parliamentary contests. I shall again. What I oppose is anybody's effort to *compel* me to pay for the propagation of Romanist or any other Church doctrines, or to use the Parliament of the people for that purpose. Against that I have battled, and will whilst I have breath, for I am sure it cannot be right for me to force one citizen to pay another for calling him a 'schismatic,' assuring him that 'he has committed a very grievous sin in forsaking the services of Westminster Abbey or Westbourne Park Chapel,' and that his preachers are all unauthorised, that his 'Church' is no Church of Christ at all, and that if he gets to heaven at last it will be on some broken raft, and not on a good Church ship. No, I do not think you ought to force me to pay for that; and if you try, you will discover that you have for once undertaken an impossibility.

But that is precisely what this Act is doing for Romanism. Romanist schools are on the rates. I do not complain. They have a right to be there according to the law. Romanist training colleges are on the rates. Notices are printed in the papers announcing new schools for 'teaching the doctrines of the Roman Catholic denomination.' For educational work they are not needed; there are places in other schools where the Roman Catholic atmosphere does not exist; but the Romanists have abundant money, and they are erecting new schools and applying to the educational authorities to have them recognised as public elementary schools, and to place them upon the rates. The Romanists are not lacking in wisdom or wealth, and no doubt within the next few years these schools will spring up in great abundance.

Is it surprising that the Passive Resistance Movement grows? Would it not be astonishing if legislation so diametrically opposed to the eternal principles of justice and liberty, of democracy and progress, did not stir every reflective Englishman to do his utmost to accomplish its removal at the earliest possible moment, and many others to say, come what will, 'We will not submit'?

117) 'School Question in Great Britain', in *New Encyclopedia of Social Reform* (Funk & Wagnalls, 1908), 1099–1100.

The Non-Conformists claim that from rates which all rate-payers are compelled to pay, no matter what their religious or lack of religious view, the government has no right to support schools in which the denominational teaching of any church or churches may be forced upon the children of the State. The Non-Conformists stand (1) for the application of the principle of the total severance of the functions of Parliament and of religious societies to all State education. They stand (2) for the entire control of national education by the people, and the exclusion of churches as churches, and priests as priests, and ministers as ministers, and parents as parents from such control, and for the admission of parents, ministers, and priests as citizens and only as citizens. They stand (3) for the complete exclusion of all theological and ecclesiastical tests for teachers and require only drilled capacity and character.

Resolutions of Dec. 20, 1905, of the General Committees of the National Council of Free Evangelical Churches declare that the aim of State education should be:

(1) To secure a truly national and efficient system of education.

(2) To secure justice to every citizen.

(3) To wound no conscience.

(4) To bring about a lasting educational peace.

The basis of the system should be exclusively civic, exclude preferential treatment for any person or persons, clergy or teachers; and for any institution theological or ecclesiastical. It should cast the entire responsibility for theological and ecclesiastical teaching on the home and the Church.

This means—

(1) That no change in the number of managers—such as substituting two for four, or electing representatives of parents, and the like—will suffice.

(2) That the non-provided schools must either be trans-

ferred to the State or be maintained by the denomination as denominational schools; for as State schools they must cease, and no arrangements for sectarian teaching should have any place whatever in the State system.

(3) That it should be the aim of the government to secure the provision of public schools (purely civic schools) at positions convenient for the children all over the land; for it is certain that educational peace will not be secured until the education given by the State is carried on in non-ecclesiastical buildings owned by the public.

(4) That those provided school buildings only should be purchased which are found after careful and competent investigation to be suitable as to structure and condition to become public property for educational purposes and should not be rented for a longer period than five years.

(5) That the utmost care should be given to secure such schools as belong, or in part belong, to the public for the public.

(6) That State education should return to some form of the *ad hoc* system. That cooptation should cease. That women shall be eligible for election on the local education authority on the same terms as men. That the administrative breakdown of the present arrangement should be met by recognizing: (a) That the county areas are in most cases far too large. (b) That local interest in education is being destroyed. (c) That areas of suitable size should be substituted for county areas. (d) That such local authorities might have power given them to combine for specific purposes, e.g., secondary education.

Non-Conformists cannot on any account admit the principle that (a) the churches have the right to give, or (b) the parents a right to demand, any denominational teaching whatever in connection with public school life.

That the entry of sectarian teachers into State schools and training colleges *during the hours allotted for State work* should be absolutely forbidden as fatal to the efficiency of the teaching, disturbing to the order of the school, and productive of religious strife.

That in case public school buildings are used, by permission of local authority, for imparting dogmatic and ecclesiastical teaching to the children attending the school outside school hours, a payment should be made by the denomination so using the buildings to cover the expenses connected therewith.

That no denomination shall be allowed to, use the

teachers or other officers or machinery of the State for such denominational teaching.

The foregoing provisions also have reference to secondary education as far as they may be applicable.

Not for a very lengthened period has the Free Church mind been so deeply moved as upon this question.

The root of all the evil is to be found in the existence of a Church establishment. There is general agreement among Free Churchmen as to the origin of the two pernicious educational measures which they have so justly denounced. For some years past a section of the supporters of the Established Church have been persistently undermining the Act of 1870. When the time appeared to be ripe for the purpose, the two Anglican convocations formulated their demands and urged them upon the government. These were, with one exception, acceded to, and formed the basis of the Education Bill of 1902. Still further concessions were made to the Church of England during the passage of the bill, and notably as the result of the action of the bishops in the Lords.

Solicitude for religious education has been exprest in justification of this course; but few will doubt that the struggle has been mainly one for the retention and the strengthening of the Church establishment. Had that institution not existed, and had its bishops no seats in Parliament, such bills would never have been introduced.

The force we are fighting, then, is not primarily political. Parliament is only its tool. It is ecclesiastical. 'Clericalism is the enemy.' The reversal of the broader and more just educational policy initiated in 1870, and the return to the clericalism of the beginning of the last century, is due to the change which has taken place in the Anglican Church, in its ideas and spirit, its temper and aims. It is not the tolerant and inclusive Church of the days of Lord Shaftesbury, but the bigoted and persecuting Church of the times of Laud and Whitgift. It is a Romanized church; and in and by the English Church Union it is becoming increasingly Romanist. It is that section—the large and dominating section of twentieth-century Anglicanism—that has given us these acts. It is the victory of the High Church party.

It has been said there is taught now in the council schools of London and in the 'unsectarian' or 'provided' schools of the country, 'a new-fangled faith', an 'unsectarian religion', which 'is only another expression of non-conformity', 'a novel form of religion, whose only recommendation is that it pleases Dr. Clifford and his friends', and we are told that what Romanists and Anglicans have secured by their prolonged efforts in the Education Acts of 1902 and 1903 is the opportunity of giving 'our poorer brothers a way of escape from the threatened universal domination of modern unsectarianism' or of the Free Churches.

According to the 'London syllabus,' children are taught at the expense of the State Psalm xxiii, the Ten Commandments, the Lord's Prayer, the Beatitudes, the blessedness of hunger for what is right and just, of making peace between individuals and nations, of purity of thought and spirit—in short, the religion which consists in 'doing justly and loving mercy, and walking humbly with God.' They are introduced, not to the whole of the Bible, but only to those portions of the Testament best suited to their capacity, and least likely to suggest controversy; to the purest ethic, the most quickening poetry, the most inspiring biography, i.e., to the most potent character-building literature the world contains; and I confess that to me it appears that if Parliament undertakes the education of the children of the nation it ought not to fail to open the doors for them into this all-hallowing temple of truth and justice, liberty and progress.

I know this is not 'teaching religion' in the sense of the High Church party; but in my judgment it is all the State is competent to do, and all it can attempt without inflicting injustice upon some portion of its members.

Against being compelled to support schools where principles are taught they cannot in conscience accept, very many Non-Conformists have felt it their duty to refuse to pay their full education rates and inaugurate a policy of 'passive resistance to the payment of the sectarian patron'.

Over 400 imprisonments have taken place and more than 100,000 distraints of goods have been carried out. The reasons given in court for resistance were:

(1) That the Education Acts of 1902 and 1903 compelled him to pay for teaching on the deepest subjects of the inward and religious life; subjects with which the State, or Parliament, or Borough Council has no right whatever to deal. They are personal, individual, and the State ought to leave them to

every man's conscience. Complete freedom in this thing is the right of every British citizen, a right he would enjoy if he dwelt under the British flag in Canada or Australia, and a right he cannot surrender because he lives in England.

(2) That the law attempts to coerce him to pay for teaching children doctrines and practises he holds to be distinctly opposed:

1. To the teaching of Christ;
2. To the well-being of the child; and
3. To the happiness and prosperity of the nation.

(3) That by this law he is compelled to pay, that the children of England may be taught that the doctrines he has held and taught for nearly fifty years are false, and that the Free Churches, to which he is grateful to belong, are heretical and to be avoided as the plague.

Non-Conformists cannot and will not accept any such legislation. Let others teach them if they so believe, but let them not compel me to do so.   JOHN CLIFFORD

118)   Margaret McMillan, *The Child and the State* (National Labour Press, 1911), x–xiii, 26–8.

No one, however poor and faltering his work, can write of the higher education of the masses to-day without waking some thrill of interest and hope in everyone who thinks at all of his race or its future. This question is a new one. To-day thousands of workpeople awaken almost as if from sleep. In a single year the number of Tutorial Classes for working people has more than doubled.

Every tutor knows perfectly well that the waking of any one of his working-class students to-day is an event quite other than is the smooth progress of even the most brilliant under-graduate. To begin with, the worker's eyes are opened in an hour when Science is laying bare the effects of balked youth and despoiled childhood, and is proving that long hours of labour without mental progress mean nothing more or less than mutilation, and that of the saddest kind. The 'prizes' of life beckon the selfish and even the unselfish. But life itself takes on a different hue to those who *know* at last what they and theirs have paid for our modern civilisation. And meantime every week and month sees the army of serious students growing—sees miners, dockers, railway men, drivers, spinners, and even the unemployed forging their way across barriers that were yesterday believed to be impassable by them. There may be, and indeed there are, two opinions as to whether they are taking the right road. Still they are finding a road—and the goal before them is clear enough. It is Higher Education for all.

The world has never seen a large, highly educated Democracy—a Democracy scorning the notion of slavery. The world has never seen, and I do not pretend to say whether it will ever see it, for Higher Education does not depend merely on leisure, and access to Universities and tutors, but on the will and power to go through a great deal of hard and long drudgery. One thing, however, is growing clearer every day, viz., that a great number of working people are willing to go through this immense drudgery, and more, to welcome trouble of every kind, in order to win the knowledge that is power. . . .

Within the next twenty years the struggle for efficiency will be carried on with a new earnestness in every civilised land. There will be a demand (which we try to re-inforce) for better technical education. But this new efficiency, while it benefits the ruling class may do very little indeed for the people. Efficient workmen have been slaves in the past, and may be worse than slaves in the future. Something more is wanted. If the working class is not to be content to be educated *as a subject race,* then they must enter on a new struggle—a struggle for Higher Education. . . .

There are successful cases that show up all the tragic elements in thousands of difficult and seemingly hopeless cases.

A miserable little boy, deaf, almost inarticulate, undersized, unable to read even the smallest words is allowed to receive treatment. Two months later he is full of eager desire to learn. He attacks the reading book and begins to master the new art, draws vigorously, wants to model, to work, to play—asks endless questions. In short, awakens to life and all its joys. It is not possible to think that the treatment which thus opens the doors of life is a thing altogether apart from 'Education,' and that an inspector, a teacher, or parent is to think of it as something for which the school has no responsibility at all. One might as well say that a violinist should not think of his violin —but only of his score.

There are many schemes already drawn up by medical officers and administrators for meeting the need of suffering children. Some of these (like Dr. Barwise's Provident Club scheme in Derbyshire) fall back on voluntary subscriptions and contributions from parents. Only one quarter of all those needing treatment and reported on could be dealt with in the first year. In London, the Education Authority falls back on the hospitals—which, however, were never intended to deal with school children at all. Diseases that do not interfere with school-going are not only, in some cases infectious. They are nearly all very stubborn and need routine treatment. Their cure is largely a matter of the forming of new habits. Education, as well as medical care, is needed, in order to put an end to them. But, of course, no hospital can take the place of school, and no doctor can do the work of a teacher or highly skilled mother.

The well-to-do mother perhaps need not fear when the worst is over and the doctor comes no more. In her home she has a nursery, and many 'helps'. All the routine of prevention can go on merrily—bathing, dressing, exercise, eating, sleeping at regular hours. And by these the old evil is chased away every day and every night.

Why did this private nursery come into existence? Because it was needed. The school nursery must come into existence for the same reason. Nurseries are needed also for the children of the masses. That same routine of washing, dressing, play in cheerful healthy space, is necessary for the prevention of illness in the case of the poor as of the rich; and opportunities for these must be forthcoming if the new medical service is to be of any practical service to rich or poor.

The School Health-centre is an extension of the Home Nursery—no more and no less. As the school family is immense, however, and as its needs are various, the Head of the School Nursery-Clinic must be a doctor, and his assistants must be trained hospital nurses (without ceasing to be home nurses first and foremost). The school is not home. No, and yet it must supply something that will be found one day in every home. It must be built to supplement the poor shelters of to-day.

119)   C. Booth, *Life and Labour of the People in London*, final volume (Macmillan, 1902), 143–8.

I myself advocate as a third element the introduction of Old Age Pensions, contributed directly from the national purse, not so much in aid of poverty as of thrift; but acting directly and indirectly in relief both of the Poor Law and of private charity; simplifying the problems which each has to treat; and making concerted action on their part in dealing with destitution and distress more practicable and more efficacious.

To this end the recipient of a pension must have kept in the main clear of poor relief; otherwise the fewer the conditions imposed the better. The coming of the pension at a fixed age must be certain, provided independence has been maintained before. Under these two fundamental conditions the expectation of the pension will surely stimulate individual effort to hold out till it comes and to add something to its meagre provision. Thrift tests are unnecessary and delusive. To adopt them is to drop the reality in catching at the apparent, like the dog in the fable.

As my plan bears closely on the administration both of the Poor Law and of private charity, I will venture to recapitulate it.[1] I would make seventy the age at which a free and honourable pension should be granted to everyone who up to then had not received poor relief (other than medical), and I put the amount at seven shillings per week, in place of the more generally adopted proposal of five shillings a week at sixty-five. Proof of age, nationality, and residence in England during the working years of life would be required. There would be no restriction as to earnings (if at seventy any are still possible); nor as to amount of savings: the seven shillings would be in addition to whatever the recipient had or might earn, but would be drawn weekly by personal application, or in cases of debility or illness by some accredited relative or friend. If on this system any who did not exactly need the money, should still collect it, so much the better for maintaining the dignity of the rest; as one may welcome a bishop or a lord who deigns to travel third class.

At and after seventy most of the difficulties and, I think, all the dangers of a universal pension system melt away. Its cost is no longer prohibitive, while the coming of the pension would be of untold value in limiting the liabilities which prolonged life entail, not only on the individual, but on thrift agencies and on charitable funds, and would lift from very many old hearts the fear of the workhouse at the last.

It is, however, before seventy, and mainly between sixty and

[1] *Old Age Pensions and the Aged Poor—a proposal.* Macmillan, 1899.

seventy, that the battle of independence has to be fought; and it is to the beneficial effect of a coming pension on the lives of the people, especially during this period, that I attach especial importance. It is this effect, moreover, which brings the subject definitely within the range of the subject I am now discussing.

To those who demand that the State provision should begin at sixty, and who claim that it is impossible for working men to save enough for maintenance in old age, I would say that most could provide enough to eke out the earnings which are still possible between sixty and seventy; and that their clubs could more easily assist them in this if relieved of all liability for those whose lives are prolonged. To those again who take their stand on sixty-five as the right pension age, with five shillings as the amount, I can only say that in my view, seven shillings at seventy provides a more practical scheme. The cost would be substantially less, and the difficulties, both economic and administrative, very much so. The future seven shillings coming at the age of seventy would, perhaps, loom as large in the imagination of a man of fifty or sixty, as would five shillings accruing at sixty-five. Up to seventy he would have to provide for his life; beyond that age he need not worry, though few who save at all would limit their action so closely or be content when seventy was at last reached, if they had not some funds in hand to help out the pension allowance. The motive to save up to the time of the pension and beyond it would be strong; as also, too, would be the motive with those living nearer the line of pauperism, to avoid application to the Poor Law. The effect of looking forward to a pension would be the exact opposite to that of the anticipation of Poor Law relief, any claim to which must rest upon absolute destitution.

It is a mistake to suppose that no advantage would come except to those who live beyond seventy. The provident would feel the benefit at once through the decreased rate of contribution for remote benefits, which would be possible if their clubs could omit old age in their calculations, while the effective value of any other savings they are able to make will be immediately increased, in so far as the possible years of extreme old age can be dropped out of financial count. For very many, the one doubt as to being able to escape the workhouse would be removed. And even those who largely trust to others to do their saving for them, would find it far easier to obtain aid from some old employer, or friend, or relative, or even child, if the liability were limited to a definite term. Those of the improvident class who lived past seventy, might still find themselves stranded, without friends, in their old age; but, to parody an old rhyme—

> 'When friends are gone, and money spent,
> Then Pensions are most excellent'

and the certainty of a pension accruing would often bridge the gulf, enabling those who might otherwise have been abandoned to the Poor Law, to maintain a decent home outside.

My plan goes still a little further, and it is at this point particularly that united action between the Poor Law and private charity becomes essential. There will be cases unsuited for the Poor Law, for which it may be nevertheless difficult to secure sufficient private assistance; cases in which a small pension is clearly the form in which assistance could be given most judiciously. Such may occur at almost any age, but it is more usually after sixty that, failing other help, the workhouse comes so near. It would then seem very hard that the pension assured to any who live till seventy, should not in some way be made available; and I suggest that with the co-operation of the Guardians, who are directly interested in keeping people off the rates, a case might be made out for an *immediate pension at a permanently lower rate*, which would be actuarially equivalent to the value of the deferred pension, provided the recipient can by some means be assured a total income from all sources sufficient for independent maintenance. The object would be to prevent the dissipation of savings, and to rouse in time the effort that is needed to secure an adequate provision for life. Practically no one would be likely to ask this accommodation who would not otherwise become a pauper; charity would find its opportunity, and while the national exchequer would hardly suffer at all, the rates would profit.

If the separate spheres of Poor Law and charity were distinctly recognised, and pensions, thus adapted, were available to assist voluntary effort of all kinds, out-relief could and should be abolished. With its abolition all difficulty of deciding what agency ought to be employed in the relief of poverty would pass away. Evidently no case ought to be relegated to the workhouse which could be satisfactorily dealt with outside. Those who are abandoned to that last resource, because from sickness or infirmity they are unfitted for any home that is open to them, would be cared for in one building, while the destitute who come upon the Poor Law from any other cause would be accommodated in another building and altogether differently regarded.

It is commonly said that few of the old who are now inmates of workhouses could, if a pension were granted, find any home outside. That may be so, but it hardly affects the question. The object of the pension, actual or prospective, is to *maintain* a home, which is a very different thing from suddenly *finding* one. The pension itself is only one factor out of many that would be found working with it in this direction. The preservation of the homes would exercise a constant wholesome influence on family relations as well as on thrift. The young would look to the old, instead of only the old looking to the young. Some, doubtless, might be completely stranded in old age, and might be glad to abandon their pension for the haven of the workhouse, and there would be others whose tempers made home life impossible; but I cannot doubt that if they were no longer a financial burthen, most old people whose health permitted it would remain outside. For the most part they do so now where out relief is given, though the amount allowed them is very small. It is only those whose infirmities are such that they require a nurse's care who ought to be recommended to give up home and pension in favour of the workhouse infirmary. Such as these should, indeed, be encouraged to do so, but it would be the work of charitable and friendly kindness to minister to the comfort and happiness of all such as can remain in the world outside.

120)   R. S. Churchill, *Winston S. Churchill*, volume II, companion, part 2 (Heinemann, 1969), 863–4.

CHURCHILL TO ASQUITH, 29 DECEMBER 1908

I have been revolving many things during these few days of tranquillity & I feel impelled to state to you the conviction that has for a long time past been forming in my mind. There is a tremendous policy in Social Organisation. The need is urgent & the moment ripe. Germany with a harder climate and far less accumulated wealth has managed to establish tolerable basic conditions for her people. She is organised not only for war, but for peace. We are organised for nothing except party politics. The Minister who will apply to this country the successful experiences of Germany in social organisation may or may not be supported at the polls, but he will at least have left a memorial which time will not deface of his administration. It is impossible to under-pin the existing voluntary agencies by a comprehensive system—necessarily at a lower level—of state action. We have at least two years. We have the miseries which this winter is inflicting upon the poorer classes to back us. And oddly enough the very class of legislation which is required is just the kind the House of Lords will not dare to oppose. The expenditure of less than ten millions a year, not upon relief, but upon machinery, & thrift-stimuli would make England a different country for the poor. And I believe that once the nation begins to feel the momentum of these large designs, it will range itself at first with breathless interest & afterwards in solid support behind the shoulder of the Government. Here are the steps as I see them.

1. Labour Exchanges & Unemployed Insurance:
2. National Infirmity Insurance etc:
3. Special Expansive State Industries—Afforestation—Roads:
4. Modernised Poor Law i.e. classification:
5. Railway Amalgamation with State Control and guarantee:
6. Education compulsory till 17.

I believe there is not one of these things that cannot be carried & carried triumphantly & that they would not only benefit the state but fortify the party. But how much better to fail in such noble efforts, than to perish by slow paralysis or windy agitation.

I say—thrust a big slice of Bismarkianism over the whole underside of our industrial system, & await the consequences whatever they may be with a good conscience.

Pray forgive the vehemence and frankness of this letter. I would not write it to you did I not feel confident you would receive it in an equal mood of earnestness.

121) *Report of the Royal Commission on the Poor Laws and Relief of Distress* (HMSO, 1909), Cd. 4499, Majority Report, 78, 644.

It is very unpleasant to record that, notwithstanding our assumed moral and material progress, and notwithstanding the enormous annual expenditure, amounting to nearly sixty millions a year, upon poor relief, education, and public health, we still have a vast army of persons quartered upon us unable to support themselves, and an army which in numbers has recently shown signs of increase rather than decrease. To what is the retrogression due? It cannot be attributed to lack of expenditure. Is this costly and elaborate machinery we have established defective, and if so where does it fail to accomplish its end? Is the material upon which this machinery operates becoming less amenable to the remedies applied?

The recommendations we shall make in later stages of this Report will furnish the reply to these interrogations, but the statistical review of the expenditure incurred and of the results attained by it prove that something in our social organisation is seriously wrong, and that whatever may be the evils, they are not of such a nature as to be improved or removed by the mere signing of cheques or the outpouring of public funds. . . .

'Land of Hope and Glory' is a popular and patriotic lyric sung each year with rapture by thousands of voices. The enthusiasm is partly evoked by the beauty of the idea itself, but more by the belief that Great Britain does, above other countries, merit this eulogium, and that the conditions in existence here are such that the fulfilment of hope and the achievement of glory are more open to the individual than in other and less favoured lands. To certain classes of the community into whose moral and material condition it has been our duty to enquire, these words are a mockery and a falsehood. To many of them, possibly from their own failure and faults, there is in this life but little hope, and to many more 'glory' or its realisation is an unknown ideal. Our investigations prove the existence in our midst of a class whose condition and environment are a discredit, and a peril to the whole community. Each and every section of society has a common duty to perform in combating this evil and contracting its area, a duty which can only be performed by united and untiring effort to convert useless and costly inefficients into self-sustaining and respectable members of the community. No country, however rich, can permanently hold its own in the race of international competition, if hampered by an increasing load of this dead weight; or can successfully perform the role of sovereignty beyond the seas, if a portion of its own folk at home are sinking below the civilization and aspirations of its subject races abroad.

122) *Report of the Royal Commission on the Poor Laws and Relief of Distress* (HMSO, 1909), Cd. 4499, Minority Report, 430–2, 684–9.

Deferring our proposals with regard to the whole of the Able-bodied until Part II of the present Report, we recommend:—

1. That, except the 43 Elizabeth, c. 2, the Poor Law Amendment Act of 1834 for England and Wales, and the various Acts for the relief of the poor and the corresponding legislation for Scotland and Ireland, so far as they relate exclusively to Poor Relief, and including the Law of Settlement, should be repealed.

2. That the Boards of Guardians in England, Wales and Ireland, and (at any rate as far as Poor Law functions are concerned) the parish Councils in Scotland, together with all combinations of these bodies, should be abolished.

3. That the property and liabilities, powers and duties of these Destitution Authorities should be transferred (subject to the necessary adjustments) to the County and County Borough Councils, strengthened in numbers as may be deemed necessary for their enlarged duties; with suitable modifications to provide for the special circumstances of Scotland and Ireland, and for the cases of the Metropolitan Boroughs, the Non-County Boroughs over 10,000 in population, and the Urban Districts over 20,000 in population, on the plan that we have sketched out.

4. That the provision for the various classes of the Non-Able-bodied should be wholly separated from that to be made for the Able-bodied whether these be unemployed workmen, vagrants or able-bodied persons now in receipt of Poor Relief.

5. That the services at present administered by the Destitu-

tion Authorities (other than those connected with vagrants or the able-bodied) — that is to say, the provision for: —

   (i) Children of school age;

  (ii) The sick and the permanently incapacitated, the infants under school age, and the aged needing institutional care;

 (iii) The mentally defective of all grades and all ages; and

  (iv) The aged to whom pensions are awarded —

should be assumed, under the directions of the County and County Borough Councils, by: —

   (i) The Education Committee;

  (ii) The Health Committee;

 (iii) The Asylums Committee; and

  (iv) The Pension Committee respectively.

6. That the several committees concerned should be authorised and required, under the directions of their Councils, to provide, under suitable conditions and safeguards to be embodied in Statutes and regulative Orders, for the several classes of persons committed to their charge, whatever treatment they may deem most appropriate to their condition; being either institutional treatment, in the various specialised schools, hospitals, asylums, &c., under their charge; or whenever judged preferable, domiciliary treatment, conjoined with the grant of Home Aliment where this is indispensably required.

7. That the law with regard to liability to pay for relief or treatment received, or to contribute towards the maintenance of dependents and other relations, should be embodied in a definite and consistent code, on the basis, in those services for which a charge should be made, of recovering the cost from all those who are really able to pay, and of exempting those who cannot properly do so.

8. That there should be established in each County and County Borough one or more officers, to be designated Registrars of Public Assistance, to be appointed by the County and County Borough Council, and to be charged with the threefold duty of: —

  (i) Keeping a Public Register of all cases in receipt of public assistance;

 (ii) Assessing and recovering, according to the law of the land and the evidence as to sufficiency of ability to pay, whatever charges Parliament may decide to make for particular kinds of relief or treatment; and

(iii) Sanctioning the grants of Home Aliment proposed by the Committees concerned with the treatment of the case.

9. That the Registrar of Public Assistance should have under his direction (and under the control of the General Purposes Committee of the County or County Borough Council) the necessary staff of Inquiry and Recovery Officers, and a local Receiving House for the strictly temporary accommodation of non-able-bodied persons found in need, and not as yet dealt with by the Committees concerned.

10. That the present national subventions in aid of the Destitution Authorities should be replaced by Grants-in-Aid of the expenditure on the whole of the services to be administered by the Health Committees of the County and County Borough Councils, subject to the administration of these services up to, at any rate, a National Minimum of Efficiency; the aggregate amount of such Grants-in-Aid for the United Kingdom and their allocation as between England (including Wales), Scotland and Ireland being fixed, and subject to revision only every seven years; but the distribution of this total among the several County and County Borough Councils being made, according to the plan we have specified, in proportion to their several gross expenditures on these services, and at the same time in such a proportion to the poverty of their districts as will enable the National Minimum of Efficiency to be everywhere attained without anywhere exceeding the Standard Average Rate.

11. That the Local Authorities in England and Wales, in respect of the services administered by each Committee, be placed under the supervision of a single Department or Division of a Department of the National Government, which shall itself administer the Grants-in-Aid of its particular services, issue its own regulative Orders, and have its own technically qualified Inspectors; the Education Committees in England and Wales being thus responsible, for the efficiency of all their services to the Board of Education; the Mentally Defectives (or Asylums) Committees to the proposed Board of Control, in succession to the Lunacy Commissioners; the Pension Committees to whatever Department is deputed to take charge of the administration of the Old-age Pensions Act of 1908; and the Health Committees, with regard to all their

enlarged range of functions, to a separately organised and self-contained Public Health Department, whether this is organised as a separate Division of the Local Government Board or made a distinct Department. The determination of appeals from the decisions of the Registrar of Public Assistance, and whatever national supervision may be exercised over the grant of Home Aliment to the Non-Able-Bodied, should, we suggest, be entrusted to another separately organised and self-contained Department or Division of a Department which, if it can be dissociated from the Local Government Board, might, with advantage, be placed, along with the Department or Division dealing with Audit, Loans and Local Finance generally, in close connection with the Treasury.

12. That a temporary Executive Commission be appointed to adjust areas, boundaries, assets and liabilities; and to allocate buildings and officers among the future Local Authorities. . . .

'UTOPIAN?'

This elaborate scheme of national organization for dealing with the grave social evil of Unemployment, with its resultant Able-bodied Destitution, and its deterioration of hundreds of thousands of working class families, will seem to many persons Utopian. Experience proves, however, that this may mean no more than that it will take a little time to accustom people to the proposals, and to get them carried into operation. The first step is to make the whole community realise that the evil exists. At present, it is not too much to say that the average citizen of the middle or upper class takes for granted the constantly recurring destitution among wage-earning families due to Unemployment as part of the natural order of things, and as no more to be combated than the east wind. In the same way, the eighteenth century citizen acquiesced in the horrors of the contemporary prison administration, and in the slave trade, just as, for the first decades of the nineteenth century, our grandfathers accepted as inevitable the slavery of the little children of the wage-earners in mines and factories, and the incessant devastation of the slums by 'fever'. Fifty years hence we shall be looking back with amazement at the helpless and ignorant acquiescence of the governing classes of the United Kingdom, at the opening of the twentieth century, in the constant debasement of character and *physique,* not to mention[the perpetual draining away of the nation's wealth that idleness combined with starvation plainly causes.]

The second step is for the Government to make a serious endeavour to grapple with the evil as a whole, on a deliberately thought-out plan.

What has been effected in the organisation of Public Health and Public Education can be effected, if we wish it, in the Public Organization of the Labour Market.

Summary of Proposals

We therefore recommend:—

1. That the duty of so organising the National Labour Market as to prevent or to minimise Unemployment should be placed upon a Minister responsible to Parliament, who might be designated the Minister for Labour.

2. That the Ministry of Labour should include six distinct and separately organized Divisions, each with its own Assistant Secretary, namely, the National Labour Exchange, the Trade Insurance Division, the Maintenance and Training Division, the Industrial Regulation Division, the Emigration and Immigration Division, and the Statistical Division.

3. That the function of the National Labour Exchange should be, not only (*a*) to ascertain and report the surplus or shortage of labour of particular kinds, at particular places; and (*b*) to diminish the time and energy now spent in looking for work, and the consequent 'leakage' between jobs; but also (*c*) so to 'dovetail' casual and seasonal employments as to arrange for practical continuity of work for those now chronically Under-employed. That whilst resort to the National Labour Exchange might be optional for employers filling situations of at least a month's duration, it should (following the precedent of the Labour Exchange for seamen already conducted by the Board of Trade in the Mercantile Marine Offices) be made legally compulsory in certain scheduled trades in which excessive Discontinuity of Employment prevails, and especially for the engagement of Casual Labour.

4. That in our opinion no effective steps can be taken towards the 'Decasualisation of Casual Labour,' and the Suppression of Under-employment, without simultaneously

taking action to ensure the immediate absorption, or else to provide the full and honourable maintenance at the public expense, of the surplus of labourers that will thereby stand revealed.

5. That, in order to secure proper industrial training for the youth of the nation, an amendment of the Factory Acts is urgently required to provide that no child should be employed at all below the age of fifteen; that no young person under eighteen should be employed for more than thirty hours per week; and that all young persons so employed should be required to attend for thirty hours per week at suitable Trade Schools to be maintained by the Local Education Authorities.

6. That the terms of the Regulation of Railways Act, 1893, should be so amended as to enable the Minister of Labour to require the prompt reduction of the hours of duty of railway, tramway, and omnibus workers, if not to forty-eight, at any rate, to not more than sixty in any one week as a maximum.

7. That all mothers having the charge of young children, and in receipt, by themselves or their husbands, of any form of Public Assistance, should receive enough for the full maintenance of the family; and that it should then be made a condition of such assistance that the mother should devote herself to the care of her children, without seeking industrial employment.

8. That we recommend these reforms for their own sake, but it is an additional advantage that they (and especially the Halving of Boy Labour) would permit the immediate addition to the number of men in employment equal to a large proportion of those who are now Unemployed or Under-employed.

9. That in order to meet the periodically recurrent general depressions of Trade, the Government should take advantage of there being at these periods as much Unemployment of capital as there is Unemployment of labour; that it should definitely undertake, as far as practicable, the Regularization of the National Demand for Labour; and that it should for this purpose, and to the extent of at least 4,000,000*l.* a year, arrange a portion of the ordinary work required by each Department on a Ten Years' Programme; such 40,000,000*l.* worth of work for the decade being then put in hand, not by equal annual instalments, but exclusively in the lean years of the trade cycle; being paid for out of loans for short terms raised as they are required, and being executed with the best

available labour, at Standard Rates, *engaged in the ordinary way.*

10. That in this Ten Years' Programme there should be included works of Afforestation, Coast Protection and Land Reclamation; to be carried out by the Board of Agriculture exclusively in the lean years of the trade cycle; *by the most suitable labour obtainable taken on in the ordinary way,* at the rates locally current for the work, and paid for out of loans raised as required.

11. That the statistical and other evidence indicates that, by such measures as the above, the greater bulk of the fluctuations in the aggregate volume of employment can be obviated; and the bulk of the surplus labour manifesting itself in chronic Under-employment can be immediately absorbed, leaving, at all times, only a relatively small residuum of men who are, for various reasons, in distress from want of work.

12. That with a lessened Discontinuity of Employment, and the Suppression of Under-employment, the provision of Out-of-Work Benefit by Trade Unions would become practicable over a much greater range of industry than at present; and its extension should, as the best form of insurance against Unemployment, receive Government encouragement and support. That in view of its probable adverse effect on Trade Union membership and organization, we are unable to recommend the establishment of any plan of Government or compulsory Insurance against Unemployment. That we recommend, however, that following the precedents set in several foreign countries, a Government subvention not exceeding one-half of the sum actually paid in the last preceding year as Out-of-Work Benefit should be offered to Trade Unions or other societies providing such Benefit, in order to enable the necessary weekly contributions to be brought within the means of a larger proportion of the wage-earners.

13. That for the ultimate residuum of men in distress from want of employment, who may be expected to remain, after the measures now recommended have been put in operation, we recommend that Maintenance should be freely provided, without disfranchisement, on condition that they submit themselves to the physical and mental training that they may prove to require. That it should be the function of the Maintenance and Training Division of the Ministry of Labour to establish and maintain Receiving Offices in the various centres of population, at which able-bodied men in distress could

apply for assistance, and at which they would be medically examined and have their faculties tested in order to discover in what way they could be improved by training. They would then be assigned either to suitable Day Training Depôts or residential Farm Colonies, where their whole working time would be absorbed in such varied beneficial training of body and mind as they proved capable of; their wives and families being, meanwhile, provided with adequate Home Aliment.

14. That no applicant for employment or man out of work need be legally required to register at the National Labour Exchange, or to attend or remain in any Training Establishment, so long as he abstained from crime (including Vagrancy and Mendicity), and maintained himself and his family without receiving or needing Public Assistance in any form; but that such registration, and, if required, such attendance, should be legally enforced on all men who fail to fulfil any of their social obligations, or are found houseless, or requiring Public Assistance for themselves or their families.

15. That the Maintenance and Training Division should also establish one or more Detention Colonies, of a reformatory type, to which men would be committed by the Magistrates, and compulsorily detained and kept to work under discipline, upon conviction of any such offences as Vagrancy, Mendicity, neglect to maintain family or to apply for Public Assistance for their maintenance if destitute, repeated recalcitrancy or breach of discipline in a Training Establishment, &c.

16. That for able-bodied women, without husband or dependent children, who may be found in distress from want of employment, there should be exactly the same sort of provision as for men. That for widows or other mothers in distress, having the care of young children, residing in homes not below the National Minimum of sanitation, and being themselves not adjudged unworthy to have children entrusted to them, there should be granted adequate Home Aliment on condition of their devoting their whole time and energy to the care of the children. That for the childless wives of able-bodied men in attendance at a Training Establishment, adequate Home Aliment be granted, conditional on their devoting their time to such further training in domestic Economy as may be prescribed for them.

17. That upon the establishment of the Ministry of Labour,

and the setting to work of its new organisation, the Unemployed Workmen Act of 1905 should cease to apply; and the
Local Authorities should be relieved of all responsibilities with
regard to the Able-bodied and the Unemployed.

18. That upon the necessary legislation being passed, a
small Executive Commission be empowered to effect the
necessary transfer to the Ministry of Labour of the functions
with regard to the Able-bodied and the Unemployed at
present performed by the Poor Law Authorities and the
Distress Committees under the Unemployed Workmen Act;
and to make, as from the Appointed Day, all necessary
transfers and adjustments of buildings and officers, Farm
Colonies and Labour Exchanges, assets and liabilities.

123)   W. H. Beveridge, *Unemployment, a Problem of Industry*
(Longmans, 1909), 203.

A Labour Exchange or common taking-on place for many
separate undertakings may do as between them what in a
single firm is done as between different departments. It may
become the headquarters of a compact mobile reserve of
labour, replacing and by its mobility covering the same
ground as the enormous stagnant reserve which drifts about
the streets to-day. The larger and more varied the area of
employment covered by an Exchange, the more completely
will it be able to regularise the work of this reserve, because
the more nearly will the independent fluctuations of many
businesses neutralise one another to yield a steady average.
There are, of course, limits to the movement of labour—limits
of space and limits of skill. Men cannot be transferred in a
morning from London to Glasgow or from carpentering to
bricklaying. Obstacles of space would in part yield to every
improvement of organisation; would in part have to be accepted as ultimate. As to the requirement of special skill the
important point has to be noted that, while it limits the range
of movement, it also makes a large range of movement unnecessary. It is harder to regularise skilled employment than
unskilled, but the skilled workman, because of his higher
wages, can stand greater irregularity without falling into
distress. The casual employment of the barrister or the doctor,
the artist or the journalist, does not as a rule involve chronic

distress. Moreover, it is not necessary to argue that all irregularity can be abolished by simply organising the movement
of labour, or that nothing will remain to be done later. It is
sufficient to say that each step in this direction is a step in
advance. Wherever any two wharfingers, by using a common
list of casuals, reduce the number of individuals between
whom their work is shared from fifty to forty-nine, they have
to that extent reduced under-employment.

124) W. S. Churchill, *Liberalism and the Social Problem* (Hodder
    & Stoughton, 1909), 256–7, 377–9.

Two main defects in modern industrial conditions which
were emphasised by the Royal Commission were the lack of
mobility of labour and lack of information. With both of these
defects the National System of Labour Exchanges is calculated
to deal. Modern industry has become national. Fresh means
of transport knit the country into one, as it was never knit
before. Labour alone in its search for markets has not profited;
the antiquated, wasteful, and demoralising method of personal
application—that is to say, the hawking of labour—persists.
Labour Exchanges will give labour for the first time a
modernised market. Labour Exchanges, in the second place,
will increase and will organise the mobility of labour. But let
me point out that to increase the *mobility* of labour is not
necessarily to increase the *movement* of labour. Labour Exchanges will not increase the movement of labour; they will
only render that movement, when it has become necessary,
more easy, more smooth, more painless, and less wasteful.

Labour Exchanges do not pretend to any large extent to
create new employment. Their main function will be to
organise the existing employment, and by organising the
existing employment to reduce the friction and wastage, resulting from changes in employment and the movement of
workers, to a minimum. By so doing they will necessarily raise
the general economic standard of our industrial life. . . .

A new question has arisen. We do not only ask to-day, 'How
much have you got?' we also ask, 'How did you get it? Did you
earn it by yourself, or has it just been left you by others? Was
it gained by processes which are in themselves beneficial to the
community in general, or was it gained by processes which

have done no good to any one, but only harm? Was it gained by the enterprise and capacity necessary to found a business, or merely by squeezing and bleeding the owner and founder of the business? Was it gained by supplying the capital which industry needs, or by denying, except at an extortionate price, the land which industry requires? Was it derived from active reproductive processes, or merely by squatting on some piece of necessary land till enterprise and labour, and national interests and municipal interests, had to buy you out at fifty times the agricultural value? Was it gained from opening new minerals to the service of man, or by drawing a mining royalty from the toil and adventure of others? Was it gained by the curious process of using political influence to convert an annual licence into a practical freehold and thereby pocketing a monopoly value which properly belongs to the State—how did you get it?' That is the new question which has been postulated and which is vibrating in penetrating repetition through the land.[1]

It is a tremendous question, never previously in this country asked so plainly, a new idea, pregnant, formidable, full of life, that taxation should not only have regard to the volume of wealth, but, so far as possible, to the character of the processes of its origin. I do not wonder it has raised a great stir. I do not wonder that there are heart-searchings and angry words because that simple question, that modest proposal, which we see embodied in the new income-tax provisions, in the land taxes, in the licence duties, and in the tax on mining royalties —that modest proposal means, and can only mean, the refusal of the modern State to bow down unquestioningly before the authority of wealth. This refusal to treat all forms of wealth with equal deference, no matter what may have been the process by which it was acquired, is a strenuous assertion in a practical form, that there ought to be a constant relation between acquired wealth and useful service previously rendered, and that where no service, but rather disservice, is proved, then, whenever possible, the State should make a sensible difference in the taxes it is bound to impose.

[1] We do not, of course, ask it of the individual taxpayer. That would be an impossible inquisition. But the House of Commons asks itself when it has to choose between taxes on various forms of wealth, 'By what process was it got?'

125)   H. du Parcq, *Life of David Lloyd George* (Caxton, 1913),
       IV, 687–8, 696.

LLOYD GEORGE SPEECH AT NEWCASTLE, 1909

The dukes have been making speeches recently. One
especially expensive duke made a speech, and all the Tory
Press said, 'Well, now, really, is that the sort of thing we are
spending £250,000 a year upon?' Because a fully-equipped
duke costs as much to keep up as two 'Dreadnoughts,' and
they are just as great a terror, and they last longer. As long as
they were contented to be mere idols on their pedestals,
preserving that stately silence which became their rank and
their intelligence, all went well, and the average British citizen
rather looked up to them, and said to himself, 'Well, if the
worst comes to the worst for this old country, we have always
got the dukes to fall back on.'

But then came the Budget. The dukes stepped off their
perch. They have been scolding like omnibus drivers purely
because the Budget cart has knocked a little of the gilt off their
old stage coach. Well, we cannot put them back again. That is
the only property that has gone down badly in the market. All
the rest has improved. The prospects of trade are better, and
that is the result of a great agitation which describes the
Budget as an attack on industry and on property.

Well, now, why should Liberalism be supposed to be ready
to attack property? After all, they forget this: I lay down as a
proposition that most of the people who work hard for a living
in the country belong to the Liberal party. I would say, and I
think, without offence, that most of the people who never
worked for a living at all belong to the Tory party. And
whenever you go across country you see men building up
trade and business, some small, some great, by their industry,
by their skill, by their energy, by their enterprise—not merely
maintaining themselves and their families, but putting something by for evil days—hundreds of thousands of them—not
all of them, I do not say that—but hundreds of thousands of
them belong to the Liberal party. . . .

Who talks about altering and meddling with the Constitution? The Constitutional party—the great Constitutional
party. As long as the Constitution gave rank and possession
and power to the Lords it was not to be interfered with. As
long as it secured even their sports from intrusion and made

interference with them a crime; as long as the Constitution enforced royalties and ground rents and fees and premiums and fines, and all the black retinue of exaction; as long as it showered writs and summonses and injunctions and distresses and warrants to enforce them, then the Constitution was inviolate. It was sacred. It was something that was put in the same category as religion, that no man should with rude hands touch, something that the chivalry of the nation ought to range itself in defence of. But the moment the Constitution looks round; the moment the Constitution begins to discover that there are millions of people outside park gates who need attention, then the Constitution is to be torn to pieces.

Let them realise what they are doing. They are forcing a revolution, and they will get it. The Lords may decree a revolution, but the people will direct it. If they begin, issues will be raised that they little dream of. Questions will be asked which are now whispered in humble voices, and answers will be demanded then with authority. The question will be asked whether five hundred men, ordinary men chosen accidentally from among the unemployed, should override the judgment—the deliberate judgment—of millions of people who are engaged in the industry which makes the wealth of the country.

That is one question. Another will be, Who ordained that a few should have the land of Britain as a perquisite? Who made ten thousand people owners of the soil, and the rest of us trespassers in the land of our birth? Who is it who is responsible for the scheme of things whereby one man is engaged through life in grinding labour to win a bare and precarious subsistence for himself, and when, at the end of his days, he claims at the hands of the community he served a poor pension of eightpence a day, he can only get it through a revolution, and another man who does not toil receives every hour of the day, every hour of the night, whilst he slumbers, more than his poor neighbour receives in a whole year of toil? Where did the table of that law come from? Whose finger inscribed it? These are the questions that will be asked. The answers are charged with peril for the order of things the Peers represent; but they are fraught with rare and refreshing fruit for the parched lips of the multitude who have been treading the dusty road along which the people have marched through the dark ages which are now merging into the light.

126) *The Times*, 18 November 1909.

BALFOUR SPEECH AT MANCHESTER, NOVEMBER 1909

No man who looks at the world in which we live thinks, at all events in November 1909, that there are before the country other than these two alternatives—the Budget or fiscal reform . . . you may say truly of this Budget that it is a combination of bad finance and muddle-headed Socialism. It is bad finance because, for instance, it has raised the tobacco duties to a point perfectly preposterous, and it has destroyed the spirit duties as a fiscal engine. It has imposed a gigantic burden upon the taxpayer in order to carry out a universal land survey, which is not going to bring in anything in the immediate future, and, as I believe, very little in the remote future. Some of its provisions seem to be directly calculated—some of its purely financial provisions I mean, such as the great augmentation of the old death duties—seem to be directly calculated to produce unemployment in many parts of the country. I do not see, nobody has ever explained, how you can take a great fragment of capital suddenly on the death of an individual, which may happen at any moment, and which he cannot foresee and which nobody can foresee—nobody has ever explained how you can take these great masses of capital and put them in the Exchequer without injuring the industry of the locality where that capital is invested. Well I call that bad management. But I am not going to discuss that part of the Budget which deals with bad finance. I am going to deal with that part of it which I have described as muddle-headed Socialism. Now, ladies and gentlemen, there is more than one part of the Budget which comes under that description. I think, for example, that the method of dealing with licenses is abominably unjust. . . .

I am going to talk about what I am told is the popular part of the Budget, the land taxes. I am told that is the only popular part of the Budget, that those who like nothing else about the Budget like that. . . . There are people who tell you that the land of the country belongs to the people. When you ask them what they mean by that, they do not mean that it should belong to the people of the country, they think it ought to belong to a department or some public office which is to manage the whole land of the country; in other words, that the land of the country is not to belong to any individual in the

country at all. I do not think that is a reasonable way of
looking at land, and it is not the way that any progressive
community has ever looked at land. I think land, personally,
ought to be in private ownership, and the wider the ownership
is extended the better I am pleased. I do not want all the land
of the country to belong to the Woods and Forests, I want it to
be distributed as far as possible in private ownership, and that
it should be regarded as a favoured investment by building
societies, that it should be regarded as a perfectly safe way of
investing benefit funds, that it should be regarded as a legitimate way in which friendly societies might put those great
resources which the thrift of the community has committed to
their care.

And I wish also to see that the business in land should be
like any other business, freely transacted without perpetual
interference of a department or a valuer or an inspector or
anybody else. I am, of course, in favour of land being taken
compulsorily for public purposes, and taken at the full valuation, of course. I am one of those who are most anxious to see
small agricultural ownership greatly increased. One of the
reasons why I am anxious to see it is because ownership, not
ownership of the State but ownership of the individual, carries
with it now, and has carried with it through all history, a
stimulus to energy and to self-sacrifice that nothing else will
give. . . .

I venture to assert that no competent authority has ever
suggested that the treatment which land near towns is receiving under this Budget will not diminish enterprise in that land,
because it diminishes security. . . . The taxation of land values
for rating purposes is legitimate, if it can be shown that the
value which you desire to reach are values which are not
paying their fair share of the local rates. . . . But that is not
the doctrine of the Budget. The doctrine of the Budget was
(loud cheering, as Mr. Balfour emphasized the past tense) —
the doctrine of the Budget was (renewed cheers) that all these
land values should be taxed, not for the benefit of the rates,
but for the benefit of the Exchequer. . . .

What the Budget does is to select a particular form of
property—it may belong to the rich, it may belong to the poor,
it may belong to any class of the community at all—to isolate
it, and put on a special taxation. Let me tell you, ladies and
gentlemen, that you cannot do that avowedly, of set purpose,

as a principle of your Budget, without endangering the security which is the very basis of all enterprise. . . .

A correspondent was kind enough to send me this morning an extract from a Socialist newspaper of repute, which seems to me to bear upon this point. . . . 'The Liberal party', says this Socialist organ, 'is digging its own grave by using arguments against landowners which are at least as applicable to capitalists.' I do not think Socialists are practical, but they are logical, and there is not the slightest doubt that what the Socialist organ says is absolutely true. . . . If you think the rich man ought to pay more than he does to the national need, tax him according to his wealth, but do not tax him according to the kind of property in which his wealth happens to be. Nothing will justify that, nothing will justify it in policy. It is very difficult to frame a system of taxation which shall be absolutely fair all round, but these people are doing it on purpose. It is not an unhappy incident of their Budget; it is the object of the Budget. And I say that an object like that destroys all security. . . . I feel that it is this part of the Budget, the so-called popular part of the Budget, which requires the serious attention of the working classes more than any other part. . . . Do not let them entertain the folly of supposing that they are attacking the rich classes. They are doing nothing of the kind. They are first of all attacking the mortgagee. If you attack the mortgagee you attack the debenture holder, and by attacking the debenture holder you attack the shareholders, and so through the whole rather complicated system of modern industry that feeling of insecurity which you have rashly produced at the base of your fabric will spread by inevitable law through every vein and every nerve of the system. . . .

Compare the treatment which two successive Governments have given to two great fiscal issues. The fiscal controversy, as you all know, was raised before the late Government left office. We always said it had never been put before the people; that the country never had an opportunity of pronouncing upon it, and that it would have been a misuse of the majority which we were given in 1900, if that majority had been used to press forward tariff reform. . . . We say that this Government had not the smallest right to come forward with these novel and, as I think dangerous proposals, and to force them through the House of Commons after endless sittings, and then to make them law before the people of this country had had a word to say upon the subject. For my own part, therefore, I rejoice to see that Lord Lansdowne has embodied in one concise and complete phrase the whole doctrine which I have been endeavouring to preach to you. . . .

The object of a second Chamber is not, and never has been, to prevent the people, the mass of the community, the electorate, the constituencies determining what policy they should pursue; it exists for the purpose of seeing that on great issues the policy which is pursued is not the policy of a temporary majority elected for a different purpose, but represents the sovereign conviction of the people for the few years in which it carries their mandate . . . its mission and great function is to see that the Government of this country is a popular Government. What it has to do on these fortunately rare, but all the more important, occasions is not to insist that this or that Minority, powerful for the time, once powerful perhaps, no longer powerful it may be, is to be clothed with all the tyrannical powers which we have done so much to prevent anybody in the State, any element in the State, exercising. The object is to see that there shall be referred to the people that which concerns the people; and that the people shall not be betrayed by hasty legislation, interested legislation, legislation having, it may be, some electoral object in view, or some vindictive policy to carry out.

127)   *The Times,* 11 December 1909.

ASQUITH SPEECH AT THE ALBERT HALL, LONDON, DECEMBER 1909

Sickness, invalidity, unemployment—these are spectres which are always hovering on the horizon of possibility, I may almost say of certainty, to the industrious workman. We believe here also the time has come for the State to lend a helping hand. That is the secret, or at least it is one of the secrets, of the Budget of this year . . . it was a Budget which sought by taxes on the accumulations of the rich and the luxuries of the well-to-do, and by a moderate toll on monopoly values which the community itself has, either actively or passively, created, to provide the sinews of war for the initiation and the prosecution of what must be a long, a costly, social campaign. That was the Budget put forward on the authority of a united Cabinet—passed after months of by no means fruitless discussion by the House of Commons—rejected in a week, and at a single blow, by the House of Lords. And that, gentlemen, is primarily why we are here to-night.

The immediate, the actively provoking cause of what is rightly called a constitutional crisis is the entirely new claim put forward by the House of Lords, not only to meddle with, but, in effect, to control and to mould our national finances. . . . This year, by one stroke, they have taken upon themselves to shatter the whole fabric of the year's taxation. This, I repeat, is a new and entirely unexpected danger to popular liberties. Two years ago it was as undreamt of as would have been, and as it is to-day, the revival by an arbitrary Minister of the veto of the Crown. . . .

We are indeed . . . suddenly confronted with no less than three constitutional innovations. In the first place we have the claim of the Upper House, not as an archaic legal survival, but as a living and effective right, to control the levying of taxation. In the second place we have the claim of the same House—a body which cannot itself be dissolved—to compel a dissolution of the popular Chamber. And, lastly, as a consequence and a corollary of the other two, we have the assertion of its power to make or to unmake the Executive Government of the Crown. Every one of these revolutionary pretensions we shall withstand for all we are worth. The result is what at first sight seems rather like a paradox, that we, the progressive party, find ourselves here to-day, in the first place, occupying Conservative and constitutional ground, defending the liberties which have been transmitted to us from the past against invasions and usurpations which have for the first time received the official countenance of the Tory party. Gentlemen, what has been done once may be done again. I do not say that it will be; but I do say this, that it becomes our first duty to take effective steps to make its recurrence impossible. We shall therefore demand authority from the electorate to translate the ancient and unwritten usage into an Act of Parliament, and to place upon the Statute-book the recognition, explicit and complete, of the settled doctrine of our Constitution, that it is beyond the province of the House of Lords to meddle in any way, to any degree, or for any purpose, with our national finance. . . .

So far we are on the defensive. But at the same time and by

the same action the House of Lords has not indeed raised but has hurried on for prompt decision a larger issue still. I tell you quite plainly and I tell my fellow-countrymen outside that neither I nor any other Liberal Minister supported by a majority in the House of Commons is going to submit again to the rebuffs and the humiliations of the last four years. We shall not assume office, and we shall not hold office, unless we can secure the safeguards which experience shows us to be necessary for the legislative utility and honour of the party of progress. . . . I myself, and I believe a large majority of the Liberal party, are in favour of what is called the bicameral system. I see nothing inconsistent with democratic principle or practice in a Second Chamber as such. On the contrary, I see much practical advantage that might result from the existence side by side with the House of Commons of a body, not, indeed, of co-ordinate authority, but suitable in its numbers and by its composition to exercise impartially in regard to our ordinary legislation the powers of revision, amendment, fuller deliberation, and, subject to proper safeguards, of delay. . . . Those are both useful and dignified functions. Yes, gentlemen, but we have got to deal with a present and an immediate necessity. . . . Our present position gives us all the drawbacks, with few, if any, of the advantages of a Second Chamber. For what is our actual Second Chamber? It is a body which has no pretensions or qualifications to be the organ or the interpreter of the popular will. It is a body in which one party in the State is in possession of a permanent and overwhelming majority. It is a body which, as experience has shown, in temper and in action is frankly, nakedly partisan. It is a body which does not attempt to exercise any kind of effective control over the legislation of the other House when its own party is in a majority there. It is a body which, when the conditions are reversed, however clear and emphatic the verdict of the country has been, sets itself to work to mutilate and to destroy democratic legislation, and even in these latter days it lays a usurping hand on democratic finance. That is a plain, literal, unvarnished picture of what everyone knows to be the fact.

We are going to ask the country to give us authority to apply an effective remedy to these intolerable conditions. Here, again, what is to be done is to be done by Act of Parliament. The time for unwritten convention has, unhappily, gone by. . . . we are going to ask the electors to say, that the

House of Lords shall be confined to the proper functions of a Second Chamber, which I enumerated to you a few moments ago. The absolute veto which it at present possesses must go. The powers which it claims from time to time of, in effect, compelling us to choose between a dissolution and, as far as main projects are concerned—legislative sterility—that power must go also. The people in future when they elect a new House of Commons must be able to feel what they cannot feel now, that they are sending to Westminster men who will have the power not merely of proposing and debating but of making laws. The will of the people, as deliberately expressed by their elected representatives, must, within the limits of a single Parliament, be made effective.

128)   H. du Parcq, *Life of David Lloyd George* (Caxton, 1913), IV, 792–3.

LLOYD GEORGE SPEECH AT KENNINGTON, 1912

So long as the head of the family is in good health, on the whole with a fierce struggle he can keep the wolves of hunger in the vast majority of cases from the door; but when he breaks down in health, his children are at the mercy of these fierce ravaging beasts, and there is no one there to stand at the door to fight for the young. What happens in these cases? In hundreds of thousands there is penury, privation, everything going from the household, nothing left unpawned, except its pride. On Monday next an Act of Parliament comes into operation that abolishes that state of things for ever. Twenty-seven millions of money raised as a fund—raised as a parapet between the people and the poverty that comes from sickness and unemployment! I worked hard at that parapet. Gentlemen, that is the crime for which I stand arraigned. I do not say that it will ensure an era of abundance, but it will inaugurate it. I do not say that it is the Millennium, but it brings it nearer. That is one parapet. Another parapet was Old-Age Pensions, and between them they will help millions of people from stumbling, slipping, and struggling into the dark flood of wretchedness which flows beneath.

The Prime Minister did me the honour of appointing me to be foreman of that job in building these two parapets. While I was helping my colleagues to build them, missiles and mud have been flung at the workers by men who have never carried a hod, who have never done any good work for their fellows. Our Chairman has told you that at first the Tory Press, without exception, received this measure with acclamation. Why, the 'Times' in its leading article to-day says that when I first announced my intention of committing this crime, when I gave particulars of the way I was going about it, they received it with a genuine and sincere welcome. These are their words: 'An act of oppression, of tyranny, that is wrecking the interests of the nation and crushing everybody,' and yet when it appeared the 'Times' boasts to-day that it welcomed it with sincere and genuine gratification. What altered their attitude? Why did they depart from their more generous position? Why did they abandon their nobler impulses? I will tell you. They found that, although people may approve of a great scheme, there is just one little kink in human nature that always prefers that somebody else should pay for it. They found suspicion and selfishness arrayed against it; formidable foes, very formidable, and they could not resist the temptation to take advantage of it. I have found a good many men on the other side who always measure schemes for the improvement of the condition of the masses by their electioneering value, and if you say to them, 'We are doing this because we think it will relieve distress, will chase away hunger, will cure the consumptive, will lighten the burden of the workers,' they say, 'Ah! Don't you talk to us like that, we know better. When we bring in housing schemes we do it for none of these reasons, but because our papers say that we must have a programme to please the working classes.' They are firmly convinced that we are just the same. Let them speak for themselves. When the Insurance Bill came on first of all, they were full of acclamation. Then they found misunderstandings. It was not a good electioneering measure, and now they are saying, 'Thank God that Act is a failure. Why, it lost the Radicals the Manchester election.' (A voice: '*It will win many more.*') I quite agree with my friend there. We are a little more far-sighted than they are. We live on a higher ground, and can see much further ahead.

129)   *The Times*, 30 November 1911.

ALBERT HALL DEMONSTRATION, NOVEMBER 1911

The Dowager Lady Desart, in opening the proceedings, said their organization had been accused of being one of rich people seeking to prevent benefits reaching the poor. On the contrary, they were fighting in defence of the hard-come-by earnings of the poor. The highly-trained, highly-paid servants would scarcely suffer under this Bill, and well-to-do mistresses would sooner pay the double contribution than lose the servants to whom they owed most of the comforts and half the luxuries of their lives. This tax was of no importance to the rich, but it was of vast importance to those who were not rich. They were met to fight the battle of the small house-holder, the battle of the rank and file of servants, the battle of the socially, physically, or mentally handicapped. Small householders called upon to pay 26s. a year for the servants they employed, would either have to take the amount out of their wages or do without them. In either case the poorer of the two parties, the maid, would suffer most.

It was true that an enormous percentage of the patients in infirmaries and hospitals were servants, but that percentage would remain just as high if the clauses were carried. The servants were in those institutions because there they stood the best chance of recovering and got the best nursing. These clauses would not merely inflict increased hardship on the most defenceless portion of the servant industry; they were calculated to set class against class—to prevent in future any appeal to friendship, let alone that beautiful intimacy which had hitherto so often existed between mistresses and servants. By what right did Mr. Lloyd George decree that every mistress was to be a tax-gatherer? Not only had she to collect his tax, but she had to decide on whose shoulders that tax should fall, with a moral, but no legal power to enforce her decisions.

130) *Parliamentary Debates, House of Commons,* fifth series, **XXVII** (1911), 1393–1400.

SNOWDEN ON THE NATIONAL INSURANCE BILL, 1911

The practice of requiring a direct contribution for social services has been gradually abandoned during the last thirty years, because it was both expensive and ineffective. I submit working people cannot afford to pay the contribution which is to be exacted from them under this Bill. . . .

My second objection was that it is irritating and cumber-some. I am quite sure if this Bill passes into law the compulsory deduction every week from the wages of workmen will be very much resented. I remember, when the Chancellor of the Exchequer was speaking on the Old Age Pensions Bill, and was dealing with the German system, he brushed that aside as un-English. . . . The case I shall attempt to put against imposing a direct contribution on the employer is because I feel it will prove disastrous to working men themselves. I really cannot imagine any sensible reason why an employer should be called upon to make a direct contribution for the support of his workpeople during times of sickness. The obligation to improve the condition of work-people, especially in such a matter as this, is not on the employer, it is on the community, and to put the obligation of supporting his workpeople during sickness on the employer is going back to the days of the patriarchs. . . . We are told that the Chancellor of the Exchequer cannot find the money. Of course he can do so, if he is so disposed. . . . The right hon. Gentleman told us, during his speech in introducing the Bill that during the tenure of office of this Government £12,000,000 had been added to our naval expenditure. The right hon. Gentleman had no difficulty in finding that money, and it would be just as easy for him to find money for this purpose as it is to find it for the purposes of destroying life. . . . He had an interview with some Socialists a few weeks ago, and in the course of his conversation with them he stated that it would mean an Income Tax of 7d. in the £ if the State assumed entire responsibility for this. He is going to place upon the employers under this Bill a sum which eventually will be equal to 3d. or 4d. in the £ of Income Tax at the present rate of the yield of Income Tax. Therefore it would not make any difference to the employer if he paid directly in his Income Tax, but in putting it upon the Income Tax and upon Death Duties it will be much more difficult to shift the incidence of such a tax. It would be then not a tax upon the cost of production. It would be a tax on property. . . .

I am quite sure if the Bill passes into law the agitation in favour of a non-contributory scheme will grow in volume, and that within the next generation we shall do what we have done in regard to national education and other services which have come to be recognised as national in their character, and the State will accept entire responsibility and will spread the burden as equitably as possible over every section of the community.

131) D. Lloyd George, *The Rural Land Problem* (Liberal Publication Dept., 1913).

LLOYD GEORGE SPEECH AT BEDFORD, OCTOBER 1913

Landlordism is the greatest of all monopolies in this land. Not only is it the greatest of all monopolies, it is the least controlled of all monopolies. I want to know the reason why, and I think the time has come to inquire. . . . I wonder how many people there are who realise what gigantic powers those who own the land possess upon the life of the nation. The Sovereign of this Empire has no power over his subjects comparable to the power which the landlord has over his subjects. What can he do? The landowner can devastate the countryside. He can sweep every cottage away and convert it into a wilderness. He can do what no foreign invader is permitted to do now by the laws of civilised warfare—destroy cottages and drive the peasantry away to exile, convert the land into a desert. He can do more than a foreign enemy. Even in the old barbarous days of warfare, the moment the invader had retired the peasants returned to their homes, rebuilt their cottages, tilled their land, and the country assumed its normal appearance of industry and of thrift. Landlordism can by legal process not merely ordain a wilderness, it can maintain a wilderness. . . .

The workman is worse off than he used to be. There was a time when he had an interest in the land—a freehold interest. The labourer was a freeholder in the land. He had his commons. There he could graze a cow to give him butter and milk for himself and his children. There was a little patch where he could raise corn to feed them. There he had his poultry, his geese, his pigs—a patch of land where he could raise green produce for his table. He was a gentleman. He was independent. He had a stake in the country. His title was as ancient and apparently as indefensible as that of the lord of the manor. Where has it gone to? Stolen! Landlord Parliaments have annexed Naboth's vineyard. There is now occasionally a little garden. Sometimes, as a matter of grace, he has a little row of potatoes, but he has no longer a right in the soil as his fathers had. He has been converted from a contented, well-fed, independent peasant to a hopeless, underpaid, landless drudge on the soil.

His wages are less to-day in proportion to their purchasing power than they were in the reign of Henry the Seventh.

That is what we have done with him, and the land system is responsible for it. The labourer has no real access to the owner of the soil, and the responsibility must lie with the owner. . . . Land ownership is not merely an ownership; it is a steward-ship. How idle it is to talk about the ownership of land as if it were something you were putting your money in and had no responsibility for! Land ownership has always through its history been established, maintained, and continued as stewardship for the State of that particular plot of British soil. It is enforced by ownership. Ownership is its condition. Ownership is its reward. In essence it is a trust. The land-owners of England are responsible not merely for the farmers that till their soil, but for the labourers as well. . . .

It is not enough to deal with the state of things temporarily and tentatively. You must deal with it thoroughly. You must do what business-men do. When a business gets into a thoroughly bad condition through long years of mismanage-ment, it is no use tinkering here and mending there. You must recast it and put it on a thoroughly good basis and deal boldly with it. . . .

Walking along the principal streets of our great cities you will see displayed advertisements calling attention to the allurements of Canada, Australia, and New Zealand, for British labour. There you will find a picture of a nice home, with most beautiful surroundings. . . . Do you know when the land question will be settled in England, and Scotland and Wales? It will be when similar advertisements, setting forth the attractions of settlement on British soil will be displayed in some of the most prominent windows of the streets of every city and town in the land.

132)   Lloyd George/C. P. Scott conversation on the land campaign, 16 January 1913 (British Museum Add. Mss. 5091).

He would not however start on his campaign till he had £50,000 at his back. For it was not a case for speeches alone; the country must be flooded with pamphlets and relevant facts. Asked how long the campaign could be effectively kept up he said he thought as much as two years. No attempt should at first be made to formulate a scheme of reforms, but the evils of the existing conditions should be explained and enforced and out of the discussions thus raised a scheme of reform could gradually be evolved.

But he was already clear as to the general lines on which it should proceed. (1) Wages of agricultural labourer must be raised. 14/- to 18/- a week was not a living wage. This was already recognised in the fact that the labourer was not asked to pay an economic rent for his cottage. There must be a minimum wage and this would help to solve (2) the Housing question. This was vital. Present conditions as shown e.g. in report of Diocesan Committee for diocese of Carlisle, make decency and morality practically impossible. A case of 14 people of all ages living practically in one room and girl of 14 pregnant. These horrors difficult to speak of in public but it must be done. (3) The Use of the Land in the public interest. At present three dominant objects of landlord class were first Power, then Amenity, last profitable use of the land in the public interest. The order must be reversed.

He touched on two points (a) Game Preserving. Sport in the old style was all right where a man was content to follow the dogs and come back with a modest bag but the battue with all that it involved was a monstrosity and bred mischief. (b) The system, almost universal in England, of annual tenancies was inconsistent with good husbandry. In farming a man ought to be able to look ten years ahead and to have full security. The evidence already in his hands on all these matters was overwhelming. It was directed not against individuals but against a system.

His Personal Position. He had no idea now, as he had when I last saw him, of leaving the Cabinet in order to have a free hand. He counted confidently on carrying the Cabinet with him. There were of course people in the party who in their hearts hated all reforms and he constantly came across nominal Liberals whose one cry was 'Why not let it alone?' They did not realise that for Liberalism stagnation was death. The worst kind of Tory was the nominal Liberal.

CHAPTER ELEVEN

Labour versus Capital

Conflict between labour and capital was welcomed as inevitable by Edwardian socialist theorists (133). Though most Edwardian workmen were little interested in theory, the pressures and aspirations of everyday life made many of them willing to strike, chiefly for higher wages (134, 135). Hostility towards the ruling and owning classes was intensified by the Taff Vale (136) and Osborne judgements (137), threatening the legal position of trade unions. An extreme industrial policy was offered by the syndicalist authors of *The Miners' Next Step* (138), a policy which was misleadingly publicized as posing a serious threat of revolution in Britain (139). The guild socialists subsequently offered a rather less strident English version of syndicalism (140). *The Times* attempted a well-meaning discussion of 'labour's share' and 'the living wage', but came only to a meaningless conclusion, reflecting the bafflement of upper- and middle-class opinion at the confusion of strikes, demands and aspirations (141). One thing was certain, emphasized H. G. Wells, 'the slack days for rulers and owners are over' (135).

133) G. D. H. Cole, *The World of Labour* (Bell, 1913), 285–8.

In these 'pacifist' days, the word 'war' has an ugly sound. 'Peace', on the other hand, sounds sweetly on a modern ear: 'peace', 'love' and 'brotherhood' are surely what we are all out to realise. How nice then to realise them here and now! Social peace! A country without strikes! Co-partnership and co-operation of worker and employer! How delightful, and how soothing to the troubled social conscience!

When all this is hypocrisy, it is bad enough; when it is mere stupidity, it is even worse. There are, unfortunately, people who really believe in social peace from disinterested motives, and are earnestly engaged in its furtherance. They have been deceived by the nonsensical or hypocritical talk of those who pretend that 'the interests of Capital and Labour are identical', and that all that is needed is 'a better understanding of economic truths on both sides'—especially on the side of Labour. Let it be understood once for all that the interests of Capital and Labour are diametrically opposed, and that although it may be necessary for Labour sometimes to acquiesce in 'social peace', such peace is only the lull before the storm.

Proposals for conciliation, arbitration, State interference in Labour disputes and the like, are almost always made in the name of 'social peace'. Strikes affect the public as well as the masters and workers directly concerned; they affect other masters and, still more nearly, other workers. There is on this account a *prima facie* case in favour of all attempts to put an end to strikes and lock-outs, and this *prima facie* case is run for all it is worth by the capitalist press, whenever a big strike occurs. Before, however, we need accept any argument based on this line of reasoning, on the inconvenience caused to the public, the 'consumer', by industrial disputes, there are certain general considerations we may take into account. The employer runs his business for a profit: therefore it is to the employer's advantage to keep his business going, that is, to avoid strikes. It may be answered that the worker lives by selling his labour, and that it must be to his advantage always to find a buyer: but the crucial difference between them is that Capital exploits while Labour is exploited. If both started fair, they would have an equal interest in securing smooth running and avoiding unnecessary friction; but as it is, one starts with everything, and the other with nothing. The worker has gradually to gain, by his own efforts, the position in which he should, in fairness, have been all along. The worker is on the offensive; the capitalist is only trying to keep his place, though he seems, from the rise in profits and the fall in real wages, to be doing rather more than that just at present. The continuance of the *status quo* is, then, the capitalist's constant object, and it follows that a continued state of 'social peace' is just what suits him most, and the worker least. 'Social peace' is a sham and a trick; how far 'social truces' may be necessary in the social war we shall see later on.

What is here being attacked is not the habit of negotiation between the Unions and the employers, but the attempt to represent the success of this negotiation as implying that the interests of both parties are the same. It proves, at most, only the superiority of a disciplined campaign over guerilla warfare. As we have seen, industrial diplomacy, the use of collective bargaining, may and usually does amount merely to a trial of strength, or of estimated strength, between the parties concerned. The avoidance of conflict by such means may be highly desirable, whereas the abandonment of the method of collective bargaining involved in arbitration and in a good deal of conciliation is certainly not so.

In asking, then, whether either conciliation or arbitration is desirable at all, we shall be asking not whether the Labour movement can be drugged into accepting a 'social peace' based on the present system, but whether the recognition of the class-struggle implies war to the death without truce or negotiation. We shall find that, though there is a real class-war, the whole social system does not rest solely upon it, and that, provided the Labour movement keeps its ultimate revolutionary aim clearly in sight, it will get on far better with discipline than without it—far better by negotiating as well as striking than by striking alone. Conciliation, *backed by the threat of a strike*, has a very useful function; conciliation that is disguised arbitration is Capital's latest sleeping-draught for Labour. The arguments for truceless war are very largely arguments really against compulsory arbitration, sectional and long agreements, and veiled arbitration. Get rid of all these, and the residuum of pure conciliation is a useful method of saving strike pay and suffering.

Industrial peace, then, must not be permanent. There is a real class-antagonism, a quarrel that can only be adjusted by the overthrow of capitalist society. The fact that strikes inconvenience the public and are 'brutal' in their effects is an argument, not for prohibiting strikes, but for altering the social system. A public that acquiesces in exploitation has no rights against workers who are up in arms against it: the State has no right to intervene *as an impartial person*. The State should represent the moral sense of the community, and for the moral sense of the community to be 'impartial' in the great war between justice and injustice is for it to forfeit its right as a community.

134) B. S. Rowntree, *The Way to Industrial Peace and the Problem of Unemployment* (Fisher Unwin, 1914), 8–12.

A SAMPLE OF THE DISCONTENTED

Picture a young labourer with wife and three or four children dependent on him. He is of ordinary intelligence and has some acquaintance, often fairly accurate, though gleaned from fiction and the evening paper, with what life may be under more favourable circumstances. Think of him as he returns after work to the one living-room of his badly furnished house, perhaps clean, perhaps the reverse, half the week redolent of washing day; the older children playing in the streets for want of a better playground, the younger clamouring around his wife, who is harassed, anæmic, and prematurely old —although in years no older than the lovely heroine of his newspaper serial. Follow his train of thought. His wage, say 25*s.* (about a third of the adult male workers in the United Kingdom receive no more, while over one-tenth have less than a pound a week) is only sufficient to pay for the necessities of physical efficiency, even when work is quite regular. If he would indulge in the slightest luxury—buy his children nice clothes for the Whit Monday procession, or take his wife to the theatre or a concert—he can, if he has as many as three children dependent on him, only do so at the cost of physical efficiency. 'The poor have no exchequer except the exchequer of the belly.'

The children are growing rapidly, and need more food and clothes year by year. If ever he has to stay off work through illness, or loses his job, they face starvation. His younger brothers who occasionally helped when times were bad, are all married now, and have children of their own. The cheap furniture bought at marriage, and paid off on the instalment plan, is getting very shaky, and will soon be worthless. The clock, the china tea-service, and other simple wedding presents were pawned when he was off work last winter for a few weeks with 'blood-poisoning' and will never be redeemed. He may have spent a few pence in the week on tobacco and beer; he may have lent a 'bob' occasionally to a mate who was worse off than himself; he may have taken his wife for a holiday in the first year of their marriage, but he can think of no serious extravagance with which to reproach himself.

Perhaps our friend has attended a health lecture, and learned the value of light and air, and he may know of a cottage to let which has a little garden, at a rent not much higher than he is paying now. He could grow a few vegetables, and the children would soon be 'different beings.' But how could he get a bicycle, even a second-hand one, to carry him to and from his work? There is something still owing at 'the corner shop', that trusted them during his illness.

Again, he may possibly have to read about the nutriment necessary to maintain the body in full physical efficiency, and whether he has read about it or not, he knows quite well that he and his are inadequately fed, in spite of all his wife's economies. Then he reads of the immense growth of the national wealth—from £8,548,000,000 in 1875 to £13,986,000,000 in 1905, and sees on every hand the increase of luxury. What wonder if the doctrine of discontent finds in him a ready echo? This doctrine is preached to him by every reformer, or would-be reformer, whether his motto be 'tariff reform and higher wages,' 'tax the land and free the people,' or 'socialism and plenty for all.' As years go by, and matters do not improve, his discontent becomes more firmly rooted, and when the day comes for decision, he will be one of the many men determined to 'down tools,' even if the issue of the conflict be very doubtful, and his accredited leader deprecates hasty action.

135)   H. G. Wells, 'The Labour Unrest' in *What the Worker Wants* (Hodder & Stoughton, 1912), 9–11.

A new generation of workers is seen replacing the old, workers of a quality unfamiliar to the middle-aged and elderly men who still manage our great businesses and political affairs. The worker is beginning now to strike for unprecedented ends —against the system, against the fundamental conditions of labour, to strike for no defined ends at all, perplexingly and disconcertingly. The old-fashioned strike was a method of bargaining, clumsy and violent perhaps, but bargaining still; the new-fashioned strike is far less of a haggle, far more of a display of temper. The first thing that has to be realised if the Labour question is to be understood at all is this, that

THE TEMPER OF LABOUR HAS CHANGED

altogether in the last twenty or thirty years. Essentially that is a change due to intelligence not merely increased but greatly stimulated, to the work, that is, of the board schools and of the cheap Press. The outlook of the workman has passed beyond the works and his beer and his dog. He has become— or, rather, he has been replaced by—a being of eyes, however imperfect, and of criticism, however hasty and unjust. The working man to-day reads, talks, has general ideas and a sense of the round world; he is far nearer to the ruler of to-day in knowledge and intellectual range than he is to the working man of fifty years ago. The politician or business magnate of to-day is no better educated and very little better informed than his equals were fifty years ago. The chief difference is golf. The working man questions a thousand things his father accepted as in the very nature of the world, and among others he begins to ask with the utmost alertness and persistence why it is that he in particular is expected to toil. The answer, the only justifiable answer, should be that that is the work for which he is fitted by his inferior capacity and culture, that these others are a special and select sort, very specially trained and prepared for their responsibilities, and that at once brings this new fact of a working-class criticism of social values into play. The old workman might and did quarrel very vigorously with his specific employer, but he never set out to arraign all employers; he took the law and the Church and State craft and politics for the higher and noble things they claimed to be. He wanted an extra shilling or he wanted an hour of leisure, and that was as much as he wanted. The young workman, on the other hand, has put the

WHOLE SOCIAL SYSTEM UPON ITS TRIAL

and seems quite disposed to give an adverse verdict. He looks far beyond the older conflict of interests between employer and employed. He criticises the good intentions of the whole system of governing and influential people, and not only their good intentions but their ability. These are the new conditions, and these middle-aged and elderly gentlemen who are dealing with the crisis on the supposition that their vast experience of Labour questions in the 'seventies and 'eighties furnishes valuable guidance in this present issue are merely bringing the gunpowder of misapprehension to the revolutionary fort. . . .

HOW IS CONFIDENCE TO BE RESTORED?

The real task before a governing class that means to go on governing is not just at present to get the better of an argument or the best of a bargain, but to lay hold of the imaginations of this drifting, sullen, and suspicious multitude, which is the working body of the country. What we prosperous people, who have nearly all the good things of life and most of the opportunity, have to do now is to justify ourselves. We have to show that we are indeed responsible and serviceable, willing to give ourselves, and to give ourselves generously, for what we have and what we have had. We have to meet the challenge of this distrust.

The slack days for rulers and owners are over. If there are still to be rulers and owners and managing and governing people, then in the face of the new masses, sensitive, intelligent, critical, irritable, as no common people have ever been before, these rulers and owners must be prepared to make themselves and display themselves wise, capable, and heroic—beyond any aristocratic precedent. The alternative, if it is an alternative is resignation—to the Social Democracy.

136)   *1901, The Law Reports, House of Lords* (Council of Law Reporting, 1901), 438–40.

TAFF VALE DECISION (LORD MACNAGHTEN)

The substantial question, therefore, as Farwell J. put it, is this: Has the Legislature authorized the creation of numerous bodies of men capable of owning great wealth and of acting by agents with absolutely no responsibility for the wrongs they may do to other persons by the use of that wealth and the employment of those agents? In my opinion, Parliament has done nothing of the kind. I cannot find anything in the Acts of 1871 and 1876, or either of them, from beginning to end, to warrant or suggest such a notion. It is perhaps satisfactory to find that nothing of the sort was contemplated by the minority of the members of the Royal Commission on Trade Unions, whose views found acceptance with the Legislature. In paragraph 4 of their report they say: 'It should be specially provided that except so far as combinations are thereby exempted from criminal prosecution nothing should affect . . . the liability of every person to be sued at law or in equity in respect of any damage which may have been occasioned to any other person through the act or default of the person so sued.' (1) Now, if the liability of every person in this respect was to be preserved, it would seem to follow that it was intended by the strongest advocates of trade unionism that persons should be liable for concerted as well as for individual action; and for this purpose it seems to me that it cannot matter in the least whether the persons acting in concert be combined together in a trade union, or collected and united under any other form of association.

Then, if trade unions are not above the law, the only remaining question, as it seems to me, is one of form. How are these bodies to be sued? I have no doubt whatever that a trade union, whether registered or unregistered, may be sued in a representative action if the persons selected as defendants be persons who, from their position, may be taken fairly to represent the body. . . .

The further question remains: May a registered trade union be sued in and by its registered name? For my part, I cannot see any difficulty in the way of such a suit. It is quite true that a registered trade union is not a corporation, but it has a registered name and a registered office. The registered name is nothing more than a collective name for all the members. The registered office is the place where it carries on business. A partnership firm which is not a corporation, nor, I suppose, a legal entity, may now be sued in the firm's name. And when I find that the Act of Parliament actually provides for a registered trade union being sued in certain cases for penalties by its registered name, as a trade union, and does not say that the cases specified are the only cases in which it may be so sued, I can see nothing contrary to principle, or contrary to the provisions of the Trade Union Acts, in holding that a trade union may be sued by its registered name.

I am, therefore, of opinion that the appeal should be allowed and the judgment of Farwell J. restored with costs, here and below.

137)   *1910, The Law Reports, House of Lords* (Council of Law
Reporting, 1910), 94, 97, 114–15.

THE OSBORNE JUDGEMENT

Lord Macnaghten,

It is a broad and general principle that companies incorporated by statute for special purposes, and societies, whether
incorporated or not, which owe their constitution and their
status to an Act of Parliament, having their objects and powers
defined thereby, cannot apply their funds to any purpose
foreign to the purposes for which they were established, or
embark on any undertaking in which they were not intended
by Parliament to be concerned. . . .

It can hardly be contended that a political organization is
not a thing very different from a combination for trade
purposes. There is nothing in any of the Trade Union Acts
from which it can be reasonably inferred that trade unions, as
defined by Parliament, were ever meant to have the power
of collecting and administering funds for political purposes. . . .

Lord Shaw,

In brief, my opinion accordingly is: The proposed additional
rule of the society that 'all candidates shall sign and respect
the conditions of the Labour party, and be subject to their
"whip,"' the rule that candidates are to be 'responsible to
and paid by the society,' and, in particular, the provision in
the constitution of the Labour party that 'candidates and
members must accept this constitution, and agree to abide by
the decision of the parliamentary party in carrying out the aims
of this constitution,' are all fundamentally illegal, because they
are in violation of that sound public policy which is essential to
the working of representative government.

Parliament is summoned by the Sovereign to advise His
Majesty freely. By the nature of the case it is implied that
coercion, constraint, or a money payment, which is the price of
voting at the bidding of others, destroys or imperils that
function of freedom of advice which is fundamental in the very
constitution of Parliament. Inter alia, the Labour party pledge
is such a price, with its accompaniments of unconstitutional
and illegal constraint or temptation.

Further, the pledge is an unconstitutional and unwarrant-
able interference with the rights of the constituencies of the

United Kingdom. The Corrupt Practices Acts, and the proceedings of Parliament before such Acts were passed, were but machinery to make effective the fundamental rule that the electors, in the exercise of their franchise, are to be free from coercion, constraint, or corrupt influence; and it is they, acting through their majority, and not any outside body having money power, that are charged with the election of a representative, and with the judgment on the question of his continuance as such.

Still further, in regard to the member of Parliament himself, he too is to be free; he is not to be the paid mandatory of any man, or organization of men, nor is he entitled to bind himself to subordinate his opinions on public questions to others, for wages, or at the peril of pecuniary loss; and any contract of this character would not be recognized by a Court of law, either for its enforcement or in respect of its breach.

138) Unofficial Reform Committee, *The Miners' Next Step* (Davies, printer, Tonypandy, 1912), 28–30.

The Elimination of the Employer

This can only be obtained gradually and in one way. We cannot get rid of employers and slave-driving in the mining industry, until all other industries have organized for, and progressed towards, the same objective. Their rate of progress conditions ours, all we can do is to set an example and the pace.

Nationalization of Mines

Does not lead in this direction, but simply makes a National Trust, with all the force of the Government behind it, whose one concern will be, to see that the industry is run in such a way, as to pay the interest on the bonds, with which the Coalowners are paid out, and to extract as much more profit as possible, in order to relieve the taxation of other landlords and capitalists.

Our only concern is to see to it, that those who create the value receive it. And if by the force of a more perfect organization and more militant policy, we reduce profits, we shall at the same time tend to eliminate the shareholders who own the coalfield. As they feel the increasing pressure we shall be bringing on their profits, they will loudly cry for Nationaliza-

tion. We shall and must strenuously oppose this in our own
interests, and in the interests of our objective.

Industrial Democracy the objective

To-day the shareholders own and rule the coalfields. They
own and rule them mainly through paid officials. The men
who work in the mine are surely as competent to elect these,
as shareholders who may never have seen a colliery. To have
a vote in determining who shall be your fireman, manager,
inspector, etc., is to have a vote in determining the conditions
which shall rule your working life. On that vote will depend
in a large measure your safety of life and limb, of your freedom
from oppression by petty bosses, and would give you an
intelligent interest in, and control over your conditions of
work. To vote for a man to represent you in Parliament, to
make rules for, and assist in appointing officials to rule you, is
a different proposition altogether.

Our objective begins to take shape before your eyes. Every
industry thoroughly organized, in the first place, to fight, to
gain control of, and then to administer, that industry. The
co-ordination of all industries on a Central Production Board,
who, with a statistical department to ascertain the needs of
the people, will issue its demands on the different departments
of industry, leaving to the men themselves to determine under
what conditions and how, the work should be done. This
would mean real democracy in real life, making for real
manhood and womanhood. Any other form of democracy is a
delusion and a snare.

Every fight for, and victory won by the men, will inevitably
assist them in arriving at a clearer conception of the responsibilities and duties before them. It will also assist them to see,
that so long as shareholders are permitted to continue their
ownership, or the State administers on behalf of the Shareholders, slavery and oppression are bound to be the rule in
industry. And with this realization, the age-long oppression
of Labour will draw to its end. The weary sigh of the over
driven slave, pitilessly exploited and regarded as an animated
tool or beast of burden: the mediæval serf fast bound to the
soil, and life-long prisoner on his lord's domain, subject to all
the caprices of his lord's lust or anger: the modern wageslave,
with nothing but his labour to sell, selling that, with his

manhood as a wrapper, in the world's market place for a mess
of pottage: these three phases of slavery, each in their turn
inevitable and unavoidable, will have exhausted the possibilities of slavery, and mankind shall at last have leisure and
inclination to really live as men, and not as the beasts which
perish.

139) *Parliamentary Debates, House of Commons,* fifth series,
XXXVI (1912), 558–9.

GEORGE ROBERTS (LABOUR) ON SYNDICALISM

With intellectually equipped working classes you cannot
possibly keep them back. You have gone before them a
spectacle of leisured luxury. I say again that I am speaking
without malice in my heart, but I know that. I have the
experience of my own life. Of my poor old mother sitting up
night after night in order to make us boys presentable for
school. We have seen our father working into the night, in
order that he might provide us with a little schooling so that
we might get somewhat broader aspects of life. Those who are
rendering, and willing to render, honest toil should be able to
get a fair and decent livelihood. That is a question that you
must ask yourselves, and that you have got to answer if you
desire to get rid of this unrest which has manifested itself, as I
recognise and regret, in a fashion that I do not sanction, which
I strongly regret—the Syndicalism that has been made the
subject of our speeches to-night. If we are to rid this nation of
the enemy, as you have called it, of Syndicalism, you will have
to remove its causes. Those causes are poverty, low wages,
and those incidental miseries which affect the working classes
at the present time.

140) A. R. Orage (ed.), *National Guilds, an Inquiry into the
Wage System and the Way Out* (Bell, 1914), v–vi, 281–3.

Both the present Editor of *The New Age* in an article in the
Contemporary Review of 1906, and Mr. A. J. Penty in his work
on *The Restoration of the Guild System* of the same year, put
forward the suggestion that the Guild organisation was indispensable to higher industry at any rate. The tide of Collec-
tivism, however, was then and for some years afterwards too

powerful to admit of even the smallest counter-current. Some experience of Collectivism in action and of political methods as distinct from economic methods was necessary before the mind of the Labour movement could be turned in another direction. This was brought about by the impulse known as Syndicalism which, in essence, is the demand of Labour to control its industry. At the same time that Syndicalism came to be discussed, a revival of trade-union activity took place, and on such a scale that it seemed to the present writers that at last the trade unions were now finally determined to form a permanent element in society. In short, every speculation concerning the future of industry was henceforward bound to take into account the trade unions as well as the State. Reflecting upon this in the light of a considerable experience, both theoretical and practical, the writers were driven to the conclusions herein stated. In no respect, they believe, have they written 'without their book' or in the spirit of Utopianism. The analysis of the nature of wages, here made, for the first time, the foundation of a critique of labour economics, leads inevitably to the conclusion that by no manner of means can wages generally be raised while the wage system continues. There follows from that the necessity, in the minds of real reformers at any rate, to consider the means by which the wage system itself may be abolished, in the interests, in the first instance, of the proletariat, but no less, though secondarily, in the interests of society and of civilisation. The indispensability of the State, upon which the present writers lay stress the more that the Syndicalists deny it, is affirmed and maintained at the same time that the right of Labour to control its production is throughout assumed. In the conception of National Industrial Guilds the writers believe that the future will find the solution of the problems now vexing one-twentieth of our population and ruining the remainder. . . .

Just as we anticipate a peaceful acceptance of the Guild organisation by other countries, when once it has been established in Great Britain, so also do we anticipate the final capitulation of the profiteers in our own country. After all, what have they to fight with. Against the united decision of labour never again to sell itself as a commodity how can they contend? Would they import foreign labour? Where are the ships which would bring it across the sea? If they contrived a shipload or two of foreign blacklegs, how would this help?

Falling back upon their undoubted legal rights to the instruments of production and distribution, what could they do? Force starvation upon the population? That would not help them; their dividends would be gone beyond redemption, and their property would be valued as scrap iron. No; undoubtedly they would seek for some compromise. They would adopt a policy of wise salvage. For our part, we would help them in this. We have already suggested that in exchange for their present possession of land and machinery, the State might give them, as rough-and-ready justice, an equable income either for a fixed period of years or to two generations. Actuarially, it would probably not matter which course were adopted. But all these probabilities do not absolve the unions from adopting more modern methods of industrial warfare. Strike pay to the individual, based upon contributions, must give way to rations based upon the size of each family affected by any dispute, small or great. And in every dispute the workers must decline to recognise the fundamental distinction between rent and profit. If the profiteers force industrial war, then let the warmongers suffer with them. Therefore we have advised the strikers to make it a fixed rule that during a strike or lock-out no rent must be paid, nor must the arrears be paid when peace has been proclaimed. The logic of our argument leads to another important conclusion. If wagery be the enemy, then it is futile to strike merely for some modification of it. Every strike, therefore, should specifically aim at a change of status. In practice, that means at some form of partnership. And the Guild theory involves partnership in industry by the unions and not by the individual members. In no circumstances must the individual members of the unions be permitted to detach themselves from their natural and economic affiliation by isolated profit-sharing arrangements. Not only would such a course of action dissipate the strength of the unions, but it would perpetuate wealth, interest and profits, when the true union policy must be to absorb them.

141)   *The Times*, 11 September 1911.

LEADING ARTICLE HEADED 'LABOUR'S SHARE'

Some questions and answers passed on Friday at the Railway Inquiry which touch, very lightly and briefly but distinctly, the general problem lying at the root of all the present turmoil and of much else beside. A witness expressed the opinion that labour should be paid before a dividend is declared; and, on being asked if he thought the public would be encouraged to find money for railway purposes if there were no reasonable prospect of getting any return, he replied that if trains could not be run to pay labour adequately they should not be run at all. The witness was not prepared to follow the line of reasoning any further; but it must be followed, if any solution of the great problem of our time is to be found. That problem is the equitable distribution of wealth. The civilized world, having discovered, developed, and applied the means of creating wealth without end, is now engaged in trying to determine its distribution on right principles. All the social and political movements which distinguish our age—trade unions, strikes, labour legislation, the advance of democracy, innumerable 'isms', societies and organizations, investigations and inquiries public and private, the collection of statistics, modern forms of taxation and of administration—all these, and a vast number of other things included in the comprehensive term 'social reform' are merely aspects or manifestations of the tremendous process of change that is going on and making for the redistribution of wealth. It began long ago, near the beginning of the last century, but it has gathered weight and speed with the increase of wealth. At first and for a long time it was a blind struggle between 'haves' and 'have nots'; but, though it still retains a good deal of that element, it is changing in character. The trouble that is now emerging is not the tenacity of the 'haves' or the weakness of the 'have nots', but the intrinsic difficulty of determining the true share of the several factors engaged in producing wealth. A feeling that the present distribution is inequitable prevails widely in all classes and is growing; but the problem of what the true distribution should be remains unsolved. . . .

Like other problems of social life, it is far too complex to fit any formula. The old simple ideas of Socialism have long since gone by the board, though the crude and obsolete proposition that labour produces all wealth is still used by Socialist agitators to delude the mob. . . . Labour's share according to this hoary fallacy is the whole of the product. A more moderate and acknowledged claim is that of the 'living wage'. But the word 'living', which sounds so convincing, conceals an ambiguity that really leaves the problem where it was. What is a living wage? It means, no doubt, such a wage as will keep the worker efficient—which implies not only an adequate supply of the necessaries of life, but also a certain degree of contentment. But these conditions vary indefinitely according to time, place, circumstance, personal qualities and current notions. In short, a living wage, when practically applied, does not differ appreciably from 'as much as he can get'. That leaves us with the question—What can he get? The answer depends on the claims of other factors, which also require a living wage. If they do not get it, they too go on strike, and betake themselves elsewhere. This fact, which seems to be very imperfectly grasped, was brought out by the remarks we have quoted from the Railway Inquiry. . . .

What, then, is labour's share? We do not know; but it cannot be so large that less than enough is left for the others.

CHAPTER TWELVE

'Votes for Women'

Some eminent Edwardian medical men believed that there was a physiological and psychological case against conceding votes to women (142). The suffragettes and suffragists countered that the exclusion of women from the Parliamentary franchise condemned them to political insignificance and to social and economic inferiority (143, 144). This was the original motivation behind the campaign of the WSPU, hence the adjective 'social' in its title (145). But in later years suffragette arguments and actions became emotional and irrational (146, 147, 148). Some anti-suffrage arguments were equally short of reason (149).

142) Letter to *The Times*, 28 March 1912 on 'Militant Hysteria' reprinted in Sir A. E. Wright, *The Unexpurgated Case Against Woman Suffrage* (Constable, 1913), 77–9.

Sir,—For man the physiological psychology of woman is full of difficulties.

He is not a little mystified when he encounters in her periodically recurring phases of hypersensitiveness, unreasonableness, and loss of the sense of proportion.

He is frankly perplexed when confronted with a complete alteration of character in a woman who is child-bearing.

When he is a witness of the 'tendency of woman to morally warp when nervously ill', and of the terrible physical havoc which the pangs of a disappointed love may work, he is appalled.

And it leaves on his mind an eerie feeling when he sees serious and long-continued mental disorders developing in connexion with the approaching extinction of a woman's reproductive faculty.

No man can close his eyes to these things; but he does not feel at liberty to speak of them.

For the woman that God gave him is not his to give away.

As for woman herself, she makes very light of any of these mental upsettings.

She perhaps smiles a little at them. . . .[1]

None the less, these upsettings of her mental equilibrium are the things that a woman has most cause to fear; and no doctor can ever lose sight of the fact that the mind of woman is always threatened with danger from the reverberations of her physiological emergencies.

It is with such thoughts that the doctor lets his eyes rest upon the militant suffragist. He cannot shut them to the fact that there is mixed up with the woman's movement much mental disorder; and he cannot conceal from himself the physiological emergencies which lie behind.

The recruiting field for the militant suffragists is the million of our excess female population—that million which had better long ago have gone out to mate with its complement of men beyond the sea.

Among them there are the following different types of women:—(a) First—let us put them first—come a class of women who hold, with minds otherwise unwarped, that they may, whenever it is to their advantage, lawfully resort to physical violence.

The programme, as distinguished from the methods, of these women is not very different from that of the ordinary suffragist woman.

(b) There file past next a class of women who have all their life-long been strangers to joy, women in whom instincts long suppressed have in the end broken into flame. These are the sexually embittered women in whom everything has turned into gall and bitterness of heart, and hatred of men.

Their legislative programme is licence for themselves, or else restrictions for man.

(c) Next there file past the incomplete. One side of their nature has undergone atrophy, with the result that they have

[1] In the interests of those who feel that female dignity is compromised by it, I have here omitted a woman's flippant overestimate of the number of women in London society who suffer from nervous disorders at the climacteric.

lost touch with their living fellow men and women.

Their programme is to convert the whole world into an epicene institution—an epicene institution in which man and woman shall everywhere work side by side at the selfsame tasks and for the selfsame pay.

These wishes can never by any possibility be realised. Even in animals—I say *even*, because in these at least one of the sexes has periods of complete quiescence—male and female cannot be safely worked side by side, except when they are incomplete.

While in the human species safety can be obtained, it can be obtained only at the price of continual constraint.

And even then woman, though she protests that she does not require it, and that she does not receive it, practically always does receive differential treatment at the hands of man.

It would be well, I often think, that every woman should be clearly told—and the woman of the world will immediately understand—that when man sets his face against the proposal to bring in an epicene world, he does so because he can do his best work only in surroundings where he is perfectly free from suggestion and from restraint, and from the onus which all differential treatment imposes.

143)   W. L. Blease, *The Emancipation of English Women* (Constable, 1910), 170–2.

To the early Suffragists and to their successors the Parliamentary franchise has thus been much more than a mere means of influencing Government. It has always appeared as a symbol of social worth. So long as it is enjoyed by men, and by them denied to women, so long must women be in a state of subjection and exposed to innumerable wrongs which are not directly connected with votes. The captain is not more clearly the superior of the soldier whom he commands than is the man that of the woman whose position in society he prescribes. It is useless to declaim upon the equal or superior worth of women, so long as men exercise their power to exclude them from any sphere of activity which they may desire to enter. It is useless, indeed, to declare that they are willing to admit women into everything except politics. The very declaration, even if it were true, is an assertion of their power and their intention to direct the lives of women not according to the wishes of women themselves, but according to their own. The exclusion from national politics would outweigh all the other privileges. Mere inability to obtain degrees at Cambridge, or to enter the legal profession, or to serve on juries, would be slight things in comparison. But in a country where politics bulk so largely as in England, disfranchisement stamps and brands the disfranchised with an indelible mark of inferiority. The person who, being an adult, is not fit to take part in English politics, will inevitably encounter all the consequences of subjection in education, in professional and industrial employments, and in social intercourse, whenever he or she has to do with those who are invested with all the dignity of citizenship. The disfranchisement of women is thus intimately connected not only with their remaining political and legal disabilities, but also with their inferior training, their narrower outlook upon life and their consequent defects of character, with their inadequate rewards for services, and with their purely sexual grievances of marital subjection and prostitution.

The man of exceptional generosity will always rise superior to his circumstances, as husbands of exceptional generosity rose superior to them before the Married Women's Property Acts. But the average man does not rise superior to his circumstances, he is always enslaved by them. To him, the woman upon whom he imposes taxes, the conditions of whose labour he prescribes, whom he may at his pleasure admit to or exclude from any occupation, high or low, whose government he controls at the same time that he prevents her from controlling it herself, must ever remain a person of inferior worth to himself. In the degree of each man's goodness or badness of disposition, he will always maltreat women, in some cases merely insulting them by condescension, in others depriving them of education, checking the development of their matured minds, or using them as the instruments of the vilest passions of himself and his associates.

144)   L. Baily, *B.B.C. Scrapbooks,* I (Allen & Unwin, 1966), 143.

MRS PANKHURST SPEECH FROM THE DOCK, BOW STREET, 1908

We shall submit to the treatment—the degrading treatment

—that we have submitted to before. Although the Government has admitted that we are political offenders we shall be treated as pickpockets and drunkards. I want you, sir, if you can, as a man, to realize what it means to women like us. We are driven to this. We are determined to go on with this agitation, because we feel it is our duty to make this world a better place for women than it is today. I have been in prison. I was in the hospital at Holloway, and when I was there I heard from one of the beds near me the moans of a woman who was in the pangs of childbirth. I should like you to realize how women feel at helpless infants breathing their first breath in the atmosphere of a prison. That woman was not guilty—she was finally acquitted. We believe that if we get the vote it will mean better conditions for our unfortunate sisters. Many women pass through this court who would not come before you if they were able to live morally and honestly. The average earnings of the women who earn their living in this country are only seven and sixpence a week. Some of us have worked for many years to help our own sex, and we have been driven to the conclusion that only through legislation can any improvement be effected, and that the legislation can never be effected until we have the same power as men to bring pressure to bear upon governments to give us the necessary legislation.

We have tried every way. We have presented larger petitions than were ever presented before for any other reform, we have succeeded in holding greater public meetings than men have ever had for any reform. We have faced hostile mobs at street corners, because we were told that we could not have that representation for our taxes which men have won unless we converted the whole country to our side. Because we have done this we have been misrepresented, we have been ridiculed, we have had contempt poured upon us.

No, sir, I do say deliberately to you that I come here not as an ordinary law-breaker. I should never be here if I had the same kind of laws that the very meanest and commonest of men have—the same power that the wife-beater has, the same power that the drunkard has. This is the only way we have to get that power which every citizen should have of deciding how the taxes she contributes to should be made, and until we get that power we shall be here. We are here today, and we shall come here over and over again. If you had the power to send us to prison, not for six months but for six years, or for the whole of our lives, the Government must not think that they can stop this agitation. It will go on. We are going to win.

Well, sir, that is all I have to say to you. We are not here because we are law-breakers, we are here in our efforts to become law-*makers*!

145)   Emmeline Pankhurst, *My Own Story* (Eveleigh Nash, 1914), 51–3, 57, 61–2.

This was the beginning of a campaign the like of which was never known in England, or, for that matter, in any other country. If we had been strong enough we should have opposed the election of every Liberal candidate, but being limited both in funds and in members we concentrated on one member of the Government, Mr. Winston Churchill. Not that we had any animus against Mr. Churchill. We chose him simply because he was the only important candidate standing for constituencies · within reach of our headquarters. We attended every meeting addressed by Mr. Churchill. We heckled him unmercifully; we spoiled his best points by flinging back such obvious retorts that the crowds roared with laughter. We lifted out little white banners from unexpected corners of the hall, exactly at the moment when an interruption was least desired. Sometimes our banners were torn from our hands and trodden under foot. Sometimes, again, the crowds were with us, and we actually broke up the meeting. We did not succeed in defeating Mr. Churchill, but he was returned by a very small majority, the smallest of any of the Manchester Liberal candidates.

We did not confine our efforts to heckling Mr. Churchill. Throughout the campaign we kept up the work of questioning Cabinet Ministers at meetings all over England and Scotland. At Sun Hall, Liverpool, addressed by the Prime Minister, nine women in succession asked the important question, and were thrown out of the hall; this in the face of the fact that Sir Campbell-Bannerman was an avowed suffragist. But we were not questioning him as to his private opinions on the suffrage; we were asking him what his Government were willing to do about suffrage. We questioned Mr. Asquith in Sheffield, Mr. Lloyd-George in Altrincham, Cheshire, the Prime Minister again in Glasgow, and we interrupted a great many other meetings as well. Always we were violently thrown out and insulted. Often we were painfully bruised and hurt.

What good did it do? We have often been asked that question, even by the women our actions spurred into an activity they had never before thought themselves capable of. For one thing, our heckling campaign made women's suffrage a matter of news—it had never been that before. Now the newspapers were full of us. For another thing, we woke up the old suffrage associations. During the general election various groups of non-militant suffragists came back to life and organised a gigantic manifesto in favour of action from the Liberal Government. Among others, the manifesto was signed by the Women's Co-operative Guild with nearly 21,000 members; the Women's Liberal Federation, with 76,000 members; the Scottish Women's Liberal Federation, with 15,000 members; the North-of-England Weavers' Association, with 100,000 members; the British Women's Temperance Association, with nearly 110,000 members; and the Independent Labour Party with 20,000 members. Surely it was something to have inspired all this activity.

We decided that the next step must be to carry the fight to London, and Annie Kenney was chosen to be organiser there. . . .

To account for the phenomenal growth of the Women's Social and Political Union after it was established in London, to explain why it made such an instant appeal to women hitherto indifferent, I shall have to point out exactly wherein our society differs from all other suffrage associations. In the first place, our members are absolutely single minded; they concentrate all their forces on one object, political equality with men. No member of the W.S.P.U. divides her attention between suffrage and other social reforms. We hold that both reason and justice dictate that women shall have a share in reforming the evils that afflict society, especially those evils bearing directly on women themselves. Therefore, we demand, before any other legislation whatever, the elementary justice of votes for women.

There is not the slightest doubt that the women of Great Britain would have been enfranchised years ago had all the suffragists adopted this simple principle. They never did, and even to-day many English women refuse to adopt it. They are party members first and suffragists afterward; or they are suffragists part of the time and social theorists the rest of the time. . . .

The contention of the old-fashioned suffragists, and of the politicians as well, has always been that an educated public opinion will ultimately give votes to women without any great force being exerted in behalf of the reform. We agree that public opinion must be educated, but we contend that even an educated public opinion is useless unless it is vigorously utilised. The keenest weapon is powerless unless it is courageously wielded. In the year 1906 there was an immensely large public opinion in favour of woman suffrage. But what good did that do the cause? We called upon the public for a great deal more than sympathy. We called upon it to demand of the Government to yield to public opinion and give women votes. And we declared that we would wage war, not only on all anti-suffrage forces, but on all neutral and non-active forces. Every man with a vote was considered a foe to woman suffrage unless he was prepared to be actively a friend.

Not that we believed that the campaign of education ought to be given up. On the contrary, we knew that education must go on, and in much more vigorous fashion than ever before. The first thing we did was to enter upon a sensational campaign to arouse the public to the importance of woman suffrage, and to interest it in our plans for forcing the Government's hands. I think we can claim that our success in this regard was instant, and that it has proved permanent. From the very first, in those early London days, when we were few in numbers and very poor in purse, we made the public aware of the woman suffrage movement as it had never been before. We adopted Salvation Army methods and went out into the highways and the byways after converts. We threw away all our conventional notions of what was 'ladylike' and 'good form,' and we applied to our methods the one test question, Will it help? Just as the Booths and their followers took religion to the street crowds in such fashion that the church people were horrified, so we took suffrage to the general public in a manner that amazed and scandalised the other suffragists.

146)   C. P. Scott's account of a conversation with Lloyd
        George on the suffragettes, 2 December 1911 (British
        Museum Add. Mss. 50901).

We talked almost entirely of the Women's Suffrage movement and the damage done to it by the militant outrages. I
regretted Grey's letter in yesterday's paper practically throwing up the sponge if there should be a continuance of these
proceedings, and said I supposed it was written from a sense of
loyalty (exaggerated as I thought) to Asquith on his being
attacked by the militants—a non suffragist by suffragists—and
was glad to hear that this was the case since it gave the letter
only an incidental importance. As a matter of fact the militants
did not attack Asquith as an anti-suffragist at all and liked him
better than many of the suffragist members of the Government, but simply as a member of the Government. 'But what
can they hope to achieve by attacking him?', he asked, 'they
can't expect to make him change his mind'. 'Oh! yes, they do;
they are quite hopeful of converting him'. (I had this the
previous day from Brailsford). 'Then they must be mad'.
'They are mad, Christabel Pankhurst has lost all sense of
proportion and of reality'. 'It's just like going to a lunatic
asylum', said George, 'and talking to a man who thinks he's
God Almighty'. 'Yes, very much like that.'
    Afterwards we discussed what should be done. I urged that
the militants should be ignored and the suffrage campaign
pressed on as though they didn't exist. 'That's all very well for
us', said George, 'though it's difficult. I don't mind and it
doesn't put me out much at meetings or irritate me, I'm used
to the rough and tumble and have had to fight my way, so is
Churchill (though he is sensitive about his perorations) but it's
different with Grey, he isn't accustomed to interruption and
can't do with it. But what really matters is the effect on the
audiences and on the public. At Bath I had very hard work.
The people were already irritated with previous interruptions
when I rose to speak; my task of persuasion was made very
much more difficult'. I replied that that was no doubt the case
but we were in for a fight and must go through with it. The
public would of course be furious; the problem was to turn
their fury into the right channel. At present they said 'these
people are suffragists; let us wreck the suffrage'; the reply was
'not at all; they are suffrage-wreckers; let us disappoint them'.
He agreed, but said it wasn't easy. 'Anyway,' I replied, 'it's

the best we can do; besides, after a bit people will get used to the interruptions, and when it is seen that we are going steadily on and fighting for the suffrage and that they, professed suffragists, are attacking and hindering us for doing it, the thing will become absurd and really laughable and the public will back us and help us to defeat them.' George agreed but doubted if Grey and people like that would have resolution to go through with it. 'Well, anyway,' I said, 'you've got to.' 'I see what you mean,' he replied, 'it's the compulsion of my temperament.' 'Exactly.' 'And that's the worst kind of compulsion.' So there we left it.

147) *The Times*, 7 August 1912.

LETTER FROM G. M. GODDEN ON SUFFRAGETTE LITERATURE

An examination of this literature proves the present so-called 'suffrage' movement to be deeply involved in an unnatural and indecent agitation quite distinct from purely political aims. The diffusion of such literature largely accounts, I submit, for the epidemic hysteria, with its attendant symptoms of a loss of the normal sense of decency and of the normal use of reasoning powers, now prevalent among certain sections of Englishwomen. . . .

I cannot ask you to print full quotations from these pamphlets; no paper other than the medical or scientific journals would publish such matter. But a few passages taken from the pamphlets mentioned above will suffice to justify every word. . . . Suffrage physiology teaches that 'woman's organism is more complex and her totality of function larger than those of any other thing inhabiting our earth. Therefore her position in the scale of life is the most exalted, the most sovereign one.' 'Science has abundantly proved that the male element was primarily an excrescence, a superfluity, a waste product of nature.' 'All facts point to the feminine as the primary and fundamental basis of existence.' 'Life is feminine.' These doctrines could be cited from suffrage columns *ad nauseam*. They are, moreover, disseminated from suffrage platforms and addressed to mixed audiences. To give one example: in a recent suffrage lecture at Wimbledon the speaker, a woman, asserted that 'the female part of creation was the primary, central, and fundamental element', and that 'the female was physiologically the superior of the male'.

She elaborated her point with details that the reporter evidently found unfit for publication. She then proceeded to state that it is 'to women that races and individuals owe their leading attributes', and that for centuries progress has been retarded by the 'insensate folly of man, blinded by his arrogant self-worship'. Here we have the doctrine of the superiority of woman and the inferiority and vileness of man carried to its inevitable and logical conclusion of sex war. Both the premises and the conclusion permeate the literature before me:—'No female animal has been so ruthlessly, so brutally, so generally mercilessly treated' as woman, and 'Man as a rule has not deemed his offspring worthy of the safeguard of the ape' are two of the few passages fit for quotation from an indescribable tract on gestation displayed in the suffrage shop in Kensington, and, as I have tested, sold, with no inquiry, to young girls. 'Man has sought in woman only a body.' 'From time immemorial she [woman] has served as the butt of man's contemptuous humour.' 'The suffering of woman has built the human body and the human soul'; 'man-made law' threatens 'health and home and race'. 'We need a new ethic of the sexes.' The 'whole horizon bounded by masculine limitations' must be re-made—by women. Not, be it noted, must a mere political measure of enfranchisement be passed. The so-called 'suffrage' movement affects the 'whole horizon' of religion, ethics, physiology, pathology, sociology. And herein we have the explanation of the disintegration of the whole mind and body, brain and nerves, of the victims of this teaching. As no act is too irrational for them to commit, so no statement is too absurd for them to promulgate. . . .

In literature suffrage criticism assures us that a woman wrote the Odyssey, and that Priscilla may be credited with the composition of the Epistle to the Hebrews. Suffrage theology teaches us that Adam was made of dust and to dust he will return, but that Eve was not; that, as regards the text 'male and female created He them', in 'the original the gender is here feminine, denoting Elohim the supernal Mother,' and adds, 'Woman should press for a true translation of the Bible'. It quotes approvingly the suggestion 'we have even now a new revelation, and the name of its Messiah is Woman'. . . . A mental condition which has been educated into accepting these statements is precisely that condition which confounds hammers with argument and suicide with martyrdom.

148) Christabel Pankhurst, *The Great Scourge and How to End It* (E. Pankhurst, 1913), VI–X, 99–100.

The sexual diseases are the great cause of physical, mental, and moral degeneracy, and of race suicide. As they are very widespread (from 75 to 80 per cent. of men being infected by gonorrhœa, and a considerable percentage, difficult to ascertain precisely, being infected with syphilis), the problem is one of appalling magnitude.

To discuss an evil, and then to run away from it without suggesting how it may be cured, is not the way of Suffragettes, and in the following pages will be found a proposed cure for the great evil in question. That cure, briefly stated, is Votes for Women and Chastity for Men. Quotations and opinions from eminent medical men are given, and these show that chastity for men is healthful for themselves and is imperative in the interests of the race. . . .

Regulation of vice and enforced medical inspection of the White Slaves is equally futile, and gives a false appearance of security which is fatal. Chastity for men—or, in other words, their observance of the same moral standard as is observed by women—is therefore indispensable.

Votes for Women will strike at the Great Scourge in many ways. When they are citizens women will feel a greater respect for themselves, and will be more respected by men. They will have the power to secure the enactment of laws for their protection, and to strengthen their economic position. . . .

One of the chief objects of the book is to enlighten women as to the true reason why there is opposition to giving them the vote. That reason is sexual vice.

The opponents of votes for women know that women, when they are politically free and economically strong, will not be purchasable for the base uses of vice. . . .

For several practical, common-sensible, sanitary reasons women are chary of marriage. When the best-informed and most experienced medical men say that the vast majority of men expose themselves before marriage to sexual disease, and that only an 'insignificant minority,' as the authority puts it —25 per cent. at most—escape infection; when these medical authorities further say that sexual disease is difficult, if not impossible, to cure, healthy women naturally hesitate to marry. Mr. Punch's 'advice to those about to marry—Don't!'

has a true and terrible application to the facts of the case.

Perhaps our childless and celibate Bishops may say that it is a woman's duty, faced by the prospect, if she marries, of being infected by her husband, to sacrifice herself and to marry all the same. They must not be surprised if such advice falls upon deaf ears. 'Sacrifice yourself, sacrifice yourself,' is a cry that has lost its power over women. Why should women sacrifice themselves to no purpose save that of losing their health and happiness? Now that women have learnt to think for themselves, they discover that woman, in sacrificing herself, sacrifices the race.

If the Bishops, and the whole pack of men who delight in advising, lecturing, and preaching to women, would exhort the members of their own sex to some sacrifice of their baser impulses, it would be better for the race, better for women, and better even for men.

149)   Marie Corelli, *Woman or—Suffragette? A Question of National Choice* (Pearson, 1907), 3–7.

A great question is before the country. It is this: Shall we sacrifice our Womanhood to Politics? Shall we make a holocaust of maidens, wives and mothers on the brazen altars of Party? Shall we throw open the once sweet and sacred homes of England to the manœuvres of the electioneering agent? Surely the best and bravest of us will answer No!—ten thousand times no! Rather let us use every means in our power to prevent the consummation of what would be nothing less than a national disaster. For Great Britain is already too rapidly losing many of the noble ideals and institutions which once made her the unrivalled mistress of the world; the sanctity of the private household is being exchanged for the scrambling life of public restaurants and hotels,—preachers of all creeds are reproaching women (and rightly too) for their open and gross neglect of their highest duties,—for their frivolity, waste of time, waste of money and waste of love,— the grace of hospitality, the beauty of sincerity, the art of good manners are all being forgotten under an avalanche of loose conduct and coarse speech,—and if the mothers of the British race decide to part altogether with the birthright of their simple *womanliness* for a political mess of pottage, then darker days are in store for the nation than can yet be foreseen or imagined. For with women alone rests the Home, which is the foundation of Empire. When they desert this, their God-appointed centre, the core of the national being, then things are tottering to a fall.

'Votes for women!' is the shrill cry of a number of apparently discontented ladies who somehow seem to have missed the best of life. And it is well-nigh useless to re-iterate the plain, trite truth that Woman was and is destined to *make* voters rather than to be one of them. ...

It cannot, of course, be denied that women have suffered, and still are destined to suffer, great injustice at the hands of men. But again, that is the result of the way in which mothers have reared their sons and still continue to rear them. Till they alter their rule of treatment,—which is one continuous system of spoiling, molly-coddling and baby-worship carried on into manhood,—so long must they reap what they have sown,—namely, that familiarity 'which breeds contempt.' Women have quite as good brains as men,—they can become great artists, great writers, great scientists,—that is, if they choose to practise the self-denial and endure the hardships which are the necessary accompaniments to these careers,—they might even become great musicians, if with depth of sentiment, they could also obtain self-control. ...

But sentiment apart, she always lacks the grand self-control which is the inward power of the great musician. She was born to be a creature of sweet impulses—of love—of coquetry—of tenderness—of persuasiveness,—and these things, instilled by the unconscious grace and beauty of her natural ways into the spirit of man, are no doubt the true origin of music itself—music which she *inspires*, but cannot *create*. It is the same way—to my thinking—with politics. There are certain fixed rules of Government. The Heart must not run away with the Head. The political gamut has little more than seven tones, or up and down gradations of movement,—and out of these seven must be evolved a practical working harmony for the betterment of the nation. It is largely a question of mathematics,—and woman is not—(*naturally* speaking)—a mathematician. One woman here and there may occasionally train herself to out-do the sharpest master of the science, but in the effort she will lose far more than she gains. And, as in music, so in politics,—woman's business is to illumine the background—to *inspire* the work, and let her light 'shine through' the victorious accomplishment of noble purpose.

CHAPTER THIRTEEN

Home Rule

Ireland, 'John Bull's Other Island' in the title of Shaw's play (1904) had been a trouble to its English rulers for centuries (150, 151). Yet they had remained reluctant to relax control by conceding Home Rule, which the Irish (outside Ulster) demanded (152). British Conservatives argued that Home Rule would not solve the Irish question (153), also that its enforcement would be so unjust to Protestant Ulster as to justify armed resistance (154, 155, 156). Ulstermen signed the Covenant (157), and Englishmen favourable to them produced a British Covenant (158). The Curragh 'mutiny' showed the strength of pro-Ulster feeling among many army officers (159). The Liberal Government still insisted upon Home Rule for the Catholic South (160), but by 1914 was willing to make significant concessions to Ulster (161). Agreement in detail, however, proved impossible, and towards the end of July 1914 civil war in Ireland seemed near (162).

150)   G. B. Shaw, *Prefaces* (Constable, 1934), 454–5.

PREFACE TO 'JOHN BULL'S OTHER ISLAND'

A conquered nation is like a man with cancer: he can think of nothing else, and is forced to place himself, to the exclusion of all better company, in the hands of quacks who profess to treat or cure cancer. The windbags of the two rival platforms are the most insufferable of all windbags. It requires neither knowledge, character, conscience, diligence in public affairs, nor any virtue, private or communal, to thump the Nationalist or Orange tub: nay, it puts a premium on the rancor or callousness that has given rise to the proverb that if you put an Irishman on a spit you can always get another Irishman to baste him. Jingo oratory in England is sickening enough to serious people: indeed one evening's mafficking in London produced a determined call for the police. Well, in Ireland all political oratory is Jingo oratory; and all political demonstrations are maffickings. English rule is such an intolerable abomination that no other subject can reach the people. Nationalism stands between Ireland and the light of the world. Nobody in Ireland of any intelligence likes Nationalism any more than a man with a broken arm likes having it set. A healthy nation is as unconscious of its nationality as a healthy man of his bones. But if you break a nation's nationality it will think of nothing else but getting it set again. It will listen to no reformer, to no philosopher, to no preacher, until the demand of the Nationalist is granted. It will attend to no business, however vital, except the business of unification and liberation.

That is why everything is in abeyance in Ireland pending the achievement of Home Rule. The great movements of the human spirit which sweep in waves over Europe are stopped on the Irish coast by the English guns of the Pigeon House Fort. Only a quaint little offshoot of English pre-Raphaelitism called the Gaelic movement has got a footing by using Nationalism as a stalking-horse, and popularizing itself as an attack on the native language of the Irish people, which is most fortunately also the native language of half the world, including England. Every election is fought on nationalist grounds; every appointment is made on nationalist grounds; every judge is a partisan in the nationalist conflict; every speech is a dreary recapitulation of nationalist twaddle; every lecture is a corruption of history to flatter nationalism or defame it; every school is a recruiting station; every church is a barrack; and every Irishman is unspeakably tired of the whole miserable business, which nevertheless is and perforce must remain his first business until Home Rule makes an end of it, and sweeps the nationalist and the garrison hack together into the dustbin.

There is indeed no greater curse to a nation than a nationalist movement, which is only the agonizing symptom of a suppressed natural function. Conquered nations lose their place in the world's march because they can do nothing but strive to get rid of their nationalist movements by recovering their national liberty. All demonstrations of the virtues of a foreign government, though often conclusive, are as useless as demonstrations of the superiority of artificial teeth, glass eyes, silver windpipes, and patent wooden legs to the natural products. Like Democracy, national self-government is not for the good of the people: it is for the satisfaction of the people. One Antonine emperor, one St Louis, one Richelieu, may be worth ten democracies in point of what is called good government; but there is no satisfaction for the people in them. To deprive a dyspeptic of his dinner and hand it over to a man who can digest it better is a highly logical proceeding; but it is not a sensible one. To take the government of Ireland away from the Irish and hand it over to the English on the ground that they can govern better would be a precisely parallel case if the English had managed their own affairs so well as to place their superior faculty for governing beyond question. But as the English are avowed muddlers—rather proud of it, in fact— even the logic of that case against Home Rule is not complete. Read Mr Charles Booth's account of London, Mr Rowntree's account of York, and the latest official report on Dundee; and then pretend, if you can, that Englishmen and Scotchmen have not more cause to hand over their affairs to an Irish parliament than to clamor for another nation's cities to devastate and another people's business to mismanage.

151) Yeats to Shaw, 5 October 1904 (British Museum Add. Mss. 50553).

YEATS ON 'JOHN BULL'S OTHER ISLAND'

I was disappointed by the first act and a half. The stage Irishman who wasn't an Irishman was very amusing, but then I said to myself 'What the devil did Shaw mean by all this Union of Hearts—like conversation? What do we care here in this country, which despite the Act of Union is still an island, about the English Liberal party and the Tariff, and the difference between English and Irish character, or whatever else it was all about. Being raw people, I said we do care about human nature in action, and that he's not giving us'. Then my interest began to awake. That young woman who per-suaded that Englishman, full of the impulsiveness that comes from a good banking account, that he was drunk on nothing more serious than poteen, was altogether a delight. The motor car too, the choosing the member of Parliament, and so on right to the end, often exciting and mostly to the point. I thought in reading the first act that you had forgotten Ireland, but I found in the other acts that it is the only subject on which you are entirely serious. In fact you are so serious that sometimes your seriousness leaps upon the stage, knocks the characters over, and insists on having all the conversation to himself. . . . You have said things in this play which are entirely true about Ireland, things which nobody has ever said before, and these are the very things that are most part of the action. It astonishes me that you should have been so long in London and yet have remembered so much. To some extent this play is unlike anything you have done before. Hitherto you have taken your situations from melodrama and called upon logic to make them ridiculous. Your process here seems to be quite different, you are taking situations more from life, you are for the first time trying to get the atmosphere of a place, you have for the first time a geographical conscience.

152) *Parliamentary Debates*, fourth series, CLXXIV (1907), 114–15.

REDMOND SPEECH ON HOME RULE, 1907

What we mean by Home Rule is that in the management of all exclusively Irish affairs Irish public opinion shall be as powerful as the public opinion of Canada or Australia is in the management of Canadian or Australian affairs. That is our claim; we rest that claim on historic right, on historic title, but we rest it also on the admitted failure of British government in Ireland for the last 100 years. I say admitted failure. What Unionist or Conservative statesman has gone to Ireland for the last twenty five years to carry out Unionist policy who has not frankly admitted that the state of government in Ireland was injurious to Ireland and impossible to sustain? Why, I myself heard the present Leader of the Unionist Party in the House of Lords declare a few short months ago that the system of government by Dublin Castle was an anachronism and could not continue to exist as it is to-day. What has the history been of your rule? The history of famine, of misery, of insurrection, of depopulation. These are facts that cannot be disputed. There have been three unsuccessful outbreaks of insurrection during that time, there has been one great famine which swept away in one year 1,500,000 of the Irish people by starvation. There have been famines every decade during that period, and depopulation is going on to this very moment, so that in a little over fifty years one half of the population has entirely gone. You may differ from me as to the precise cause of all these things, but you must admit that your rule has not been a success, but a failure. We have always been quite frank in these matters in the House of Commons, and I say that if your rule had been as good in the last 100 years as it has been bad, if it had led to the material advancement of Ireland—as in the case of Egypt—still our claim would have remained, because we stand by the principle enunciated by the Prime Minister himself quite recently, when he said, 'good government can never be a substitute for self-government'. No man has any doubt what our demand means, and it can only be met by full trust in the Irish people.

153)   *Opinions and Argument from Speeches and Addresses of the Earl of Balfour* (Hodder & Stoughton, 1927), 79–81.

BALFOUR SPEECH AT NOTTINGHAM, 1913

The Irish problem, now that all Irish grievances connected with land, religion, and finance have been removed, is essentially due to the exclusive and often hostile form which Irish patriotism outside Ulster has assumed.

This finds no justification either in differences of race or in the memories of native institutions destroyed by foreign usurpation.

It has its origin in the unhappy circumstances of Irish history, and especially in the inevitable fusion, both in fact and in the memory of the Roman Catholic Irish, of wrongs due to religious divisions with others that followed on the heels of rebellion and civil war.

The memory of these unhappy events was kept alive long after the events were over by the social irritation due to one of the worst systems of land tenure which has ever existed; and though this and all the other causes which have produced the Irish problem are now removed, their effects, as is inevitable, survive them.

Those who think, as I do, that these effects are diminishing, and are destined to disappear, look forward to a time when

Irish patriotism will as easily combine with British patriotism as Scottish patriotism combines now. They ask only for time, and not much of that. Although more than eighty years have passed since Roman Catholic disabilities were removed, yet it is only about a quarter of a century since the problem presented by the congested districts in Ireland began to receive special treatment; it is only about fifteen years since local government on a popular basis was set up; it is only about ten years since the land system was remodelled under the Wyndham Acts; and only about five years since provision was made to meet the special wants of the Roman Catholics in respect of University education. Measured by the standard of a nation's life such figures are insignificant. Give these remedial measures a chance, and do not in the meanwhile meddle with the constitution of the United Kingdom for other than purely administrative reasons. To those who reject this policy, who think that Irish patriotism, in its exclusive and more or less hostile form, is destined to be eternal, I would respectfully say that they must seriously face the question of giving Ireland outside Ulster complete autonomy even though this involves potential separation. Such a policy, however ruinous to Ireland, and however perilous to Great Britain, would at least satisfy the most extreme claims of Irish nationality; and nothing else will.

For these claims, if they are genuine, can never be satisfied by the Home Rule Bill; and if that Bill were really to put an end to the Nationalist agitation, it would be conclusive proof that the agitation was factitious, and that the cause of Irish patriotism in its exclusive form was already lost.

But if Home Rule cannot really satisfy Nationalist aspirations, from every other point of view it stands condemned. Financially, administratively, and constitutionally, it is indefensible; and considered from these points of view few indeed are the Home Rulers who sincerely attempt to defend it.

154)   *The Times*, 29 July 1912.

BONAR LAW SPEECH AT BLENHEIM PALACE, 1912

Eleven years ago the Prime Minister said that the Liberal Party ought not to take office in dependence on the Irish vote, but again and again during the last few weeks in critical divisions they have been supported by a majority far smaller than the number of Nationalist members who voted with them, and only the other day the Prime Minister of the United Kingdom (laughter) was led captive to Dublin to grace there the triumph of the men on whose support he ought not to depend. . . . The Parliament Bill was not carried for nothing. It was carried in order that the Government might be able to force through Parliament Home Rule proposals which at the election were carefully hidden from the people of this country, and which they did not dare even to mention in their addresses—proposals which they are trying to carry, not only without the consent, but, as we know and as they know, against the will of the people of this country.

The Chief Liberal Whip has told us also that the Home Rule Bill will be carried through the House of Commons before Christmas. Perhaps it will. I do not know. But I do know this—that we do not acknowledge their right to carry such a revolution by such a means. We do not recognize that any such action is the constitutional government of a free people. We regard them as a revolutionary committee which has seized by fraud upon despotic power. In our opposition to them we shall not be guided by the considerations, we shall not be restrained by the bonds, which would influence us in any ordinary political struggle. We shall use any means, whatever means seems to us likely to be effective. That is all we shall think about. We shall use any means to deprive them of the power which they have usurped and to compel them to face the people whom they have deceived. Even if the Home Rule Bill passes through the House of Commons, what then? I said in the House of Commons, I repeat here, that there are things stronger than Parliamentary majorities. . . .

Mr. Asquith denies that there are two nations in Ireland. How can he deny it with the fact staring him in the face? There are two nations arrayed against each other in hostile camps, and, in my deliberate opinion, in all the elements which constitute national strength the nation which refuses Home Rule is stronger than the nation which desires it. . . . Under such circumstances surely the only sane method is to make the British people arbiter between them, to have both subject to the British House of Commons, in which both are represented. . . .

Nations, and great nations, have, indeed, taken up arms to

prevent their subjects from seceding, but no nation will ever take up arms to compel loyal subjects to leave their community. I do not believe for a moment that any Government would ever dare to make the attempt; but I am sure of this—that, if the attempt were made, the Government would not succeed in carrying Home Rule. They would succeed only in lighting forces of civil war which would shatter the Empire to its foundations. On this subject I shall say one word, and one word only. While I had still in the party a position of less responsibility than that which I have now I said that in my opinion if an attempt were made without the clearly expressed will of the people of this country, and as part of a corrupt Parliamentary bargain, to deprive these men of their birth-right, they would be justified in resisting by all means in their power, including force. I said so then, and I say now, with a full sense of the responsibility which attaches to my position, that if the attempt be made under present conditions I can imagine no length of resistance to which Ulster will go in which they will not be supported by the overwhelming majority of the British people.

155)   R. Blake, *The Unknown Prime Minister, the Life and Times of Andrew Bonar Law* (Eyre & Spottiswoode, 1955), 162.

BONAR LAW'S ACCOUNT OF A CONVERSATION WITH ASQUITH, OCTOBER 1913

I pointed out to him that in our opinion the real way out was in a General Election. He then said: 'What would be the use of that?'—as Carson had clearly stated that Ulster would resist whatever happened at an Election. I said to him, that might be true, and it was obvious that Carson, or any leader of the Ulster people, must take that line because the chance of winning an Election would be increased by the strength of the belief among the people of England and Scotland that Ulster was irreconcilable in the matter. I told him, however, that since Carson had come back I had myself said to him that while we pledged ourselves to support Ulster to the utmost if there were no Election, that pledge was contingent, and if an Election took place and the Government won, our support would be withdrawn; and I added that Mr. Asquith must understand as well as I did that this made all the difference, and that it was really the certainty of British support which made the strength of the Ulster resistance. . . .

We then discussed what would happen if they went straight on with their present programme. He said that what would happen in that case was purely speculative, that no one could tell what the effect on public opinion would be if they resolutely carried out what they believed to be the law. I agreed that nobody could know in advance; but I told him that in my opinion, at bottom one of the strongest feelings in England and Scotland was Protestantism, or dislike of Roman Catholicism, and that if Protestants of Belfast were actually killed, then in my belief, the effect in Great Britain would be not only that the Government would be beaten but that they would be snowed under.

I then said to him that of course the prospect before us was not attractive. We should have to try by all means to force an Election, and to be successful we should have to take means which would be distasteful to all of us, and in saying that, I hinted at the possibility of disorder in the House of Commons, of using the letter of the Parliament Act, and as a result of all this of his finding that the Army would not obey orders. He very mildly expressed surprise that we had pledged ourselves so definitely to support Ulster in resistance. In regard to that I pointed out to him that before I had made the speech at Blenheim, which he thought so outrageous, I had carefully read what had been said on the same subject in 1886 and 1893 not only by Randolph Churchill but by Lord Salisbury, Mr. Balfour, the Duke of Devonshire and the Duke of Argyle; that in substance what I had said was simply a repetition of what had been said by them. . . .

156)   J. J. Horgan, *The Complete Grammar of Anarchy* (Nisbet, 1919) 32–5.

THE ROAD TO ANARCHY

'The Attorney-General has been reading me a lecture upon what is a serious matter, because I myself once or twice had the honour of being a law-officer of the Crown. He says that my doctrines and the course I am taking lead to anarchy. Does he not think I know that? Does he think that after coming to my time of life, and passing through the various offices and

responsibilities I have accepted, I did this like a baby without
knowing the consequences.'—*Sir Edward Carson at Glasgow,
October* 1, 1912.

THE GOSPEL OF ANARCHY

'The reckless rodomontade at Blenheim in the early summer
as developed and amplified in this Ulster campaign, furnishes
for the future a complete *Grammar of Anarchy*. The possession of
a conscience and a repugnance to obey inconvenient or objec-
tionable laws are not the monopoly of the Protestants of the
north-east of Ireland. This new dogma, countersigned as it now
is, by all the leading men of the Tory party, will be invoked,
and rightly invoked, cited, and rightly cited, called in aid, and
rightly called in aid, whenever the spirit of lawlessness, fed and
fostered by a sense whether of real or imaginary injustice, takes
body and shape, and claims to stop the ordered machinery of a
self-governing society. . . . A more deadly blow—I say it with
the utmost deliberation and with the fullest conviction—a more
deadly blow has never been dealt in our time by any body of
responsible politicians at the very foundations on which democratic government rests.'—*Mr. Asquith at Ladybank, October* 5,
1912.

'ULSTER WILL NOT STAND ALONE'

'If the Government carry the Home Rule Bill through to the
bitter end they will approach a General Election with Ulster
undoubtedly in arms, and if that arises, under the circumstances I have indicated, I tell you that Ulster will not stand
alone.'—*Mr. F. E. Smith, K.C., M.P., at Lincoln, October* 11, 1912.

'I AM GOING TO BE IN IT'

'I can assure you from my own personal knowledge that it is
not a question at which to laugh at all. Those men in the
North of Ireland are absolutely in earnest. I can assure you
that when the time comes these men will be as good as their
word. Personally they have all my sympathies, and I tell you
—and I say this very solemnly—that when the time comes if
there is any fighting to be done—I am going to be in it.'—
Colonel T. E. Hickman, M.P., in South Wolverhampton, October 25,
1912.

SIR EDWARD CARSON TELLS THE TRUTH

'The hon. and learned member for Waterford (Mr. Redmond), in his impassioned way, appeals to us and says: "Do you think we are going to pass legislation as against Protestants? Do you think that we are going to pass legislation that will be persecuting the Protestants"? Has anybody ever said that? I certainly never said that. I give my Irish fellow-countrymen credit who would be inclined, in any wise, or from any motives, to interfere with their fellow-countrymen on account of religion, that it would not be by legislation.'—*Sir Edward Carson in the House of Commons, October* 29, 1912.

THE MAJORITY MINORITY

'It is not enough in a matter of this kind to count heads. There may be a majority of the Irish people in favour of Home Rule, though even that is very doubtful. The real opinion of the Irish people is extremely difficult to get at upon such a question. But granting such a majority, there is still the fact that the minority includes all the classes upon which any Government can rely to provide the requisites for a successful State. Not even Mr. Redmond would care to undertake the Government of Ireland without being able to draw upon the resources of Ulster, and the prosperity won by the energy and capacity of Ulstermen. Such a minority is for political purposes, though not for Parliamentary purposes, a majority.'—*The Times, October* 30, 1912.

THE MORAL RIGHT TO RESIST

'The men of Ulster have a moral right to resist, and the killing of men who so resist is not an act of oppression—it is an act of murder.'—*Mr. Duke, K.C., M.P., at Exeter, October* 1912.

PASSIVE SYMPATHY AND ACTIVE HELP

'If these Ulster people will even probably resist—and I am bound to say if they do resist I think they will be right—but if they do resist, if that is the state of the facts, it is not a question that you have to consider as to whether they are right or wrong—though, as I said a moment ago, I myself think they are right—but you will have chaos and confusion in

Ireland, and not merely in Ireland, but I believe we will have at our backs, in relation to that contest, the whole body of Unionist opinion in this country, and a great many who would be willing to give us, not merely a passive sympathy, but active help.'—*Sir Edward Carson in the House of Commons, January* 1, 1913.

'I SHALL ASSIST THEM'

'If you attempt to enforce this Bill, and the people of Ulster believe, and have a right to believe, that you are doing it against the will of the people of this country, then I shall assist them in resisting it.'—*Mr. Bonar Law in the House of Commons, January* 1, 1913.

WHAT 'FOREIGN COUNTRY'?

'It is a fact which I do not think anyone who knows anything about Ireland will deny, that these people in the North-East of Ireland, from old prejudices perhaps more than from anything else, from the whole of their past history, would prefer, I believe, to accept *the government of a foreign country* rather than submit to be governed by hon. gentlemen below the gangway.'—*Mr. Bonar Law in the House of Commons, January* 1, 1913.

157)   *The Times*, 30 September 1912.

ULSTER'S SOLEMN LEAGUE AND COVENANT

Being convinced in our consciences that Home Rule would be disastrous to the material well-being of Ulster, as well as of the whole of Ireland, subversive of our civil and religious freedom, destructive of our citizenship, and perilous to the unity of the Empire, we, whose names are underwritten, men of Ulster, loyal subjects of His Gracious Majesty King George V, humbly relying on the God Whom our fathers in days of stress and trial confidently trusted, hereby pledge ourselves in solemn Covenant throughout this our time of threatened calamity to stand by one another in defending for ourselves and our children our cherished position of equal citizenship in the United Kingdom, and in using all means which may be found necessary to defeat the present conspiracy to set up a

Home Rule Parliament in Ireland; and, in the event of such a Parliament being forced upon us, we further solemnly and mutually pledge ourselves to refuse to recognize its authority. In sure confidence that God will defend the right, we hereto subscribe our names, and, further, we individually declare that we have not already signed this Covenant.

158)   *The Times*, 3 March 1914.

THE BRITISH COVENANT

I . . . of . . . , earnestly convinced that the claim of the Government to carry the Home Rule Bill into law, without submitting it to the judgement of the nation, is contrary to the spirit of our Constitution,

DO HEREBY SOLEMNLY DECLARE

that, if that Bill is so passed, I shall hold myself justified in taking or supporting any action that may be effective to prevent it being put into operation, and more particularly to prevent the armed forces of the Crown being used to deprive the people of Ulster of their rights as citizens of the United Kingdom.

159)   J. Connell, *Wavell, Scholar and Soldier* (Collins, 1964), 87–8.

WAVELL TO HIS FATHER (MAJ.-GEN. A. G. WAVELL), 23 MARCH 1914

The attitude of the majority of officers is that the Army by the action of these officers has saved the situation, won a great victory, etc. I cannot agree. I think they have won a political battle to the ruin or great danger of the Army and the country. For it is a political victory; how can you call it other when the Army refuses to enforce the *present* Home Rule Bill? It seems to me deplorable that those words should be used. And Wilson made no secret of his opinion. He actually said: 'The Army have done what the Opposition failed to do' and 'will probably cause the fall of the present Government.' What right have the Army to be on the side of the Opposition, what have they to do with causing the fall of Governments?

No, to my mind, this has been fought on the wrong issue.

The issue on which I too, I think, would have acted as the officers concerned did was the action of the Government in holding a pistol at the officer's head and trying to coerce him by threats at his pocket, saying 'You must do this or be *dismissed the Army* losing your livelihood and your pension'. It is inconceivable to me how an English Government could have done such a thing. . . .

And the attitude of Sir John French and the Army Council amazes me. Here we have a body of men at the head of the Army who acquiesce in an order like that being framed, fail to see what the effect on the officers will be, and yet submit to *pressure from their subordinates* to get the decision rescinded. . . .

How is the country going to take that state of affairs? And how are you to preserve discipline after this, how are you to use your Army to keep law and order against strikers when once the officers have successfully resisted an attempt to use them to enforce a law which they do not approve?

One lacks perspective at present of course. But I see only disaster from what has happened. We seem to have lost our balance and hard-headedness; this Ulster business should have been settled a year ago, only that it was a good weapon in the political game.

Better destroy this letter, which is written for *you alone*. Perhaps things may turn out better than I expect.

160) *Parliamentary Debates, House of Commons,* fifth series, **XXXVI** (1912), 1424–6.

ASQUITH PRESENTS THE HOME RULE BILL, 1912

I trust I have succeeded in making plain the proposals of the Government. These are the lines upon which we ask Parliament to proceed in taking the first, the most urgent and the most momentous, step towards the settlement of the controversy which, as between ourselves and Ireland, has lasted for more than a century, and of a problem—and I lay great stress on this—which, even apart from the special circumstances of Ireland, has every year, year by year, become increasingly vital to the efficiency of Parliament itself. We maintain in this Bill unimpaired, and beyond the reach of challenge or of question, the supremacy, absolute and sovereign, of the Imperial Parliament. The powers which we propose to give to Ireland of taxation, of administration, of legislation, are delegated powers, but within the limits of that delegation they embrace at once, with the exception of the reserved services, all matters of local concern. If, as we believe will be the case, as certainly has been the case elsewhere, power carries with it a sense of responsibility that will give to the Irish people a free and ample field for the development of their own national life and at the same time bind them to us and the Empire by a sense of voluntary co-operation, and, as I believe, in sincere and loyal attachment. At the same time this Imperial Parliament will have begun to break its own bonds and will be set free by the process, of which this is the first stage, for a fuller and more adequate discharge of its Imperial duties. I read a speech of the right hon. Gentleman opposite (Mr. Bonar Law), delivered to an audience in Belfast early in the present week. I gather from that speech that he can see in all the proposals of this Bill, and in the attitude and action of the Government in regard to it,

'Nothing better,'

to use his own words,

'than the latest move in a conspiracy as treacherous as has ever been formed against the life of a great nation.'

He tells us, and he told the people of Ulster—

'The present Government turned the House of Commons into a market place where everything is bought and sold.'

He added—

'In order to remain for a few months longer in office, His Majesty's Government have sold the Constitution.'

We have sold ourselves. This, Mr. Speaker, is the new style.

CAPTAIN CRAIG: It is the truth, and you do not like it.

THE PRIME MINISTER: I can understand why the party opposite are so enthusiastic—

SIR JOHN LONSDALE: Will the right hon. Gentleman finish the quotation?

THE PRIME MINISTER: Presumably because of the completeness of the contrast which it presents to anything to which they or we have hitherto been accustomed. [HON. MEMBERS: 'Limehouse.'] This is all very well for Ulster, but what about the House of Commons?

MR. BONAR LAW: I have said it here.

THE PRIME MINISTER: Am I to understand that the right hon. Gentleman repeats here, or is prepared to repeat on the floor of the House of Commons—

MR. BONAR LAW: Yes.

THE PRIME MINISTER: Let us see exactly what it is: It is that I and my colleagues are selling our convictions.

MR. BONAR LAW: You have not got any.

THE PRIME MINISTER: We are getting on with the new style. The right hon. Gentleman said that I and my colleagues are selling our convictions——

CAPTAIN CRAIG: You have sold them to Mr. John Redmond.

THE PRIME MINISTER: That we are producing a Bill which the right hon. Gentleman said, elsewhere in the same speech, does not represent our views——

MR. BONAR LAW: Hear, hear.

THE PRIME MINISTER: In order that for a few months longer we may cling to office. Does he really believe that? What have I to gain? [An HON. MEMBER: 'Office.'] What have my colleagues to gain—[An HON. MEMBER: 'Office']—by a transaction to purchase for us——

CAPTAIN CRAIG: Eighty Nationalist votes.

THE PRIME MINISTER: To purchase for us a short further spell of the burdens and responsibilities which we have borne in very difficult and troublous times, now for the best part of seven years, at the price of surrendering our convictions and soiling for all time our personal and political honour. How many people, I wonder, in this House really believe that? We put this Bill forward as the responsible advisers of the Crown as the embodiment of our own honest and deliberate judgment. What is your alternative? [HON. MEMBERS: 'Tariff Reform.'] Are you satisfied with the present system? [HON. MEMBERS: 'Quite.'] Were you satisfied with it two years ago? What do you propose to put in its place? Have you any answer to the demand of Ireland—[HON. MEMBERS: 'Yes']—beyond the naked veto of an irreconcilable minority, and the promise of a freer and more copious outflow to Ireland of Imperial doles? There are at this moment between twenty and thirty self-governing Legislatures under the allegiance of the Crown. They have solved, under every diversity of conditions, economic, racial, and religious, the problem of reconciling local autonomy with Imperial unity. Are we going to break up the Empire by adding one more? The claim comes this time, not from remote outlying quarters, but from a people close to our own doors, associated with us by every tie of kindred, of interest, of social and industrial intercourse, who have borne and are bearing their share, and a noble share it has been, in the building up and the holding together of the greatest Empire in history. [An HON. MEMBER: 'Cheering our defeats in South Africa,' and another HON. MEMBER: 'Did Lynch do that?'] That claim no longer falls on deaf ears. There has been reserved for this Parliament, this House of Commons, the double honour of reconciling Ireland and emancipating herself.

161)   *The Times*, 16 March 1914.

CHURCHILL SPEECH AT BRADFORD, MARCH 1914

Strictly speaking, no doubt, the constitutional remedy of Ulster Protestants, and of the Unionist Party, is clear and plain. They should obey the law. If they dislike the law—it is a free country—let them agitate for a majority when an election comes, and then, if they choose, they can amend, or, at the very worst, repeal a law against which the country would then have pronounced. That is a full remedy. It is the only remedy which is open to Liberals when we are in a minority and when Liberals are invaded as they have been and may be again, by reactionary or one-sided legislation in temperance, in education, on tariffs, on land, on rating, or on other grave political issues. . . .

I have always hoped, and always urged, that a fair and full offer should be made to North-East Ulster in all friendship and good will, an offer going beyond anything which, on a strict interpretation of our rights, was required of us. . . . Consider what that offer is. Any Ulster county, upon the requisition of a tenth of the electors, can, by a simple vote, stand out, for six years, of the whole operation of the Home Rule Bill and remain exactly as they are. That is to say, two General Elections in this country must take place before any county exercising its option would be compelled to change the system of government under which it has hitherto been administered. . . . Before the offer was made the Unionist Party demanded exclusion or a General Election. We have now given them both. Unless they had exclusion or a General Election, they said, there would be a civil war. They have got both, and they still say there is going to be civil war . . . to satisfy these gentry you would have not only to promise them an election, but you would have to guarantee that it will go the way they want. . . . But what is the last unmeasured infamy of Radical power of which they complain? It has all been put off for six years! They say, 'We had our rebellion all ready. It is costing us a lot of money to pay our Volunteers, and we cannot keep it up indefinitely. And now the Government have had the incredible meanness to postpone all possible provocation for six long years.' . . . If they reject the offer we have made, it can only be because they prefer shooting to voting, because they would rather use the bullet than the ballot. . . .

At any rate, when you are dealing with Orange Ulster, you are dealing with real passions and with real anxieties of real people. No such excuse is open to Mr. Bonar Law. Behind every strident sentence which he rasps out you can always hear the whisper of the party manager. 'We must have an election before the Plural Voting Bill passes into law. Ulster is our best card; it is our only card. This is our one chance to smash the Parliament Act, to restore the veto of the House of Lords, and to carry a protective tariff on the Statute Book.' . . . From the language which is employed it would almost seem that we are face to face with a disposition on the part of some sections of the propertied classes to subvert Parliamentary government and to challenge the civil and constitutional foundations of society. Against such a mood, wherever it manifests itself in action, there is no lawful measure from which the Government should shrink, and there is no lawful measure from which this Government will shrink.

Bloodshed no doubt is lamentable. I have seen some of it— more perhaps than many of those who talk about it with such levity—but there are worse things than bloodshed, even on an extensive scale. The collapse of the Central Government of the British Empire would be worse. The abandonment by public men of the righteous aims in which they are pledged in honour would be worse. The cowardly abdication of responsibility by the Executive would be worse. The trampling down of that law and order which under the conditions of a civilized State assure to millions, life, liberty, and the pursuit of happiness— all this would be worse than bloodshed. . . .

As long as it affects working men in England or Nationalist peasants in Ireland, there is no measure of military force which the Tory Party will not readily employ. They denounce all violence except their own. They uphold all law except the law they choose to break. They always welcome the application of force to others. But they themselves are to remain immune. They are to select from the Statute-book the laws they will obey and the laws they will resist. They claim to be a party in the State free to use force in all directions, but never to have it applied to themselves. Whether in office or in opposition, as they have very often told us, they are to govern the country. If they cannot do it by the veto of privilege, they will do it by the veto of violence.

162)   *The Times*, 27 July 1914.

LEADING ARTICLE HEADED 'GRAVE NEWS FROM IRELAND'

The grave news which we publish this morning from the European capitals is accompanied, we are sorry to say, by very serious intelligence from Ireland. An attempt at gun-running by the National Volunteers near Dublin yesterday morning resulted in collisions between the Volunteers, the public, the police, and the military. Four persons were killed and some sixty injured, of whom several are not expected to live. The excitement in Dublin is intense. The incident is from every point of view deplorable; but it is emphatic testimony to the true position of affairs across the Irish Channel. The nation to which a Liberal Administration was to bring a message of peace is mobilised for an internal war. The past week has seen one more hope of a settlement vanish in thin air. One spark, struck from such a momentary collision as that in Dublin yesterday, may serve, when and where we least expect it, to set in train the long-dreaded conflagration. . . .

There can no longer be the slightest doubt that the country is now confronted with one of the greatest crises in the history of the British race. The issue was not present in the minds of the electorate at the last election. It is thoroughly present now. . . . It is not clear that the Government could go to the country on the single question of Home Rule. It is clear beyond dispute that they ought to consult the electorate before taking steps which must manifestly end in civil war.

CHAPTER FOURTEEN

The Coming of War

Even before the turn of the century the *Daily Mail* was warning of German rivalry, leading perhaps one day to war (163). American rivalry, on the other hand, might be submerged in friendship, even alliance (164). But what was the extent of British commitment to France and Russia against Germany? Left-wingers wanted more Parliamentary control of foreign policy (165). Right-wingers wanted the introduction of 'national service' (166). The party leaders knew, however, that this was unacceptable to the Edwardian public, and decided that British defence needs and British opinion could best be satisfied through a large navy ('We want eight, and we won't wait' [167]) plus a small regular army backed by a volunteer force of Territorials (168). In correctly demonstrating the foolishness of war in any reasonable economic analysis, Norman Angell, though widely-read, was still unable to prevent war's coming (169). But once the fighting had begun left-wingers began to proclaim that it was a holy war, 'the war to end war' (170, 171).

163) T. Brex (ed.), *'Scaremongerings' from the Daily Mail, 1896–1914, the Paper that Foretold the War* (Daily Mail, 1914), 16–18.

A *Daily Mail* REPORTER (G. W. STEEVENS) VISITS GERMANY, SEPTEMBER 1897

Rivalry in projects of colonisation and empire—these, beyond question, are the chief springs that feed German hostility towards England.

Hostility, of course, could not have waxed and flourished as it has without a fertile soil to grow in. Competition in South Africa, or for the Peruvian export trade, is not enough to make two nations hate each other. As in England the Kaiser's tele-gram was the occasion, but the German clerk the real cause, of anti-German hatred, so with Germany the groundwork of dislike was the utter antipathy and repugnance with which the German regards our manners and national character. Both as a nation and as individuals the Germans detest us. True, they water their detestation with a sneaking admiration for our sports, our athletics, our clothes. In the German sporting papers you will meet such a sentence as 'Trainer Brown, wird die letzten Galops seiner Cracks selbst leiten; sein First-string, Little Duck, wird fur die Chesterfield Stakes starten.' But meet the man who talks this sort of language, and dresses in the nearest he can to a covert coat, and tell him he looks like an Englishman. In his heart he will rejoice, but he will pretend to be insulted. With the German Anglomaniac, as with the Kaiser, it is some of our ways, not our whole selves, that are to be imitated. . . .

External antipathy is a far more potent factor in national relations than the inner sympathy. Few experience the last; all can feel and resent the first. Therefore it is that an anti-English policy in Germany starts with the prodigiously strong leverage of national dislike. . . .

Let us make no mistake about it. It is natural to deplore the unfriendship of the two nations, but it is idle to ignore it. Hostility to England is the mission of young Germany.

It is idle to ignore it, but we need be neither furious nor panic-stricken. It is as much Germany's right to seek after the good things of the earth as it is ours. It is proper that we should be plain with ourselves, and admit that for the time Germany is our chiefest rival in all fields. We can be competitors without being enemies. Only in the honest effort to avoid enmity we need not cease to compete. Be very sure, at least, that methodical, patient, unresting Germany will make no such mistake. So, for the next ten years, fix your eyes very hard on Germany.

164)   W. T. Stead, *The Americanisation of the World or the Trend of the Twentieth Century* (*Review of Reviews*, 1902), preface.

The advent of the United States of America as the greatest of world-Powers is the greatest political, social, and commer-cial phenomenon of our times. For some years past we have all been more or less dimly conscious of its significance. It is only when we look at the manifold manifestations of the exuberant energy of the United States, and the worldwide influence which they are exerting upon the world in general and the British Empire in particular, that we realise how comparatively insignificant are all the other events of our time.

The result of the rapid survey which I have embodied in this Annual will, I trust, enable my readers to see in its true perspective the salient fact which will dictate the trend of events in the Twentieth Century.

This survey is intensely interesting to all men, but it is of transcendant importance for my own countrymen. For we are confronted by the necessity of taking one of those momentous decisions which decide the destiny of our country. Unless I am altogether mistaken, we have an opportunity— probably the last which is to be offered us—of retaining our place as the first of world-Powers. If we neglect it, we shall descend slowly but irresistibly to the position of Holland and of Belgium. No one who contemplates with an impartial mind the array of facts now submitted to his attention, will deny that I have at least made out a very strong *prima facie* case in support of my contention that, unless we can succeed in merging the British Empire in the English-speaking United States of the World, the disintegration of our Empire, and our definite displacement from the position of commercial and financial primacy is only a matter of time, and probably a very short time. If, on the other hand, we substitute for the insular patriotism of our nation the broader patriotism of the race, and frankly throw in our lot with the Americans to realise the great ideal of Race Union, we shall enter upon a new era of power and prosperity the like of which the race has never realised since the world began. But 'if before our duty we, with listless spirit, stand,' the die will be cast, and we must reconcile ourselves as best we can to accept a secondary position in a world in which we have hitherto played a leading *rôle*.

If, on the contrary, we are resolute and courageous, we have it in our power to occupy a position of vantage, in which we need fear no foe and dread no rival. We shall continue on a wider scale to carry out the providential mission which has been entrusted to the English-speaking Race, whose United States will be able to secure the peace of the World.

It is, therefore, in no spirit of despair, but rather with

joyful confidence and great hope that I commend this book to
my fellow-countrymen.

165)   H. N. Brailsford, *The War of Steel and Gold, a Study of the
Armed Peace* (Bell, 4th ed., 1915), 211–13.

There might be elected from the House of Commons by
ballot on a proportional basis, either annually or for the
duration of a Parliament, a small standing Committee for the
special consideration of foreign affairs. It should be large
enough to represent fairly every phase of opinion—seven or
eight members would be a minimum—but not so large as to
make businesslike procedure difficult. It would meet periodically at frequent intervals both during the session of Parliament and in the recess. It should be summoned if any new
situation demanded a decision which involved a departure
from a policy previously sanctioned. It should have the right to
demand the production, under the seal of confidence, of all
essential documents and despatches. The Foreign Secretary
would naturally be present at its deliberations. It would also
be useful that it should have the power to request the
attendance, on occasion, of experts in special questions, both
official and unofficial. It should be consulted in the negotiations which precede the drafting of treaties, as well as in the
later phases when the bargain is embodied in a final form of
words. It would be unwise and unnecessary formally to require
the Foreign Secretary to abide by the decision of the majority
of this Committee. That would involve too wide a departure
from our present traditions, But it should be provided that in
the event of a capital disagreement, either the Minister or the
Committee should have the right at any time to refer their
differences to the House of Commons. Over certain acts, such
as the issue of an ultimatum, a declaration of war or the
conclusion of a treaty, the Committee might be armed with a
right of veto, pending the decision of Parliament. The general
idea of such a Committee would be that it should exercise over
the Foreign Office the control which the Cabinet so rarely
exercises to any purpose. Its members would give to foreign
affairs, as the members of a Cabinet cannot, a close attention.
Most of them would be well-informed in some degree before
they were elected, and all, with these new opportunities and

new responsibilities, would tend to become expert. They would not in their debates be thinking of the fate of their own measures and the independence of their own departments as Cabinet Ministers often do. Nor would they, in the privacy of a committee room, be fettered by the party ties which oppress the private member in the division lobby. Three claims may be made for the adoption of such a system as this. It would give some guarantee, if the Committee was well selected, that the policy of the Foreign Office really reflected the will of the nation. It would place a check upon rash actions and Machiavellian designs. It would also help to secure, by the wisdom of several heads, a higher level of efficiency than the Foreign Office at present attains. There would still remain to a strong and capable Minister a considerable range of unfettered action. He would have to face the test of frequent and intimate debate. He would not be free to conclude treaties binding on his country for years to come, or to send despatches which might provoke immediate war, save with the sanction of the Committee. But over the general conduct of foreign affairs he would remain the responsible Minister, subject only to the risk that if in vital matters he ignored its opinion, the Committee would appeal against him to the House of Commons. In practice the first concern of a Minister would be to keep his Committee with him, to lead it if he were strong and capable; to follow it, if he were a man of timid character and moderate ability.

166)   Lord Roberts, *A Nation in Arms, Speeches on the Requirements of the British Army* (Murray, 1907), 143–5.

ROBERTS SPEECH AT THE ROYAL INSTITUTION, LONDON, 1906

In a few months from now it will be seven years since the first blow was struck in the South African War. It is disheartening to reflect how little has been done in that period to place ourselves in a better position than we were then, and it will take a much longer time than that to build up a sound military system, and to root in the youths of the country the aptitude for arms and a proper feeling of patriotism.

Let us see to it that the next seven years are more fruitful of good results than the last seven have been. I shall indeed have spoken in vain if I have not convinced you that, outside all that has as yet been done, there is a great and a supreme problem to be solved, and that if we hope to retain our vast possessions, and maintain the responsible position we hold amongst nations, we must have not only a powerful Fleet, but an efficient and sufficient Army, composed partly of regular troops, but chiefly of the manhood of the country.

I give place to no man in my admiration for, and my belief in, our Navy, but it seems to me little short of madness to suppose that the Navy will always, and under all circumstances, be able to prevent the invasion of these Islands, or to secure the defence of the Empire. We must, as I have just said, have, in addition, a suitable Army, and this we shall never get until the whole nation realises that it is the duty of every able-bodied citizen to fit himself to take his share in the defence of the country.

The nation must identify itself with, and take a practical interest in, the Army, and no longer look upon it as a profession with which it has nothing to do but to find the money to defray its cost.

It is because I fear that nothing short of a national disaster will make the people of this country realise this—for long years of immunity from home trouble have engendered a feeling of security which has no justification at the present day, and have induced a taste for ease and luxury to which everything must give way, and which causes the calls of duty to be felt as an intolerable interference with their pleasure and recreation—it is because of this fear that I so earnestly press for the boys and youths of Great Britain to be given an education which will teach them their duty to their country, and imbue them with that spirit of patriotism without which no nation can expect to continue great and prosperous.

Such an education as I advocate, and such a feeling as, I trust, would thereby be inculcated, would not induce the so-called jingo spirit so much dreaded. On the contrary, it would have the opposite effect, as it would bring home to every man what war would mean to himself personally and to his family, and would, I firmly believe, be the surest guarantee for peace.

My lords and gentlemen, awful as war is and much as it is to be deprecated, surely there is one thing even worse than War, and that is Defeat, with the terrible consequences to our native land that Defeat would entail.

167)   *Daily Graphic*, 26 July 1909.

After a long interval devoted to more controversial but less important subjects, the House of Commons to-day resumes the discussion of the Navy Estimates, and it is believed that Mr. McKenna will announce the decision of the Government immediately to lay down the four additional Dreadnoughts. This decision will be welcomed throughout the Empire. We should all of us be glad if it were possible to dispense with the proposed increase in the Navy, and still more glad if it were possible to reduce the present vast expenditure. But nations, like individuals, have to take facts as they find them; and the dominating fact of the existing situation is the unconcealed desire of Germany to challenge our naval supremacy. That desire is quite intelligible. The Germans are a great people, and they wish to be second to none either on sea or on land. We, however, are compelled to look at the problem from our point of view, and not from theirs. To us sea supremacy is a necessary of national life; to Germany it is a luxury of Imperial ambition. If we lost the command of the sea our commerce could be destroyed and our industries brought to a standstill, and the overwhelming German army could effect a landing where it listed. Germany runs no such risk. The utmost injury we could inflict upon her would be to blockade Hamburg and Bremen, and force her to send overland that portion of her foreign commerce which now passes through these ports. Her ordinary industrial life would continue almost unaffected. The stakes are, therefore, not even. She is playing for pride, we are playing for life—and we mean to win.

168)   General Sir I. Hamilton, *Compulsory Service, a Study of the Question in the Light of Experience* (Murray, 1910), 33–4 (from Haldane's introduction).

Suppose we raised the Home Defence Army to a million men it would cost many millions more than at present. Suppose, further, that we had been able to do this without materially impairing the industrial capacity which makes our output per head of the population greater by much than that of our competitors. Suppose all this accomplished—what then? Should we be better off with this ring of a million

bayonets bristling round the coast? They would be more, by a
long way, than was necessary to force the adversary to come
in such numbers as to constitute the requisite target for the
Navy. But what if the Navy could not command the sea? Then
we should sooner or later starve and have to submit, not the
less certainly for having the million men with us. Command of
the sea lies at the root of the whole matter. We have not a
population that can raise a home army of the magnitude that
is possible for some Continental Powers. But our wealth and
our great naval tradition make it comparatively easy for us to
keep well ahead of any possible adversary in naval strength,
at all events for many years to come, and after that the
development of the Naval and Military organisation of the
Empire ought to have done the rest. We can therefore remain
in superior power on the water, and we ought to do so; for
nothing else can give us security, and under cover of this
superiority we can easily build the relatively small military
structure that is necessary for a second line for Home defence.
I therefore dismiss, in entire agreement with Sir Ian Hamilton's
view, the proposition that an army on the Continental model
is necessary for purposes of Home defence.

169)   N. Angell, *The Great Illusion, a Study of the Relation of
       Military Power to National Advantage* (Heinemann, 1913
       ed.), vii–viii.

What are the fundamental motives that explain the present
rivalry of armaments in Europe, notably the Anglo-German?
Each nation pleads the need for defence; but this implies that
someone is likely to attack, and has therefore a presumed
interest in so doing. What are the motives which each State
thus fears its neighbours may obey?
They are based on the universal assumption that a nation,
in order to find outlets for expanding population and increasing industry, or simply to ensure the best conditions possible
for its people, is necessarily pushed to territorial expansion and
the exercise of political force against others (German naval
competition is assumed to be the expression of the growing
need of an expanding population for a larger place in the
world, a need which will find a realization in the conquest of
English Colonies or trade, unless these were defended); it is

assumed, therefore, that a nation's relative prosperity is broadly determined by its political power; that nations being competing units, advantage, in the last resort, goes to the possessor of preponderant military force, the weaker going to the wall, as in the other forms of the struggle for life.

The author challenges this whole doctrine. He attempts to show that it belongs to a stage of development out of which we have passed; that the commerce and industry of a people no longer depend upon the expansion of its political frontiers; that a nation's political and economic frontiers do not now necessarily coincide; that military power is socially and economically futile, and can have no relation to the prosperity of the people exercising it; that it is impossible for one nation to seize by force the wealth or trade of another—to enrich itself by subjugating, or imposing its will by force on another; that, in short, war, even when victorious, can no longer achieve those aims for which peoples strive.

He establishes this apparent paradox, in so far as the economic problem is concerned, by showing that wealth in the economically civilized world is founded upon credit and commercial contract (these being the outgrowth of an economic interdependence due to the increasing division of labour and greatly developed communication). If credit and commercial contract are tampered with in an attempt of confiscation, the credit-dependent wealth is undermined, and its collapse involves that of the conqueror; so that if conquest is not to be self-injurious it must respect the enemy's property, in which case it becomes economically futile.

170)   H. G. Wells, *The War That Will End War* (Palmer, 1914), 7–8, 10–11.

The cause of a war and the object of a war are not necessarily the same. The cause of this war was the invasion of Luxemburg and Belgium. We declared war because we were bound by treaty to declare war. We have been pledged to protect the integrity of Belgium since the kingdom of Belgium has existed. If the Germans had not broken the guarantees they shared with us to respect the neutrality of these little States we should certainly not be at war at the present time. The fortified eastern frontier of France could have been held against any attack without any help from us. We had no obligations and no interests there. We were pledged to France simply to protect her from a naval attack by sea, but the Germans had already given us an undertaking not to make such an attack. It was our Belgian treaty and the sudden outrage on Luxemburg that precipitated us into this conflict. No Power in the world would have respected our Flag or accepted our national word again if we had not fought. So much for the immediate cause of the war.

But now we come to the object of this war. We began to fight because our honour and our pledge obliged us; but so soon as we are embarked upon the fighting we have to ask ourselves what is the end at which our fighting aims. We cannot simply put the Germans back over the Belgian border and tell them not to do it again. . . .

Consider what the Germans have been, and what the Germans can be. Here is a race which has for its chief fault docility and a belief in teachers and rulers. For the rest, as all who know it intimately will testify, it is the most amiable of peoples. It is naturally kindly, comfort-loving, child-loving, musical, artistic, intelligent. In countless respects German homes and towns and countrysides are the most civilised in the world. But these people did a little lose their heads after the victories of the sixties and seventies, and there began a propaganda of national vanity and national ambition. It was organised by a stupidly forceful statesman, it was fostered by folly upon the throne. It was guarded from wholesome criticism by an intolerant censorship. It never gave sanity a chance. A certain patriotic sentimentality lent itself only too readily to the suggestion of the flatterer, and so there grew up this monstrous trade in weapons. German patriotism became an 'interest,' the greatest of the 'interests.' It developed a vast advertisement propaganda. It subsidised Navy Leagues and Aerial Leagues, threatening the world. Mankind, we saw too late, had been guilty of an incalculable folly in permitting private men to make a profit out of the dreadful preparations for war. But the evil was started; the German imagination was captured and enslaved. On every other European country that valued its integrity there was thrust the overwhelming necessity to arm and drill—and still to arm and drill. Money was withdrawn from education, from social progress, from business enterprise, and art and scientific research, and from every kind of happiness; life was drilled and darkened.

So that the harvest of this darkness comes now almost as a relief, and it is a grim satisfaction in our discomforts that we can at last look across the roar and torment of battlefields to the possibility of an organised peace.

For this is now a war for peace.

It aims straight at disarmament. It aims at a settlement that shall stop this sort of thing for ever. Every soldier who fights against Germany now is a crusader against war. This, the greatest of all wars, is not just another war—it is the last war!

171)   G. Murray, *The Foreign Policy of Sir Edward Grey 1906–1915* (Oxford University Press, 1915), 9–11.

Now, for my own part, if the reader will excuse some egotism, I wish to make a personal explanation. I have never held a brief for Sir Edward Grey, and do not propose to do so now. It is generally difficult for an outsider to form a considered opinion on a complicated question of foreign affairs. It is doubly difficult if your own bias of character inclines you to differ from the persons who have most knowledge. But in me that bias of character has been strong, and has resulted in pretty definite political predilections. I have been unhappy about Morocco and Persia; profoundly unhappy about our strained relations with Germany; sympathetic in general towards the Radical and Socialist line on foreign policy; and always anxious to have the smallest Navy vote that a reasonable Government would permit.

I have never till this year seriously believed in the unalterably aggressive designs of Germany. I knew our own Jingoes, and recognized the existence of German Jingoes; but I believed that there, as here, the government was in the hands of the more wise and sober part of the nation. I have derided all scares, and loathed (as I still loathe) all scaremongers and breeders of hatred. I have believed (as I still believe) that many persons now in newspaper offices might be more profitably housed in lunatic asylums. And I also felt, with some impatience, that though, as an outsider, I could not tell exactly what the Government ought to do, they surely could produce good relations between Great Britain and Germany if only they had the determination and the will.

And now I see that on a large part of this question—by no means the whole of it—I was wrong, and a large number of the people whom I honour most were wrong. One is vividly reminded of Lord Melbourne's famous dictum: 'All the sensible men were on one side, and all the d——d fools on the other. And, egad, Sir, the d——d fools were right!'

What made me change my mind was the action of the various Powers during the last ten days before the war. On July 26 or 27 I was asked to sign a declaration in favour of British neutrality in the case of a war arising between the Great Powers. I agreed without hesitation. I did not believe there would be a war; the nations were not governed by lunatics; but if by any dreadful blunder there should be war, I thought, let us by all means keep out of it. During the next week my confidence was staggered. The thing was incredible, but it looked as if Germany was deliberately refusing all roads to peace, as if she had made up her mind to have war. By the time the declaration was published—it took a week collecting signatures—my attitude had changed. For, if the war was not a mere blundering disaster, if it was a deliberate plot, a calculated policy of the strongest nation in Europe to win by bloodshed what she could not win by fair dealing, then it might be the duty of all law-abiding Powers to stand or fall together for the sake of public right. Then came more evidence: the White Book first, then the German Book, the Belgian, the French, the Russian, the Austrian. They all told fundamentally the same story. The statesman whom I had suspected as over-imperialist was doing everything humanly possible to preserve peace; the Power whose good faith I had always championed was in part playing a game of the most unscrupulous bluff, in part meant murder from the beginning.

I said something of this sort to a Radical friend. 'Yes,' he said, 'for the last twelve days Grey has been working for peace, but for the last eight years he has been making peace impossible.'

Is this a true criticism? Or is it that we Radicals judged foreign policy in part wrong, inasmuch as we did not—or would not—make enough allowance for one great factor which affected it? If German policy and Grey's policy were such as we found them in July 1914, what had they been in earlier years?

We Radicals had always worked for peace, for conciliation,

for mutual understanding. There we were right. We had argued steadily that no Power could gain and all Powers must lose by a European war. There we were right. But we had also felt a suspicion that Sir Edward Grey had persistently over-rated German hostility and thereby caused it to grow. On this point were we perhaps wrong all through, almost as much wrong on our side as the common anti-German fanatic was wrong on the other?

ACKNOWLEDGMENTS

The author is grateful to the following for permission to quote from their publications: George Allen & Unwin Ltd, for *BBC Scrapbooks* by L. Bailey; Edward Arnold (Publishers) Ltd, for *Howards End* by E. M. Forster; G. Bell & Sons, Ltd, for *National Guilds* by Orage, *South Africa Today* by Hamilton Fyfe and *The War of Steel and Gold* by Brailsford; Mrs Cheston Bennett, for *Books and Persons* by Arnold Bennett; The Clarendon Press, for *Conservation* by Lord Hugh Cecil, *The Foreign Policy of Sir Edward Grey* by Gilbert Murray and *Liberalism* by Leonard Hobhouse; Collins Publishers, for *James Ramsay Macdonald* by Lord Elton and *Wavell, Scholar and Soldier* by J. Connell; Constable Publishers, for *The Emancipation of English Women* by W. L. Blease, *The Nation and the Empire* by Lord Milner and *The Unexpurgated Case Against Woman Suffrage* by Sir A. E. Wright; Gerald Duckworth & Co. Ltd, for *Books and Things* by G. S. Street; Faber & Faber Ltd, for *Golden Cities of To-morrow* by Ebenezer Howard; Fabian Society, for *The Commonsense of Municipal Trading* by G. B. Shaw and *The Decline in Birth Rate* by Sydney Webb; Garnstone Press, for *The Psychology of Jingoism* by J. A. Hobson; William Heinemann Ltd, for *A Commentary* by John Galsworthy, *Made in Germany* by E. E. Williams and *Winston S. Churchill* by Randolph Churchill; Hodder and Stoughton Limited, for *The Temperance Problem and Social Reform* by J. Rowntree and A. Sherwell and *What the Worker Wants* by H. G. Wells; The Estate of the late Earl of Balfour and Hodder and Stoughton, for *Opinions and Argument from Speeches and Addresses of the Earl of Balfour*; Hutchinson Publishing Group Ltd, for *Arthur James Balfour* by Blanche E. C. Dugdale and *The Life of Herbert Henry Asquith* by J. A. Spender and C. Asquith; Lawrence and Wishart Ltd, for *The Ragged Trousered Philanthropists* by R. Tressell; Liberal Publication Department, for *The Rural Land Problem* by D. Lloyd George; Macmillan, London and Basingstoke, for *The Life of Joseph Chamberlain* by J. Amery, *Official Papers* by Alfred Marshall and *The Strength of the People* by Helen Bosanquet; Mrs George Bambridge and Macmillan & Co. Ltd, and the Macmillan Company of Canada Ltd, for *The Five Nations* by Rudyard Kipling; Methuen & Co. Ltd, for *Riches and Poverty* by L. G. Chiozza Money; John Murray (Publishers) Ltd, for *Compulsory Service* by Sir I. Hamilton, *Industrial Warfare* by C. Watney and J. A. Little, and *The Service of the State* by J. H. Muirhead; National Administrative Council of the Independent Labour Party, for *Socialism and Government* by Ramsay Macdonald; Thomas Nelson & Sons Limited, for *At the Works* by Lady Bell, *A History of English Literature* by A. Compton-Rickett, *How the Labourer Lives* by B. S. Rowntree and May Kendall and *Poverty, A Study of Town Life* by B. S. Rowntree; James Nisbet and Co. Ltd, for *The Complete Grammar of Anarchy* by J. J. Horgan; Routledge & Kegan Paul Ltd, for *A History of Emigration* by S. C. Johnson; The Society of Authors, for *Fanny's First Play*, *John Bull's Other Island* and *Platform and Pulpit* by G. B. Shaw; The Estate of H. G. Wells, for *Anticipations*, *New World for Old* and *An Englishman Looks at the World* by H. G. Wells.

Index